LEARN
Adobe Animate CC
for Interactive Media

Adobe Certified Associate Exam Preparation

Joseph Labrecque
with Rob Schwartz

ADOBE
PRESS

Adobe

LEARN ADOBE ANIMATE CC FOR INTERACTIVE MEDIA
ADOBE CERTIFIED ASSOCIATE EXAM PREPARATION
Joseph Labrecque
with **Rob Schwartz**

Copyright © 2016 by Peachpit Press

Adobe Press books are published by Peachpit, a division of Pearson Education.
For the latest on Adobe Press books and videos, go to www.adobepress.com.
To report errors, please send a note to errata@peachpit.com

Adobe Press Editor: Victor Gavenda
Senior Editor, Video: Karyn Johnson
Development Editor: Stephen Nathans-Kelly
Senior Production Editor: Tracey Croom
Technical Editor: Russell Chun
Copyeditor: Liz Welch
Compositor: Kim Scott, Bumpy Design
Proofreader: Kim Wimpsett
Indexer: James Minkin
Cover & Interior Design: Mimi Heft
Cover Illustration: atthameeni, Fotolia.com

ISBN 13: 978-0-134-39781-8
ISBN 10: 0-134-39781-9

2   16
Printed and bound in the United States of America

Toward enduring remains.

Acknowledgments

Flash Professional is an application that has personally (and professionally!) always been a joy to use. It is such a uniquely rich and creative environment within which to build so many different types of projects...with the ability to work with animation, design, and interactive aspects—all within a single creative environment. Like many others, I began my journey with all things "Flash" under Macromedia and have continued with it during the transition to Adobe up to the present day. Flash Professional reached superstar status at one point, and now with its rebranding as Animate CC, stands poised to reclaim its crown as the premier animation and interactive application available. We are entering a new era with Animate CC, and you, the reader of this book, get to be at the forefront.

No work of this scale can be attributed to a single individual. Thanks to Rob, who has contributed his writing to this book in order to make present a great amount of design and theory knowledge. He was also instrumental in orchestrating much of the overall work toward our unified goals with this series. Thanks to Victor at Peachpit for getting this new series of books together and working with the authors at BrainBuffet and to ensure a solid outcome. Thanks also to my editor, Stephen, and my reviewer, Russell. It would be impossible to do this correctly without you all. I'd also like to express my thanks to the wider Peachpit, Adobe Press, and Brain-Buffet teams...and special thanks to Ajay, Rich, Chris, and everyone else at Adobe who is working so hard to make Animate CC what it is today—and what it will become in the future!

In closing, I need to acknowledge the patience and support of my wife, Leslie, and of our daughters; Paige and Lily. It's a hard thing to manage a business and a family while working full time, teaching, and writing...but they make it all much, much easier.

I hope you all enjoy this book.

About the Authors

Joseph Labrecque regularly teaches classes on Flash Professional/Animate CC, web animation, graphics production, and mobile application design for the University of Denver where he is also employed by the University of Denver as a senior interactive software engineer. In that role, Joseph specializes in the creation of expressive desktop, web, and mobile solutions. His work incorporates a strong focus on the Adobe Flash Platform alongside more general web standards initiatives involving the use of HTML5, CSS, JavaScript, and related technologies.

He is also the proprietor of Fractured Vision Media, LLC; a digital media production company, technical consultancy, and distribution vehicle for a variety of creative works. Joseph authors video courses and written works through organizations which include Adobe Press, Peachpit, Lynda.com, Train Simple, Packt, O'Reilly, BrainBuffet, and video2brain. He speaks regularly at conferences such as Adobe MAX, FITC, 360|Flex/Stack, D2WC, and for a variety of local community groups.

Joseph is an Adobe Education Leader (AEL) and Adobe Community Professional. He received the Adobe Education Impact Award in 2010 and currently serves on the AEL Advisory Board. He is also an Apache Flex Committer.

Rob Schwartz (author of online chapters 9 and 10) is an award-winning teacher (currently at Sheridan Technical College in Hollywood, FL) with over 15 years experience in technical education. Rob holds several Adobe Certified Associate certifications, and is also an Adobe Certified Instructor. As an Adobe Education Leader, Rob won the prestigious Impact Award from Adobe, and in 2010 Rob was the first winner of the Certiport Adobe Certified Associate World Championship. Find out more about Rob at his online curriculum website at brainbuffet.com.

Contents

*To access your free copy of this book's Web
Edition containing more than 6 hours of video,
see the instructions on pp. xiii–xiv.

Getting Started

We design and develop a number of exciting projects which consist of vector shapes, bitmap images, text, and code to help you learn the basics of interactive media creation with Adobe AnimateCC—along with other design and project management skills that you will need for a creative career in interactive media. Adobe Animate CC (formerly known as Adobe Flash Professional CC) is a powerful program for building a wide assortment of animated and interactive project types with sophisticated transitions, effects, and interactive elements. You can use Animate CC to export projects to an ever-growing array of platforms and targets including web browsers, desktop computers, and mobile devices through a variety of native application and web technologies.

About this book and video

Learn Adobe Animate CC for Interactive Media was created by a team of expert instructors, writers, and editors with years of experience in helping beginning learners get their start with the cool creative tools from Adobe Systems. Our aim is not only to teach you the basics of the art of interactive media with Animate CC, but to give you an introduction to the associated skills (like design principles and project management) that you'll need for your first job.

We've built the training around the objectives for the Adobe Certified Associate (ACA) exam in Interactive Media Using Adobe Flash Professional CC (name correct at press time) and if you master the topics covered in this book and video you'll be in good shape to take the exam. But even if certification isn't your goal, you'll still find this training will give you an excellent foundation for your future work in video. To that end, we've structured the material in the order that makes most sense for beginning learners (as determined by experienced classroom teachers), rather than following the more arbitrary grouping of topics in the ACA Objectives.

To aid you in your quest, we've created a unique learning system that uses video and text in partnership. You'll experience this partnership in action in the Web Edition, which lives on your Account page at peachpit.com. The Web Edition contains 6 hours of video—the heart of the training—embedded in an online eBook that supports the video training and provides background material. The eBook material is also available separately for offline reading as a printed book or an eBook in a variety of formats. The Web Edition also includes about a hundred interactive review questions you can use to evaluate your progress. Purchase of the book in *any* format entitles you to free access to the Web Edition (instructions for accessing it follow later in this section).

Most chapters provide step-by-step instructions for creating a specific project or learning a specific technique. Other chapters acquaint you with other skills and concepts that you'll come to depend on as you use the software in your everyday work. Many chapters include several optional tasks that let you further explore the features you've already learned.

Each chapter opens with two lists of objectives. One list lays out the learning objectives: the specific tasks you'll learn in the chapter. The second list shows the ACA exam objectives that are covered in the chapter. A table at the end of the book guides you to coverage of all of the exam objectives in the book or video.

Conventions used in this book

This book uses several elements styled in ways to help you as you work through the projects.

Text that you should enter appears in bold, such as:

In the Link field in the Property inspector, type **http://www.adobe.com/ animate**.

Terms that are defined in the Glossary appear in bold and in color, such as:

The **web font** that's used in the header of the page is just what the client is looking for. That's a great thing.

Links to videos that cover the topics in depth appear in the margins.

▶ Video 5.1
Animating the Mask

The ACA objectives covered in the chapters are called out in the margins beside the sections that address them.

★ *ACA Objective 2.1*

Notes give additional information about a topic. The information they contain is not essential to accomplishing a task but provides a more in-depth understanding of the topic.

> **NOTE** *Notice the effect of the vanishing point, which is used to provide perspective to the artwork as it's moved through the simulated 3D environment.*

OPERATING SYSTEM DIFFERENCES

In most cases, Animate CC works the same in both Windows and Mac OS. Minor differences exist between the two versions, mostly due to platform-specific issues. Most of these are simply differences in keyboard shortcuts, how dialogs are displayed, and how buttons are named. In most cases, screen shots were made in the Mac OS version of Animate CC and may appear somewhat differently from your own screen.

Where specific commands differ, they are noted within the text. Windows commands are listed first, followed by the Mac OS equivalent, such as Ctrl+C/Cmd+C. In general, the Windows Ctrl key is equivalent to the Command (or "Cmd) key in Mac OS and the Windows Alt key is equivalent to the Option (or "Opt") key in Mac OS.

As lessons proceed, instructions may be truncated or shortened to save space, with the assumption that you picked up the essential concepts earlier in the lesson. For example, at the beginning of a lesson you may be instructed to "press Ctrl+C/Cmd+C." Later, you may be told to "copy" text or a code element. These should be considered identical instructions.

If you find you have difficulties in any particular task, review earlier steps or exercises in that lesson. In some cases if an exercise is based on concepts covered earlier, you will be referred back to the specific lesson.

Installing the software

Before you begin using *Learn Adobe Animate CC for Interactive Media*, make sure that your system is set up correctly and that you've installed the proper software and hardware. This material is based on the original 2015 release of Adobe Animate CC and is designed to cover the objectives of the Adobe Certified Associate Exam for that version of the software (as this product went to press, however, the ACA exam still bore the name "Flash Professional").

The Adobe Animate CC software is not included with this book; it is available only with an Adobe Creative Cloud membership which you must purchase or it must be supplied by your school or other organization. In addition to Adobe Animate CC, some lessons in this book have steps that can be performed with Adobe Media Encoder and other Adobe applications. You must install these applications from Adobe Creative Cloud onto your computer. Follow the instructions provided at *helpx.adobe.com/creative-cloud/help/download-install-app.html*.

ADOBE CREATIVE CLOUD DESKTOP APP

In addition to Adobe Animate CC, this training also requires the Adobe Creative Cloud desktop application, which provides a central location for managing the dozens of apps and services that are included in a Creative Cloud membership. You can use the Creative Cloud desktop application to sync and share files, manage fonts, access libraries of stock photography and design assets, and showcase and discover creative work in the design community.

The Creative Cloud desktop application is installed automatically when you download your first Creative Cloud product. If you have Adobe Application Manager installed, it auto-updates to the Creative Cloud desktop application.

If the Creative Cloud desktop application is not installed on your computer, you can download it from the Download Creative Cloud page on the Adobe website (*creative.adobe.com/products/creative-cloud*) or the Adobe Creative Cloud desktop apps page (*adobe.com/creativecloud/catalog/desktop.html*). If you are using software on classroom machines, be sure to check with your instructor before making any changes to the installed software or system configuration.

CHECKING FOR UPDATES

Adobe periodically provides updates to software. You can easily obtain these updates through the Creative Cloud. If these updates include new features that affect the content of this training or the objectives of the ACA exam in any way, we will post updated material to peachpit.com.

Accessing the free Web Edition and lesson files

Your purchase of this book in any format includes access to the corresponding Web Edition hosted on peachpit.com. The Web Edition contains the complete text of the book augmented with hours of video and interactive quizzes.

To work through the projects in this product, you will first need to download the lesson files from peachpit.com. You can download the files for individual lessons or download them all in a single file.

If you purchased an eBook from peachpit.com or adobepress.com, the Web Edition will automatically appear the Digital Purchases tab on your Account page. Click the Launch link to access the product. Continue reading to learn how to register your product to get access to the lesson files.

If you purchased an eBook from a different vendor or you bought a print book, you must register your purchase on peachpit.com:

1 Go to *www.peachpit.com/register*.

2 Sign in or create a new account.

3 Enter ISBN: **9780134397818**.

4 Answer the questions as proof of purchase.

5 The **Web Edition** will appear under the Digital Purchases tab on your Account page. Click the Launch link to access the product.

   The Lesson Files can be accessed through the Registered Products tab on your Account page. Click the Access Bonus Content link below the title of your product to proceed to the download page. Click the lesson file links to download them to your computer.

Project fonts

All fonts used in these projects are either part of standard system installs or can be downloaded from Typekit, an Adobe service which is included with your Creative Cloud membership.

Additional resources

Learn Adobe Animate CC for Interactive Media is not meant to replace documentation that comes with the program or to be a comprehensive reference for every feature. For comprehensive information about program features and tutorials, refer to these resources:

Adobe Animate CC Learn & Support: *helpx.adobe.com/animate* is where you can find and browse Help and Support content on Adobe.com. Adobe Animate Help and Adobe Animate Support Center are accessible from the Help menu in Animate CC. Help is also available as a printable PDF document. Download the document at *helpx.adobe.com/pdf/animate_reference.pdf*.

Adobe Forums: *forums.adobe.com/community/animate* lets you tap into peer-to-peer discussions, questions, and answers on Adobe products.

Adobe Animate CC product home page: *adobe.com/products/animate* provides information about new features and intuitive ways to create professional layouts for print, tablets, and eBooks.

Adobe Add-ons: *creative.adobe.com/addons* is a central resource for finding tools, services, extensions, code samples, and more to supplement and extend your Adobe products.

Resources for educators: *adobe.com/education* and *edex.adobe.com* offer a treasure trove of information for instructors who teach classes on Adobe software at all levels.

Adobe certification

The Adobe training and certification programs are designed to help designers and other creative professionals improve and promote their product-proficiency skills. The Adobe Certified Associate (ACA) is an industry-recognized credential that demonstrates proficiency in Adobe digital skills. Whether you're just starting out in your career, looking to switch jobs or interested in preparing for success in the job market, the Adobe Certified Associate program is for you! For more information visit *edex.adobe.com/aca*.

Resetting the preferences to their default settings

Animate CC lets you determine how the program looks and behaves (like tool settings and the default unit of measurement) using the extensive options in Edit > Preferences (Windows) or Animate CC > Preferences (Mac OS). To ensure that the preferences and default settings of your Adobe Animate CC program match those used in this book, you can reset your preference settings to their defaults (the Animate CC Help file calls this procedure "re-creating your preferences"). If you are using software installed on computers in a classroom, don't make any changes to the system configuration without first checking with your instructor.

To reset your preferences to their default settings, follow these steps:

1 Quit Adobe Animate CC.

2 Hold down the Ctrl + Alt + Shift keys (Windows) or Cmd + Option + Shift keys (Mac OS).

3 Continue to hold the keys and start Adobe Animate CC.

4 When the Delete Adobe Animate Preferences dialog box appears, release the keys and click OK.

The file containing your preferences will be deleted.

CHAPTER OBJECTIVES

Chapter Learning Objectives

- Meet the Animate CC workspace
- Understand the Stage and Pasteboard
- Discover the Properties and Tools panels
- Explore other commonly accessed tools
- Become familiar with the timeline and its key components

Chapter ACA Objectives

DOMAIN 3.0
UNDERSTANDING ADOBE FLASH PROFESSIONAL

3.1 Identify elements of the Flash interface and demonstrate knowledge of their functions, including Panels, the Timeline, the Property Inspector, and Document Properties dialog.

3.2 Define the functions of commonly used tools, including selection tools, the Pen tool, other drawing tools, and shape tools.

3.3 Navigate, organize, and customize the workspace.

CHAPTER 1

Welcome!

Adobe Animate CC (**Figure 1.1**) truly is a creative powerhouse. You're probably most familiar with content produced with this application served via the Adobe Flash Player web browser plug-in… but do you know that Animate CC can also be used to produce rich, creative content that targets HTML5 Canvas, WebGL, SVG, iOS, Android, and more? Animate CC is a platform-agnostic application that allows you to design assets, animation, and interactive content of all kinds for a multitude of platforms—and all with the same tools and workflows!

> **NOTE** *Adobe has rebranded Flash Professional CC as Animate CC! They are essentially the exact same application—with absolutely no differences in capability aside from features introduced in the regular update schedule. All future updates to Flash Professional CC will be known by the name Animate CC. If desired, subscribers can run multiple versions of the product—branded as either Flash Professional or Animate—but I highly recommend using the latest available version of Animate CC to take advantage of all new features.*

In this book you'll tackle some awesome projects that will introduce you to the application, learn some good practices for working on projects for others, and find tips and resources you can use to learn more on your own.

Figure 1.1 Adobe Animate CC

About Adobe Learn Books

Let's take just a second to explain what I'm trying to accomplish so I can be sure we're on the same page (pun intended!). Here's what I (and the other authors) hope to accomplish in this series.

Have fun

This is seriously a goal for me, as I hope it is for you! When you're having fun, you learn more, and you're more likely to remember what you're learning. Having fun also makes it easier to focus and stick with the task at hand.

Even if the projects you create as you complete the exercises in this book aren't the kinds of things you'd create on your own, I'll make them as entertaining and fun as possible. Just roll with it, and it will make the time you spend with this book more enjoyable. Have fun, make jokes, and enjoy your new superpowers.

Learn Adobe Animate CC

This goes along with the previous item, but when you're working on the projects in this book, you have the freedom to explore and make your projects your own. Of course you're welcome to follow along with my examples, but please feel free to change text or styles to fit your own interests. When you're sure you grasp the concepts I'm talking about, I encourage you to apply them in your own way. In some projects, you may want to even take things beyond the scope of what appears in the book. Please do so.

Animate CC vs. Flash Professional CC

In late 2015, Adobe announced a major rebrand of its longstanding animation software, Flash Professional CC. Adobe is committed to elevating Flash Professional CC as the premier animation and interaction tool–but now as a platform-agnostic creativity application not restricted to any single platform. To reinforce this renewed focus, Adobe has decided to rebrand Flash Professional CC as Animate CC.

"To more accurately represent its position as the premier animation tool for the web and beyond, Flash Professional will be renamed Adobe Animate CC, starting with the next release in early 2016." —Adobe

Flash Professional CC, as Adobe Animate CC, is now poised to regain its proper place aside such giants as Adobe Illustrator CC and Photoshop CC as a top-tier application in the Adobe Creative Cloud portfolio. A new beginning with a great legacy behind it!

Preparation for ACA exam

This book covers every objective for the Adobe Certified Associate (ACA) exam, but I won't discuss them in order or make a big point of it. The authors of this series are teachers and trainers, and we've been doing this for a long time. We'll cover the concepts in the order that makes the most sense for *learning* and *retaining* the information best. You'll read everything you need pass the exam and qualify for an entry-level job—but don't focus on that now. Instead, focus on having a blast learning Adobe Animate CC!

Developing your creative, communication, and cooperative skills

Aside from the actual hands-on work of learning Animate CC, this book explores the skills you need to become a more creative and cooperative person. These skills are critical for success—every employer, no matter what the industry, values creative people who can work and communicate well. This book describes the basics of creativity, how to design for (and work with) others, and project management.

A quick note on creativity

Animate CC is, by any definition of the term, creative software. You may have heard that creativity is something you're born with—and that some people have it and some don't. Not true! Creativity may come more naturally to some than to others, but all of us can become more creative people. It simply takes practice like anything else. The only way to get better at creativity is to practice, experiment, explore, and fail!

> **NOTE**
>
> *The important thing to remember is that Flash Player did pave the way for all the goodies we have in the native browser today. We have Flash Player to thank for advances in dynamic content, animation, audio and video playback, the browser-based canvas element, native 3D with WebGL, and much more.*

As Edwin Land said, "An essential aspect of creativity is not being afraid to fail." Failure is a *huge* part of creativity. It's a part of the process. So celebrate and enjoy your failures. Art is a very experimental activity. Even the best artists can make junk. The difference between them and the rest of us is that they learn to become comfortable with failure and recognize that it's part of the creative process. Everyone has a thousand crummy ideas in them. A creative person is just someone who's used more of them up than the rest of us!

At the end of this book you'll explore ways to build your creativity, the same way you build your muscles. So don't worry if you feel like you aren't a very strong designer. You just need to spend some time in the creative gym!

Getting Acquainted with Animate CC

One of the great things about Animate CC is how versatile its interface is. It's flexible enough to adapt to the workflow and content the user encounters in any given project, which adds to the variety of project types that users can create with this program.

For example, some people use Animate CC only to create assets for a project, such as sprite sheets for a game or a packaged SWC library for integration with a larger application. Others take advantage of the rich animation features core to the Animate CC experience. Still others develop interactive web content or even full iOS and Android apps via Adobe AIR. The creative possibilities with this application are limitless!

★ *ACA Objective 3.1*

▶ **Video 1.1** *The Animate CC Workspace*

The Animate CC workspace

The Animate interface (**Figure 1.2**) consists of a broad series of panels, tabbed windows, and specialized panels that provide the functionality you'll need to create interactive media applications, rich animations, and engaging mobile apps.

> **NOTE** *All of the videos for this book were recorded with a version of Animate CC branded as Flash Professional CC. It is important to note that everything that we demonstrate in the recordings can be applied to Animate CC—even if we refer to the application as Flash Professional. They are essentially the exact same application—with absolutely no differences in capability.*

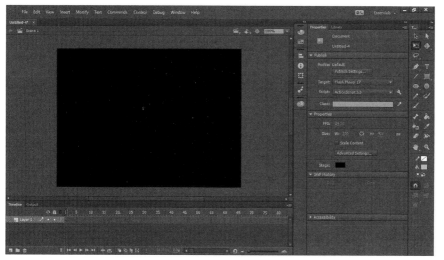

Viewing all of these options at once would fill the screen several times over. This is why it is important to learn how to manage the workspace to show only those panels that apply to the current task.

MANAGING PANELS

All individual panels or groups of panels can be minimized or maximized to make the best use of your screen area. You do this using the small double-arrow icon located in the top-right corner of the panel or panel group (**Figure 1.3**).

▶ *Video 1.2*
Managing Panels

Figure 1.3 Animate CC panels

When a panel is collapsed, the arrows will point left; clicking the arrows will expand the panel or panel group to show the full interface.

When a panel or panel group is open, clicking the arrows will collapse the panel or panel group to icon mode.

USING WORKSPACE PRESETS

▶ *Video 1.3* Using Workspace Presets

With the number of creative options available for any given project, it makes sense that certain workspace configurations and panel sets might be better suited to certain tasks. For instance, if you're working on an animation that is not going to include any interactivity or code whatsoever, it wouldn't make sense to clutter the workspace with panels for writing code or managing code snippets.

Animate CC ships with a number of prebuilt workspaces for certain tasks (**Figure 1.4**):

Figure 1.4 Workspace presets

- **Animator:** This workspace positions the timeline and Stage at dead center and includes quick access to scenes and document properties.

- **Classic:** Miss the good ol' days when Flash animation on the web was king? This workspace preset replicates the panel layout of Macromedia Flash 4…or thereabouts.

- **Debug:** This workspace is extremely important for code-heavy ActionScript projects. This preset reveals the Debug Console and Variables panel, allowing simple debugging for complex interactive content.

- **Designer:** This workspace is similar to the Animator preset, but with a greater emphasis on colors and tools.

- **Developer:** Quick access to the Components panel and a de-emphasis on the Tools panel are the hallmarks of this preset. It also makes the Compiler Errors and Output panels readily accessible.

- **Essentials:** This is the default workspace preset for Animate CC and aims to be balanced and uncluttered.

- **Small Screen:** This workspace provides a good example of how the various panels and panel groups can be collapsed. It's a good choice for screens with very little space.

CREATING A CUSTOM WORKSPACE

Sometimes the built-in workspace presets aren't enough. For instance, maybe you have a small-screen laptop or are working across multiple monitors, or maybe you have a specific task that you do frequently and requires only a few panels to be visible.

You can create a custom workspace by opening and arranging the panels to your liking and saving the layout as a custom workspace.

1   To begin, modify the set of panels and panel groups you'd like to include in your custom workspace.

2   Choose New Workspace from the Workspace drop-down menu.

3   Enter a unique name for the new workspace and click OK (**Figure 1.5**).

Now you'll be able to easily recall this particular workspace setup through the Workspace drop-down menu.

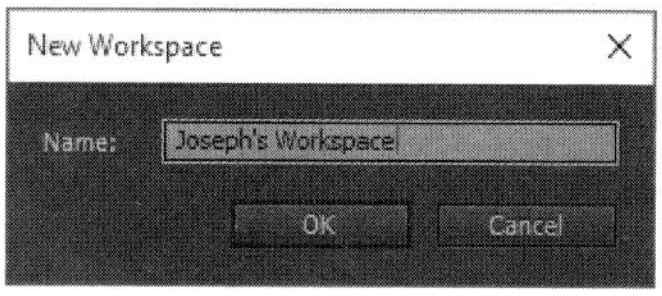

Figure 1.5 Naming a custom workspace

When customizing your workspace or simply working with panels, you should take note of a few things. The panels in the Animate CC interface have tabs that can be used to assign the panel to a group or quickly maximize and minimize the contents of the panel without collapsing the entire group.

Here are options for organizing and accessing custom workspaces:

▪ Drag tabs into a group to make that panel part of the group. If you drag the panel tab next to another tab, it will create a tab group.

▪ Drag the panel above or below another tab or tab group to create an accordion arrangement. Double-click a tab to collapse the contents of that panel vertically. Double-click again to expand the panel.

▪ You can also choose to lock any panel through its options menu. This prevents the panel from being moved around by mistake.

Major Interface Features

It's a good idea, before delving into any project, to familiarize yourself with the various panels and tools within Animate CC. Although many interface panels will not be needed at all times, some areas of the interface are so important that no matter what sort of project you are working with, you need to have them visible.

★ ACA Objective 3.1

The Stage and Pasteboard

The Stage (**Figure 1.6**) is the main visual layout area for the project. Objects that appear on the Stage at any given frame will be visible when someone runs the project outside of Animate CC, whether it is an HTML5 Canvas, WebGL, Adobe AIR, or Flash Player project.

Figure 1.6 The Stage and Pasteboard

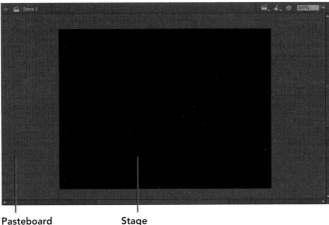

Pasteboard   Stage

The Stage has a number of important aspects you should be aware of. Let's start with the stage resolution in width and height. The default resolution is 550px wide by 400px in height. Getting the Stage size right—or at least giving it an appropriate aspect ratio—is crucial when beginning a new project. The background color determines the default Stage color when there are no other elements obscuring it. The background color of the Stage is always a solid color.

The pasteboard consists of the space surrounding the Stage. You can use the pasteboard as a scratch area or a drawing surface, or even include visual elements off the Stage that will animate into the Stage at a later time. Anything on the pasteboard will still be included in the compiled files—and will add to the overall file size—so be careful. It is a versatile tool that you should definitely make use of.

The Properties panel

Interactive media elements in Animate CC have properties that you can freely adjust and animate, depending on your needs. These properties can refer to position, color, transparency, publish settings, and more.

▶ *Video 1.4 The Properties and Tools Panels*

Use the Properties panel to modify the properties of your selected object. It's a *smart* palette, so the options presented will change to reflect the interactive media element type you have currently selected.

Figure 1.7 shows the content of the Properties panel when a movie clip symbol instance is selected. Because the Properties panel adapts to reveal the properties of any given element, you won't always see so many options available for modification.

Figure 1.7 The Properties panel

The Tools panel

The Tools panel (**Figure 1.8**) provides a variety of tools for creating and manipulating graphics and images within a project.

The panel is divided by horizontal rules into subsections that group the tools roughly by function. Options for any selected tool will vary.

Notice the tiny triangles on the bottom-right corner of some of the icons. These triangles indicate that clicking the tool will bring up an additional tool selection option. This lets you access more tools that are grouped within the visible tool and switch easily between them.

For instance, all the 3D tools are grouped together, but you will only ever see either the 3D Translation or 3D Rotation tool within the panel at one time—never both, since they are grouped.

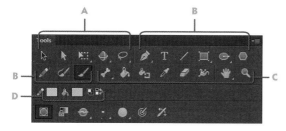

Figure 1.8 The Tools panel

A (left to right) Selection, Subselection, Transform, Gradient Transform, 3D Rotation, 3D Transform, Lasso, Polygon, and Magic Wand

B (left to right) Pen and Anchor, Text, Line, Rectangle, Rectangle Primitive, Oval, Oval Primitive, Polystar, Pencil, Paint Brush, and Brush

C (left to right) Bone, Bind, Paint Bucket, Ink Bottle, Eyedropper, Eraser, Width, Hand, Rotation, and Zoom

D (left to right) Stroke Color, Fill Color, Black and White, and Swap Colors

Commonly accessed tools

★ ACA Objective 3.2

I'll describe most of the tools in Animate CC as you come across them in working through the various projects this book covers. A few tools are universal in terms of when you would access them, so I'll briefly describe them now.

- **Hand tool** (　): Use this tool to pan around the Stage. Just select the Hand tool and then click and drag on the Stage to pan around.

- **Rotation tool** (　): This is a new tool in Animate CC. It allows you to rotate the Stage if you're using a tablet or similar device, giving you a more natural angle at which to create assets. To use this tool after selecting it, click anywhere on the Stage to set a pin, and then click and drag to rotate to your desired viewing angle.

- **Zoom tool** (　): As you may surmise from its name, the Zoom tool allows you to quickly zoom in and out of the Stage. Select the tool and then click either the icon marked with a + (plus sign) to zoom in or the icon with a – (minus sign) to zoom out. With either of these selected, clicking the Stage or dragging a selection rectangle with the tool will perform the requested zoom.

- **Stroke Color** (　) **and Fill Color** (　): When dealing with shapes and text, you can define both stroke and fill colors separately. Clicking either swatch here will summon a color picker that lets you can redefine the selected color or even generate a new, specific color choice.

- **Black and White** (　): Clicking this icon once replaces the currently defined fill and stroke colors for a white fill and black stroke.

- **Swap Colors** (　): Clicking this icon swaps the Fill and Stroke colors. Click again to reverse.

- **Options area**: This is the area below the color tools that changes based on the currently selected tool. Notice when the Zoom tool is selected, for instance, how the + and – options then appear. Keep a close eye on this area as you work through the projects with various tools selected.

The timeline

▶ Video 1.5 The Animate CC Timeline

The Timeline panel (**Figure 1.9**) provides a frame-based animation and organizational structure for the interactive media authoring environment. There are a number of concepts to take note of here: layers, frames, and keyframes.

Keyframes　　　　　　**Frames**

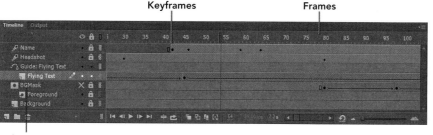

Layers

Figure 1.9 The Timeline panel

- **Layers:** Much like in other programs such as Adobe Photoshop or Adobe Illustrator, layers in Animate CC are an organizational construct that allows you to stack content vertically on the Stage. Content in the uppermost layers will obscure content it overlaps with in layers below.

- **Frames:** Since animation in Animate CC is measured in frames per second (fps), you can imagine that frames themselves play a big role in working with the timeline. Frames are added to the timeline across layers and determine how long the animation sequence will play, based on the project fps.

- **Keyframes:** These are special frames that contain information about a change in the properties of the object within that layer.

You can place assets in keyframes on the timeline by dragging instances from the library or by importing them to the Stage with that particular keyframe and layer selected. These assets will activate when the playhead of the animation reaches that point.

Keyframes that include visual content will appear with a small, filled circle within them. Keyframes with no content, or blank keyframes, appear similarly but the small circle is unfilled.

> **TIP**
>
> *When animating content, pay close attention to be sure that each object to be animated is on its own unique layer.*

> ▶ *Video 1.6 Common Keyboard Shortcuts*

Let's Get Going!

Okay—that's everything you need to know going in. You'll complete six separate projects in this book that cover all the basics of using Animate CC for creating content targeting Flash Player, HTML5, Adobe **AIR**, iOS, Android, and more. The creative possibilities are truly endless—so let's get started!

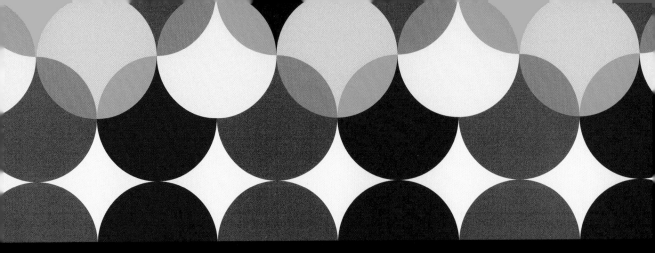

CHAPTER OBJECTIVES

Chapter Learning Objectives

- Create and prepare documents
- Create shape assets
- Manage the timeline
- Animate objects with keyframes and tweening
- Emulate natural movement through easing
- Publish a project

Chapter ACA Objectives

DOMAIN 3.0
UNDERSTANDING ADOBE FLASH PROFESSIONAL

3.2 Define the functions of commonly used tools, including selection tools, the Pen tool, other drawing tools, and shape tools.

3.6 Demonstrate knowledge of layers and masks.

DOMAIN 4.0
CREATING INTERACTIVE MEDIA CONTENT USING FLASH PROFESSIONAL

4.1 Create a new project.

4.5 Create animations (changes in shape, position, size, color, and transparency).

DOMAIN 5.0
TESTING, PUBLISHING, AND EVALUATING INTERACTIVE MEDIA ELEMENTS USING FLASH PROFESSIONAL

5.4 Publish and export Flash documents.

CHAPTER 2

Design a Vector Animation

Adobe Animate CC can be used for a wide range of project types, but at its core it remains a highly capable vector animation tool. This initial project is designed to ease you into Animate CC's interface and tools in order to complete a series of tasks focused on vector animation.

When you're finished with this project, you will have created a short animation of a ball bouncing on a floor. Although this may not be the most exciting of projects, it will introduce you to many of Animate CC's **vector** drawing tools along with animation techniques you can use across just about every other project in this book.

One thing that Animate CC is often used for in educational settings is to create simulations for classes or reference materials. Think of this project as the simulation of a bouncing ball (because that's basically what it is).

This project will incorporate many of the fundamental concepts you'll encounter when working with animated vector content. This includes creating and preparing documents; creating shape assets; managing the timeline; animating through frames, keyframes, and tweening; making animation more natural and pleasant; and publishing your project.

NOTE

Adobe has rebranded Flash Professional CC as Animate CC! They are essentially the exact same application, with absolutely no differences in capability aside from features introduced in the regular update schedule. All future updates to Flash Professional CC will be known by the name Animate CC. If desired, subscribers can run multiple versions of the product—branded as either Flash Professional or Animate—but I highly recommend using the latest available version of Animate CC to take advantage of all new features.

Video 2.1 *Project Overview*

Keeping this project small in scope will leave us room to go over some of the other tools you might find useful when creating and working with vector shapes in Animate CC (**Figure 2.1**). These include the Pen tool, Brush tool, Pencil tool, and various selection and management tools. I'll discuss these tools as they become useful in the project.

Figure 2.1 Vector animation in Animate CC

NOTE

All of the videos for this book were recorded with a version of Animate CC branded as Flash Professional CC. It is important to note that everything that we demonstrate in the recordings can be applied to Animate CC—even if we refer to the application as Flash Professional. They are essentially the exact same application—with absolutely no differences in capability.

Creating the Project Document

Although any Animate document will be in the form of a common FLA file, the capabilities and options available to you when working on a project will depend on the specific target platform.

Whereas Animate CC used to be used solely for the creation of content that will run inside of the browser-based Flash Player runtime, Adobe has been positioning the application in recent years to allow for an infinite number of target platforms. Some of the platform targets that ship natively with Animate CC are **HTML5 Canvas**, **WebGL**, ActionScript 3.0 (targeting Flash Player or Adobe AIR runtimes), plus an array of custom platforms.

Whichever document type you choose to create, there are a number of other publish options that are platform agnostic. These can include **SVG**, **bitmap**, **spritesheets**, and more.

The Animate document file

Before even concerning yourself with the specific properties of a document, you need to choose your eventual target platform for the current project. You have a number of great choices with Animate CC, and they all share a common document format: the FLA file.

Animate CC creates an FLA file whenever you open a new document. It acts as a package to hold the internal assets and to keep your project organized. A simple project can consist of a single FLA file that holds all necessary artwork, sound, and code. This is one of the major strengths of Animate CC: the tight integration of design and development.

In recent versions of Animate CC, the FLA file type has become an archive containing individual files and folders along with information about how a project is organized. Opening an FLA with a file archive utility allows you to view what is stored within and can teach you how Animate CC organizes content behind the scenes.

Animate CC uses a variety of file types in the process of creating and displaying interactive media applications. Some of the file types are specific to the Animate CC environment; others are more generic file types, including those used for images and audio.

NOTE

An FLA is a compressed file type, meaning that all the files and folders it contains have been written to a single file. An XFL is uncompressed and exists as a series of exposed files and directories.

The ActionScript 3.0 document

Animate CC has deep roots in **ActionScript** and the Adobe Flash runtimes: Flash Player and Adobe AIR. This should come as no surprise. For the majority of its lifetime, ActionScript was Animate CC's only supported platform. As a result, choosing any of the AS3-based document types allows for the fullest set of creative tooling and the use of a deeply mature programming language, ActionScript 3.0.

★ *ACA Objective 4.1*

For this project, you will create a new ActionScript 3.0 document. You'll explore other document types throughout this book, but since the idea with this project is to start off simple and explore core, traditional functionality, it makes sense to employ the document type that Animate CC is most comfortable with.

NOTE

Any Animate document, no matter what the target platform, will take the form of an Animate Document file with the extension of .fla (or .xfl, if that is your preferred format).

Setting document type and properties

▶ *Video 2.2* *Creating a New ActionScript 3.0 Document*

The first thing to do when creating a new Animate CC project is to make some decisions about document type and properties. The main properties of an Animate document include the stage size, frame rate, background color, guides, and ruler units. These properties are usually set when the document is first created, but sometimes it's necessary to adjust them afterward.

In this exercise you'll create your first Animate document and explore some basic properties settings.

1   Start Animate CC. If you're opening the application for the first time, you should see the **Welcome Screen** (**Figure 2.2**). You can disable this feature if you like, but it provides a useful display of all the choices you can make when starting off a new project, or even continuing a project you've already been working on.

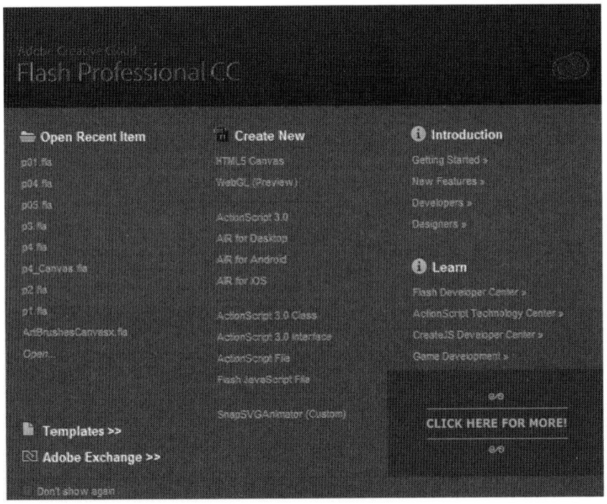

Figure 2.2 The Welcome Screen

2   In the center column, under the Create New heading, click ActionScript 3.0, which is the third option from the top.

You will immediately be taken to a new Animate document that you can modify however you like (**Figure 2.3**).

Before continuing, let's try another way to create a new document that you can do directly from the Animate CC workspace without the Welcome Screen open. Creating a new document in this way allows you to set some basic settings, like width and height, before Animate CC opens the new document.

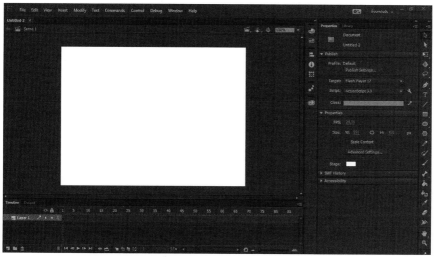

Figure 2.3 A new Animate document

3 Choose File > New from the application menu.

The Document Properties dialog box opens (**Figure 2.4**). From here, you can modify some document properties and then save your document as a file.

Figure 2.4 The Document Properties dialog box

- The default width and height for a new document is 550px wide by 400px tall. This is fine for the current project. Leave these values as they are.

- The default frames per second (fps) is set at 24. This is also fine for now.

4 Choose a background color for your stage. I nearly always choose black, but you can pick whatever color you like.

Now you have a new document with some basic stage properties configured.

5 Choose File > Save from the application menu to save your document. Note that you have two options here: FLA and XFL (**Figure 2.5**). An FLA file is the easiest to manage, since it's a neat little bundle and all you need to worry about is a single file. Stick with FLA, type a name for your file, and then click Save.

★ *ACA Objective 5.2*

File name:	Project01	⌄
Save as type:	Flash Document (*.fla)	⌄
	Flash Document (*.fla)	
	Flash Uncompressed Document (*.xfl)	
▲ Hide Folders		Save Cancel

Figure 2.5 Choosing a file type

WHAT ARE XFL DOCUMENTS?

Recent versions of Animate CC not only allow the creation of Animate CC authoring files in FLA format but also can save projects in XFL, a format that's much easier to edit outside of Animate CC or to use with a version control system like Subversion or Git. The proper name for the file format is Flash Uncompressed Document, shortened to XFL with the X standing for XML and the FL for Flash.

The XFL file format is an alternative to the packaged FLA format, which represents a Animate CC project as an XML document alongside a set of other folders and files. Each XFL structure has, at its heart, a file called DOMDocument.xml. If you open this file in a text editor, you'll see all of the information for your document, including timeline data, code, motion paths, and so on.

Remember that the FLA file format is simply an archived version of the XFL structures and documents.

ADJUSTING DOCUMENT PROPERTIES AFTER FILE CREATION

Even with the best planning, it is sometimes necessary to make adjustments to a Flash file's document properties after it has been created. This can be due to changes in delivery platform or performance issues.

The simplest way to do this is to access the Document Settings dialog box by choosing Modify > Document. This will present a dialog box with the same information that was presented when a new document was created.

You can also access this information via the Properties inspector after first clicking a blank area of the Stage.

★ *ACA Objective 3.4*

▶ **Video 2.3**
*Preparing the
Project Stage
and Timeline*

Preparing the project Stage and timeline

Before moving on to creating some vector shapes and moving them around, you'll do a little project preparation to organize your document.

Almost always, I find it useful to have snapping enabled in my projects. Snapping will enable to application itself to "snap" objects to x and y coordinates based on a number of selectable settings. It can make positioning objects in a precise way much easier. Animate CC offers a number of snapping options, and I enable them all. Whether you benefit from snapping or not will depend on how precise you like things to be managed on the Stage.

To enable or disable various snapping options, choose View > Snapping from the application menu (**Figure 2.6**).

TIP

You can also enable both rulers and the grid from the same View menu. Experiment with all these options to see what works best for your work style.

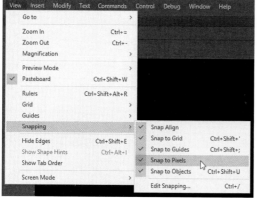

Figure 2.6 Choose Snapping options here.

Let's have a look at the timeline (**Figure 2.7**). You'll notice that within the timeline itself, a system of frames extends horizontally across the timeline depending on how long it is, and a series of layers run vertically down the timeline. Note that in a new document such as you have here, you have one layer (called Layer 1) and a single frame (on Frame 1).

Figure 2.7 The Animate CC timeline

1   To begin, double-click the "Layer 1" text to make its name editable, and type in **Floor**. You'll use this layer to hold the vectors drawn to represent the solid floor of the bouncing ball simulation.

2   Next, click the New Layer (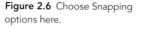) icon at the bottom of the timeline—it looks like a sheet of paper.

    This creates a new layer in the timeline, again with a default name.

3   Double-click the layer name and type **Circle** to rename it. This is the layer within which you'll draw out your bouncing ball vector shape.

Controlling layers and folders

Besides the ability to create new layers, you have a number of other options at the bottom-left side of the timeline that you can use to manage layers and related items (**Figure 2.8**):

- Use the page icon (🗏) to create a new layer.
- Use the folder icon (📁) to create folders for grouping layers.
- Use the trash can (🗑) icon to delete unneeded layers.

Figure 2.8 Click these three icons to manage layers.

Layer management icons

Rearrange layers by dragging them above and below each other in the timeline layer stack. This will also affect the Z-order of the content on the Stage (for an explanation of Z-order—the ordering of overlapping objects in an interface—see the sidebar "Arranging stacking order").

Setting layer properties on the timeline

★ ACA Objective 3.6

Layers have several properties that can be set directly on the timeline or by using a right-click.

To set the visibility of a layer, click the bullet below the eye icon. By default, Animate CC will still publish hidden layers, so this is not a way of hiding content at runtime. You might use this method when you need to focus on editing one particular set of elements by temporarily hiding the rest. If you want to toggle visibility for all layers, just click the lock icon (🔒).

Clicking the bullet below the lock icon will lock everything within the layer. This locks only the artwork; you can still edit the keyframes within the timeline. You can also lock an element or unlock all elements from this menu by clicking the lock icon.

The bullet below the outline icon toggles the object display between normal and wireframe. Wireframe view can be useful when you're working with objects that are completely covered by other objects. It allows you to see exactly where the borders of objects lay in perspective to one another regardless of stacking order.

Right-clicking a layer will reveal more layer options (**Figure 2.9**). These include options for copying, cutting, pasting, duplicating, and working with guides. Animate CC offers a ton of options for working with layers—and a lot of them can be accessed from this menu.

Turning on the Guide property will allow the layer to show up and function normally during authoring but prevent that layer from showing up in the published file. It's used only as a guide within the authoring environment itself, and it's never a part of the published project.

> **NOTE** *Flattened template images of an interface are often imported to a guide layer to provide a reference for placing actual interactive media elements.*

You'll see a lot of these other options as we go about creating and modifying our projects. One additional right-click menu option to note is the Layer Properties. Clicking this menu item brings up a dialog box where you can manage a lot of these properties through a single, unified screen (**Figure 2.10**). You can even set the outline color through the Properties dialog box!

Drawing Vector Assets

Okay! That should be enough background to get you going. Now that you have your Stage set up along with a number of layers in the timeline, you can begin creating your visual elements. Animate CC is not restricted to vector shapes, but it works with vectors very, very well. One of the original purposes of using vectors was to keep the distributable file size as low as possible. This still holds true today.

Figure 2.9 The Layer Options menu

Figure 2.10 The Layer Properties dialog box

Rectangle and Oval tools

You can create standard rectangles and ovals in Animate CC by accessing their respective tools in the Tools panel. You can set properties for these objects before you create them on the Stage or modify them later, either by selecting the objects and changing the settings within the Properties inspector or by changing the properties at the bottom of the Tools panel.

Pressing the Shift or Alt/Option key while drawing these objects constrains the drawing as follows:

- Pressing the Shift key forces the Rectangle tool to draw a perfect square.
- Pressing the Shift key constrains the Oval tool to perfect circles.
- Pressing the Alt/Option key causes any of these shapes to be created from the center out rather than from corner to corner. You can combine Shift keys and Alt/Option keys as necessary.

Rectangle and Oval Primitive tools

In addition to the standard Rectangle and Oval tools, Animate CC offers two tools that create primitive versions of the same shapes, with characteristics that can be modified in the Properties inspector (**Figure 2.11**). When using the Rectangle tool, you have an option to create rounded corners through the Properties panel before drawing the shape or even while drawing the shape by pressing your arrow keys. Unfortunately, you cannot edit this property after you've created the shape. This is where the primitive tools come into play.

Figure 2.11 The Rectangle Primitive Tool Properties inspector

The Rectangle Primitive tool lets you create a shape object that has editable corner-rounding. This is a great feature for customizing rounded tabs; without it, you would need to keep guessing at the proper rounding value as you redrew rectangles.

The Oval Primitive tool lets you select starting angles and ending angles that create a pie-chart–type graphic. You can also specify an inner radius to create a donut shape. This feature is often used to make elements for circular arrows that frequently show up in artwork used for preloading interactive media elements.

Merge drawing vs. object drawing

By default, the shape tools in Animate CC draw objects in standard Merge Drawing mode. The problem with drawing in this standard mode occurs when you have shapes that overlap each other. In Merge Drawing mode you draw all shapes on the same level, and new shapes delete anything underneath them. You can get around this by choosing Modify > Group from the application menu to group shapes as you create them. Alternatively, you can draw all of them on separate layers.

Another solution is to draw your objects in Object Drawing mode. You can toggle this mode on and off by clicking the circular icon (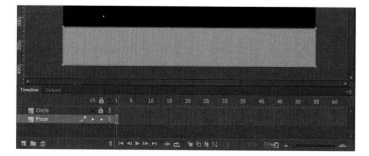) at the bottom of the Tools panel. Turning on this option forces Animate CC to draw every new shape as a separate object that is very similar to a grouped object. If you need to modify a base shape created using Object Drawing mode, first you need to double-click that object with the Selection tool to move inside the object. Once inside the object, the familiar shape controls should be available.

TIP

You can keep track of your current location in the document hierarchy by looking at the breadcrumb trail in the top-left corner of the Document window, just below the menu.

Drawing shapes

Now let's draw some shapes.

▶ **Video 2.4** *Drawing the Floor*

1 To draw out the Floor layer contents, do one of the following (or if you have the time, try both):

   ▪ Choose the Rectangle tool and be sure that Object Drawing mode is turned on.

   ▪ Choose the Rectangle Primitive tool for this project.

2 Regardless of which tool you've chosen, click the Floor layer to select it (**Figure 2.12**).

Figure 2.12 Selecting the Floor layer

3 Drag across the Stage to form a rectangular floor shape. Don't worry about the color of your assets right now—you can change that later.

4   Lock down this layer so you don't accidentally modify it.

▶ **Video 2.5** *Drawing a Ball*

5   Choose one of the oval shape tools and select the Circle layer (**Figure 2.13**).

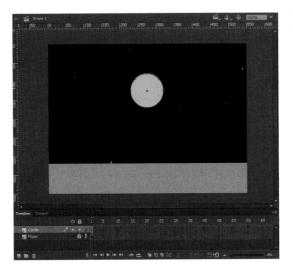

Figure 2.13 Circle layer selected

6   Hold down the Shift key; then click and drag a circle on the Stage. Don't make it too big—about 80–100 pixels should do fine.

▶ **Video 2.6** *Use the Align Panel*

7   If the Align panel isn't visible in your current workspace configuration, choose Window > Align in the application menu to access it.

8   Center the ball vertically on the stage and then align it with the top as well. Then scoot it down about 10 pixels after aligning it to the top.

▶ **Video 2.7** *Testing the Project*

9   Now that you have drawn all of your elements, preview the content by choosing Control > Test.

ARRANGING STACKING ORDER

You can also manage the depth of interactive media elements within a single layer on the timeline. You can do so by adjusting what is often referred to as the Z-order: elements can be shifted forward or back one step at a time, or they can be forced to the front or back at once. You do this by choosing Modify > Arrange or by right-clicking an object on the Stage.

When working with simple vector shapes in Animate CC, depths are automatically flattened. This can cause problems when dealing with overlapping shapes on a single layer, as they will delete portions of one another. To prevent this, you can turn on Object Drawing mode at the bottom of the Tools panel before you create basic shape elements.

Additional vector creation tools

In this project you're using only a few of the vector creation tools available in Animate CC. Before moving on, let's have a quick look at some of the additional tools at our disposal.

★ ACA Objective 3.2

LINE TOOL

The Line tool (![line tool icon]) creates a shape that is entirely composed of a single stroke. There is no fill whatsoever when you're working with the Line tool. Holding down the Shift key ensures that the line you create is completely straight along the horizontal axis, along the vertical axis, or at a 45-degree angle.

PENCIL TOOL

Just as is the case with the Line tool, using the Pencil tool (![pencil tool icon]) creates a shape consisting of one stroke only. The major difference is that the Line tool produces only straight lines and the Pencil tool is much more freeform in execution.

At the bottom of the Tools panel, you will find a Pencil Mode icon (![pencil mode icon]), which provides options to straighten, smooth, or ink the stroke created with the Pencil tool. Choosing the Straighten option tells Animate CC to guess what type of line you were attempting to create and automatically straighten things out. The Smooth option softens the curves and smooths out your line. The Ink option creates a line exactly where you drag.

BRUSH TOOL

Similar to how the Pencil tool and Line tool will create vector shapes consisting of strokes, the Brush tool (![brush tool icon]) creates a shape that has no stroke and only fill. It works in a freeform way similar to the Pencil tool in that you can draw all sorts of forms with it.

At the bottom of the Tools panel you'll find options for the Brush tool that let you modify the brush size and shape (**Figure 2.14**). These options also let you selectively create the fill based on what is already on the screen. You can choose to paint only behind the current artwork or only within a selection.

A final option on the Brush tool is the option to lock the fill. Choosing this causes a fill to be shared between multiple brushstrokes. How this works should be apparent when you use a bitmap fill or a gradient fill with the Brush tool.

Figure 2.14 Brush tool options

PAINT BRUSH TOOL

This is a brand-new tool to Animate CC that expands the creative possibilities available to you. When you use the Paint Brush tool (), Animate CC creates a stroke and then maps vector artwork onto that stroke. The Paint Brush tool uses art brushes from the Brush Library panel (**Figure 2.15**), or you can import art brushes from the CC Libraries panel after creating them with the Adobe Capture mobile app.

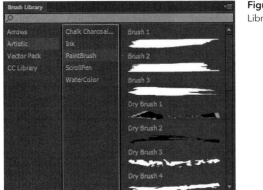

Figure 2.15 The Brush Library panel

PEN TOOL

The Pen tool (⬤) is the basic tool for creating and editing Bézier curves. It works in conjunction with the Subselection tool (⬤) to modify existing paths. It takes a while to master the Pen tool, but the power and control it allows make learning this tool worth the effort.

To create a curve, you can simply click your way around to create straight corner points, or you can drag a little at each anchor point to create a curved path. Clicking and holding the Pen Tool icon in the Tools panel will reveal additional editing options such as the Add Anchor Point tool and Delete Anchor Point tool.

ADD ANCHOR POINT TOOL

The Add Anchor Point tool (⬤) adds anchor points when you click the edge of a curve. This allows heavy modification of paths through increased complexity.

DELETE ANCHOR POINT TOOL

The Delete Anchor Point tool (⬤) removes anchor points from a curve when you click them.

CONVERT ANCHOR POINT TOOL

The Convert Anchor Point tool ( ) turns a curved anchor point into a straight anchor point with a click. You can also turn a straight anchor point into a curved anchor point by clicking the anchor point and dragging out a set of handles for further manipulation.

POLYSTAR TOOL

The PolyStar tool ( ) gives you the ability to create a shape in the form of either a polygon or a star. When using this tool, you can specify many aspects of the shape, such as how many points you want the star to have or how many sides you want the polygon to have. The resulting shape consists of both stroke and fill.

Working with Vector Shapes

Animate CC has an interesting quirk that isn't seen in many other artwork programs. When a vector object is created, it can be made up of a fill and/or a stroke. Most programs treat the fill and the stroke as a single object. Animate CC lets you access the fill, the stroke, or both, depending on how you select the objects.

Similarly, there are various tools that deal specifically with either fills or strokes. Let's have a look at some of them now.

Selecting visual elements

Animate CC has a variety of tools for enabling the selection of entire elements, or even the partial selection of certain elements. For instance, you can use the Selection tool to select a stroke or fill, the Lasso tool to perform a more freeform and precise selection, or the Magic Wand to choose calculated portions of an element.

SELECTION TOOL

The Selection tool ( ) provides several ways to modify an existing shape. You can select the stroke, the fill, or both, and drag them around the Stage. By selecting these objects, you can also access properties within the Properties inspector and modifiers at the bottom of the Tools panel.

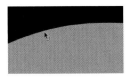

Figure 2.16 Shape-tweaking with the Selection tool

Another, less obvious use of the Selection tool involves hovering over an unselected stroke. A cursor will appear, indicating that you can bend the stroke. Pressing and dragging when you see this cursor will bend the stroke and take the fill along for the ride (**Figure 2.16**).

SUBSELECTION TOOL

Working with vectors can take some practice, but it is a skill that is absolutely essential for any interactive media producer. To edit a vector using the Subselection tool, you need to understand that there are two types of points that define a vector.

The first is an anchor point: a square point that lies directly on the edge of an object. You can move anchor points by clicking and dragging.

The other type of point associated with vector drawings is the control point. Control points are shown as dots on the end of a line attached to the anchor point. Moving the control points around determines how the curve will pass through the anchor point.

LASSO TOOL

The Lasso tool ( ) in Animate CC lets you select content by looping the cursor around shapes or portions of shapes. The ability to do this with vector objects isn't common in creative applications, but it does show up in other Adobe products such as Illustrator.

POLYGON TOOL

The Polygon tool ( ) is similar to the Lasso tool but allows the creation of straight-edged selections. These are formed by clicking the mouse rather than dragging around the area to select. The clicks are joined by a straight-edged selection to create a polygon. You can finalize the selection by double-clicking.

MAGIC WAND

The Magic Wand ( ) lets you click an area of a shape and select all similarly colored, contiguous shapes. You can access settings to adjust the allowable color variation and overall smoothing by clicking the options setting button, directly below the Magic Wand setting.

> **NOTE**
>
> *Using the Selection tool to bend strokes isn't usually the best way to approach the problem. Modifying the vectors with Bézier curves using the Subselection tool provides more precise control over the resultant curve.*

Modifying shape color

Whether you're changing the color of a fill or a stroke, Animate CC is certainly not afraid to provide you with enough tools to get the job done. A number of tools in the Tools panel allow you to select and modify color. If that isn't enough, two panels are dedicated to this effort as well.

PAINT BUCKET TOOL

The Paint Bucket tool ( ) lets you fill or modify the fill of an existing shape with the current fill color as determined in the Properties inspector or at the bottom of the Tools panel. Simply select a color in either of these areas, and click the area to be filled or the existing fill. Keep in mind that this will work only on a shape and only on a shape that is not currently selected.

INK BOTTLE TOOL

The Ink Bottle tool ( ), accessed by clicking and holding the Paint Bucket tool icon in the Tools panel, does exactly the same thing as the Paint Bucket tool but affects only strokes.

EYEDROPPER TOOL

The Eyedropper tool ( ) lets you select an existing fill or stroke and automatically sets up either a Paint Bucket tool or an Ink Bottle tool with the same settings as the shape element that you clicked.

THE SWATCHES PANEL

By default, the Swatches panel (**Figure 2.17**) is preloaded with the 216-color web-safe palette plus a few specialty fills, but it can be modified to hold only the colors or fills associated with a particular job. Pressing Ctrl/Command while clicking a color will remove a swatch, and going to a blank area of the Swatches panel with a color defined within the Color panel will let you drop that color into the Swatches panel.

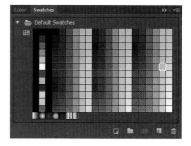

Figure 2.17 The Swatches panel

> **NOTE** *The swatch settings are stored with the FLA file, so there's no need to reload them every time you open the file.*

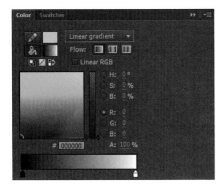

Figure 2.18 The Color panel

THE COLOR PANEL

The Color panel in Animate CC (**Figure 2.18**) allows you to accurately specify colors as well as more complex fills like gradients and bitmap-based fills. Notice that the areas for defining the fill and the stroke are separate. It's a common mistake to be adjusting the stroke and get frustrated when the fill color isn't changing.

In addition to holding simple colors, the Color panel lets you create gradients. You can add color stops within the gradient by clicking beneath the gradient window of the Color panel. Double-clicking the small square under the color stop will allow you to select the color for that area of the gradient. Dragging a color stop off the panel will delete it.

You can also use the Color panel to load bitmaps as fill areas. This lets you set an image as a fill style. Just choosing the bitmap fill from the drop-down menu will prompt you to select a bitmap image. If bitmaps are already loaded into your Library, they'll be available as possible fill selections.

Time to Animate!

★ *ACA Objective 4.5*

Now you'll add some animation to your project. Since you're dealing with vector shapes, you'll be using a *shape tween* to perform the animation. When you declare a shape tween across a span of frames, you need at least two keyframes defined. This is how Animate CC knows to fill in the between frames: it calculates motion based on the change in properties between keyframes.

Frames are the basic building blocks of a timeline. They represent chunks of time defined by the frame rate of the document. If the frame rate is 24 frames per second (fps), then the playhead will move through 24 of the small squares per second. This determines the speed of the animation.

Keyframes are special frames that contain information about new visual content, or changes in existing content present within previous keyframes. Animate CC provides two main methods of animating content: using a frame-by-frame approach or through the Animate CC tweening system.

NOTE

Keep in mind that only a keyframe can contain content. You cannot place content in a timeline without first inserting a keyframe. That keyframe can be stretched across multiple frames of the timeline.

▶ *Video 2.8 Frames and Keyframes*

A keyframe with no content is called a **blank keyframe** and is represented by a frame with an unfilled circle.

Inserting a frame span

You'll continue building this bouncing-ball project by inserting a frame span.

1   Using the mouse, select frame 30 across both the Circle and Floor layers. To do this, click the topmost frame and drag down to the bottom one.

   Frame 30 of each layer should be highlighted.

2   In the application menu, choose Insert > Timeline > Frame.

   Animate CC not only inserts a frame at frame 30 (**Figure 2.19**) but also fills in the entire span of frames up to that point. Since we begin on frame 1 with a keyframe and there's content in that keyframe, that content is visually represented across the entire span of frames from 1 to 30. You can confirm this by scrubbing the playhead through the frames in the span.

Figure 2.19 Frames inserted

Making use of keyframes

The tweening engine in Animate CC requires you to define at least two keyframes. Keyframes are special frames that hold information about shape and instance properties. In this project, you'll modify the y position of your circle shape. Animate CC will examine the number of frames between each pair of keyframes and calculate the properties for the object on each frame, based on the difference in properties between the two declared keyframes.

1   To insert a keyframe into the project, move the playhead to frame 15, making sure the Circle layer is selected.

2   Frame 15 is the midpoint of the bounce animation, so you'll move the ball shape down until it is resting on the floor. To do this, choose Insert > Timeline > Keyframe from the application menu.

   Animate CC inserts a new keyframe, identical to the existing keyframe (**Figure 2.20**).

Figure 2.20 Keyframes created

3   Choose the Selection tool. Use this tool to select the circle shape on frame 15 and drag it down to the bottom of the Stage until it rests visually on the floor shape.

Copying and pasting keyframes

You now have the properties set for the start and midpoint of your animation. Next, you need to take care of the end. If you want the animation to loop smoothly, then you'll need the properties of your shape on the ending keyframe to match the starting one. You could select the shape present on frame 1 and take notes regarding the positioning properties to copy bit by bit into the closing keyframe—but there's a simpler way: paste in place.

1   Move the playhead to frame 30.

2   Making sure the Circle layer is selected, choose Insert > Timeline > Blank Keyframe from the application menu to insert an empty keyframe just waiting for you to paste in some content.

3   Move the playhead back to frame 1 and use the Selection tool to select the shape present there. Right-click and choose Copy.

4   Move the playhead back to frame 30, right-click the Stage, and choose Paste in Place (**Figure 2.21**).

Animate CC pastes in the shape with all of its properties, filling the keyframe.

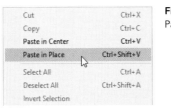

Figure 2.21 Choosing Paste in Place

Alternatively, you can copy the frame itself. To do this, right-click a keyframe and choose Copy Frames. Now you can select any frame on the timeline, right-click, and choose Paste and Overwrite Frames. It's that easy!

Creating a shape tween

Now that you've established all of your keyframes, it's time to tell Animate CC to fill in the frames between those keyframes.

1 Click and drag across both frame spans—that is, some frames before frame 15 and some after.

2 Right-click the selected frames and choose Create Shape Tween.

The frames in question turn a green color with a thin arrow pointing from left to right. This tells us that the shape tween has been created successfully (**Figure 2.22**).

Figure 2.22 Shape tween created

USING SHAPE HINTS

Unfortunately, shape tweens don't always take the route from one shape to another that you might have had in mind. Sometimes it's necessary to give the shapes some guidance.

You can find shape hints in the Modify > Shape > Add Shape Hints menu. This option allows you to place alphabetical reference points on both ends of the tween to anchor areas of the shape and control the path of the shape transition. Normally, you'd need to do this only when tweening from one shape to another.

▶ **Video 2.9**
Animating with Shape Tweens

NOTE

If you try to apply a motion tween to a shape, Animate CC will prompt you to convert that shape to a symbol first. This is not a great idea, since it will create a bunch of elements in your library named symbol #. Elements without descriptive names can be hard to track as the project grows.

FRAME-BY-FRAME ANIMATION

Frame-by-frame animation is the simplest and most primitive form of animation used in interactive media applications. This type of animation is similar to that of old-school animation techniques—created keyframe by keyframe. Just as in traditional hand-drawn animation, the background can be used for numerous animation cells through the use of layers.

The upside to frame-by-frame animation is that anything that can be drawn can be animated. The downsides include larger files when compared with those created using other animation methods. Frame-by-frame animation can also be tedious and time-consuming to produce.

Modify Animation through Easing

If you preview the animation right now, it appears stiff and lifeless even though there's constant motion. The animation appears mechanical because it is: based on the instruction we've given it so far, Animate CC is simply calculating the motion in a strictly linear fashion to achieve the animation. You can make the animation appear much more dynamic and lifelike by taking both the easing and overall timing into consideration.

Adding some impact

▶ **Video 2.10** *Squish the Ball on Impact*

Now you'll squish your circle as it impacts against the floor using the Free Transform tool. You use this tool to scale, skew, rotate, and even reposition elements on the Stage.

1   Select the Free Transform tool from the Tools panel and use it to click the circle shape at frame 15. Frame 15 is a keyframe and the content is, during this frame, in visual contact with the floor.

USING THE FREE TRANSFORM TOOL

The Free Transform tool enables you to transform a shape in four essential ways.

- **Scaling** is accomplished by dragging the square dots along a shape's edges and corners. If you drag a corner point while holding down the Shift key, you preserve the aspect ratio of the original element. In other words, it will be scaled the same amount in both the horizontal and vertical directions.

- **Skewing** is achieved by dragging the edges in between the dots. The cursor changes into a skewing icon as you roll over an edge.

- **Rotation** is done by moving the cursor just off the corner points until it changes and then dragging to rotate. Holding down the Shift key will constrain the rotation to 45-degree increments. Moving the round dot in the middle of the transformation selection allows you to adjust the axis of rotation. For example, you'd use this technique to rotate the hands of a clock by moving the dot to the bottom of the clock hand.

Clicking and dragging anywhere on the graphic element other than the control edges or points allows the Free Transform tool to act just like the Selection tool.

2   Drag the small white circle at the center of the shape to the bottom of the shape. Known as the *transform point*, this allows transforms to be pinned to that specific point.

3   Next, grab the small square that appears at the top center of the transform rectangle and pull it toward the transform point to "squish" the circle to some extent (**Figure 2.23**).

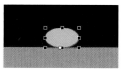

Figure 2.23 Circle squished with the Free Transform tool

MAKING USE OF ONION SKINNING

Animate CC has two options that let you visualize animations across frames. Onion skins and wireframes, both found in the Timeline panel, serve a similar purpose by allowing you to see ghosted or outlined versions of a selected range of frames within an animation. These techniques work for all timeline animation types.

> ▶ *Video 2.11 Using Onion Skinning*

Adding and adjusting keyframes

By default, tweens work in a linear fashion; in other words, halfway through the tween span, the properties are exactly halfway between the start and finish values. If you preview the animation, you'll notice that even though the shape does squish at frame 15, every other frame includes at least some bit of squish to it, and that's just unnatural.

1   To remedy this, insert blank keyframes at frames 14–17.

2   Copy the circle shape from frame 1 and use the Paste in Place command to place the circle within both of the empty keyframes you just created (**Figure 2.24**).

Figure 2.24 Circle placed

3   In each instance, move the shape down to the top of our floor.

Now when you preview, you can see that the shape is placed in the coordinates where it would be expected to be at that frame. It can take some interpretation, so use your eye!

Applying easing for a more natural look

▶ **Video 2.12** *Apply Easing to a Tween*

Applying an ease can add a nice touch to make a tween sequence look even more natural. Easing is used to determine how the properties are tweened from beginning to end. The ease will indicate whether the animated sequence will speed up, slow down, or remain steady throughout the length of the animation.

NOTE

Ease values range from –100 to 100. When you select a high positive ease value for the tween, the properties will change quickly in the beginning and then slow down at the end. Selecting a negative value will cause the changes to accelerate through the span of the tween.

1 To apply the ease to the first frame span (1–13), select any of the frames in that span, and adjust the Ease value in the Tweening Properties panel to –60 (**Figure 2.25**).

Figure 2.25 Adjusting the Ease value in the Tweening Properties panel

2 For the second lengthy frame span, which covers frames 17–29, repeat step 1, applying an Ease value of 60.

3 Preview the nearly completed animation. Everything should loop in a natural and believable way, simulating a bouncing ball on a hard surface.

Adjusting the overall frame rate

▶ **Video 2.13** *Adjusting the FPS*

The overall frame rate of a Animate CC project determines how quickly the playhead will move through the frames of the timeline. You set the frame rate at the bottom of the timeline or through the Properties inspector (**Figure 2.26**).

TIP

Never go beyond the frame rate that can be played on the target output device, or your animation will become choppy. Another common mistake is adjusting the timing of an individual animation by adjusting the overall frame rate. Although this will work, it will cause any other animations to speed up or slow down. Use keyframes and your timeline to modify the duration of an animation.

Figure 2.26 Setting frames per second (FPS) in the Properties inspector

Your choice of frame rate depends on target the playback device(s) and the nature of the interactive media content. Although higher frame rates should produce smoother animations, the use of higher frame rates can also create larger files and more work when using frame-by-frame animations.

Play around with the project frame rate to see how adjusting the fps affects the look of the animation. If you want to adjust the timing of your animation, the best way to do so is to adjust the number of frames across the timeline, effectively lengthening or shortening the animation. When you're pleased with everything, feel free to move on to publication.

Publishing the Animation for Flash Player

Once you've created your Animate document, you can preview it within the authoring environment only by using the Control > Test Movie menu option. At this point, the project is still just an authoring file and people will not be able to view your FLA project unless they have Animate CC installed on their machine as well. For most of your target audience, this will certainly *not* be the case!

So how do you get your awesome project out to the world? It's really quite easy— you need only publish the project in a widely consumable format. This could be Flash Player, Adobe AIR, or even HTML5 Canvas or WebGL. Since this project was built with Flash Player in mind, we'll focus on that target platform.

Publishing for Flash Player

The primary output for an ActionScript document type in Animate CC is the browser-based Flash Player (**Figure 2.27**). Software that runs within Flash Player is packaged as a compiled SWF file. The acronym SWF comes from ShockWave Flash. "Shockwave" refers to the web-distributable file type for projects created for the web with Adobe Director—an older application that had a number of similarities, initially, to Animate CC. The SWF file is typically embedded within an HTML structure and delivered via a web page.

★ *ACA Objective 5.4*

Figure 2.27 Adobe Flash Player

Different web browser and operating systems can handle Flash Player very differently. For instance, if you're using the Microsoft Windows 10 Edge browser or Google Chrome, Flash Player is built in as a part of the native experience. If you're using the OS X Safari browser or Mozilla Firefox, you'll have to install Flash Player and manage it as a separate extension.

Most mobile web browsers do *not* support Flash Player in any form. If you're targeting mobile browsers via Animate CC, you should consider using HTML5 Canvas or WebGL document types. You also have the option of creating a native mobile app using Adobe AIR, but not all content is suitable as an app.

As of this writing, Flash Player is at version 19. Adobe continues to improve Flash Player features with quarterly major updates along with smaller security updates at shorter intervals to address specific problems that may arise.

ActionScript 3.0 Publish Settings

The first publishing target we'll look at in this book is for ActionScript 3.0 documents. You might be a bit confused about the naming convention here—isn't ActionScript a programming language? Yes, but it also provides the core target platform for Flash Player as well as Adobe AIR for Desktop, for Android, and for iOS.

Generally, if you've chosen to create an ActionScript 3.0 document in Animate CC, you're targeting the browser-based Flash Player runtime. However, you can easily switch between ActionScript-based targets by switching the Target property of the document in the Properties panel.

The Publish Settings dialog box (**Figure 2.28**, accessed from the File menu) lets you specify how Animate CC will create the output file of an interactive media application. This dialog box lets you select the format and versioning information necessary to deliver your interactive media application to a wide variety of platforms and formats.

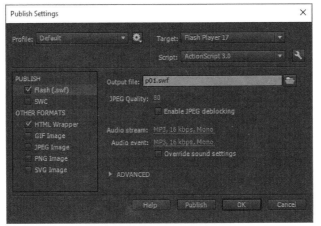

Figure 2.28 The Publish Settings dialog box

PROFILE SETTINGS

The Profile section of the Publish Settings dialog box is a huge timesaver for those who regularly publish to a variety of devices and platforms. Getting your settings just right can often require you to publish your document several times as you tweak the options of the Publish Settings dialog box.

By saving a profile with a descriptive name, you can quickly access those settings at a later date. For instance, you could be creating an Adobe AIR application for delivery to Mac and Windows desktop computers. Once you get the settings working properly, saving the profile as **AIR for Desktop** would allow you to quickly recall the settings that worked for you in the past.

TARGET SETTINGS

The Flash Player runtime and Adobe AIR platforms are constantly being updated to provide improved performance, capabilities, and security. Both of these playback engines attempt to update themselves continually to remain current. Adobe currently releases a major new version of the runtimes every quarter, with smaller security and stability updates in between.

Unfortunately, not all internal networks let users automatically update their software. In these cases, it may be necessary to select the lowest common denominator within an organization. Some organizations have a vetting process that a software update must go through before it is deployed to the entire network, so they might not be using the most current playback software.

SCRIPT SETTINGS

Flash Player uses a programming language called ActionScript to create interactivity within an interactive media application. This language has gone through several iterations; the latest is ActionScript 3.0.

ActionScript 3.0 can be a little more verbose than previous versions of ActionScript, but the performance and capabilities of this latest version make upgrading well worth the effort. Using ActionScript 3.0 will let you deliver to a wider variety of platforms, while also enhancing performance and security.

Animate CC no longer supports older versions of ActionScript. If you need to work with files created with an earlier version of ActionScript, you must use an older version of Animate CC.

NOTE

When targeting HTML5 Canvas or WebGL, the programming language you'll use will be JavaScript since you're targeting the web browser itself.

OUTPUT FILE OPTION

The Output File option in the Publish Settings dialog box lets you select the location and name of the output SWF file. This location defaults to the same directory as the FLA file.

JPEG QUALITY

Bitmaps within Animate CC are published using a version of JPEG. This format is a lossy compression scheme that decreases file size by sacrificing quality. When you publish a SWF file, all included images are compressed to keep everything nice and tidy. Setting the quality here will affect the quality of only the images included in the SWF file; lowering the image quality in the Publish Settings will have no effect on the quality of the images currently being stored as part of the FLA document.

An additional Enable JPEG Deblocking option is also available. This option helps minimize the blocky JPEG artifacts that can occur when you select lower-quality JPEG settings.

These settings affect only images that do not have a custom JPEG quality selected within the Bitmap Properties settings (which you access by right-clicking a bitmap file within the Library panel).

AUDIO QUALITY

You can set the quality of audio events and streams at publish time, just as you set the quality of a bitmap image. You can set compression schemes and compression values to make the files smaller.

Just as with bitmaps, you can use a custom setting for the audio or force all audio files to use the global settings in the Publish Settings dialog box.

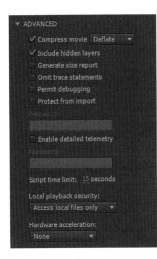

Figure 2.29 Advanced publish settings

ADVANCED PUBLISH SETTINGS

It's good to familiarize yourself with the specifics of the advanced settings as they can help increase security, performance, and search engine visibility if used correctly.

The Advanced settings (**Figure 2.29**) include these options:

- **Compress movie:** This option compresses the SWF file to enable faster downloads.

- **Include hidden layers:** Unlike other Adobe products, Flash automatically includes hidden layers in the final output.

- **Generate size report:** This option generates a report detailing the file size and download requirements of the output.

- **Omit trace statements:** Trace statements are often used for debugging during Flash development. Omitting trace statements prevents the results of the trace statements from showing up in an output window. This output window is usually not available to the end user anyway, so it isn't a huge issue.

- **Permit debugging:** This option allows the output to be viewable using the Flash debugger.
- **Protect from import:** Password-protecting your final output prevents another Flash user from loading and decompiling your Flash project.
- **Script time limit:** This setting caps the amount of time that a script can run. This can prevent an excessive or infinite loop in the code from locking up an end user's player. Good design should prevent the need to address this option.

PLAYBACK SECURITY

The Flash Player Publish Settings also include two options that directly relate to network security and performance: "Local playback security" and "Hardware acceleration."

The "Local playback security" option determines if the interactive media application can access files that are local to the published file or files that are contained within a different domain space. You must choose one or the other, since allowing Flash Player to reach across from local to remote domains could result in serious security issues.

Hardware acceleration determines what level of access the interactive media application has to the end user's local hardware. Your options are as follows:

- **None:** Select this option to prevent the interactive media application from accessing additional hardware that would enhance performance; this option provides the highest level of security.
- **Level 1: Direct:** This option lets the Flash Player bypass the browser and draw directly on the screen. Performance is enhanced, but the direct access could be a security issue.
- **Level 2: GPU:** This option not only allows direct access but also allows the Flash Player to use the graphics processing unit (GPU) on the end user's video card to help manage the graphics on the screen. Depending on the video card, this can be a huge improvement when working with video or other processor-intensive animations. Directly accessing the video card may present security concerns, but the added performance might be worth the risk.

PUBLISH SETTINGS: HTML

When publishing a standard Flash Player SWF file for use in a web environment, it's always a good idea to include a sample HTML file. You can customize this file to specify how the movie is displayed on the page.

NOTE

This approach does not apply to publishing in an HTML5 format. This applies to SWF files embedded in HTML only.

Setting these custom values and publishing the document will create an HTML document that you can study to determine how the SWF file was embedded and the results of the various embedding parameters.

Publishing a SWF

There are numerous ways in which a SWF can be published, based on the defined Publish Settings, for any Animate CC project targeting Flash Player. In fact, if you've previewed the animation at all up to this point through the application menu command Control > Test, you've already done so!

▶ ***Video 2.14*** *Publish for Flash Player*

To publish a SWF in a more intentional and direct way, you can use the File > Publish command or choose Publish from the Publish Settings dialog box.

Generating a projector

▶ ***Video 2.15*** *Generate a Projector*

Animate CC lets you create self-contained applications called projectors. These projectors can be created for both Mac OS and Windows platforms from either Mac OS or Windows versions of Animate CC. To generate a projector, choose Commands > Export as Projector from the application menu (**Figure 2.30**).

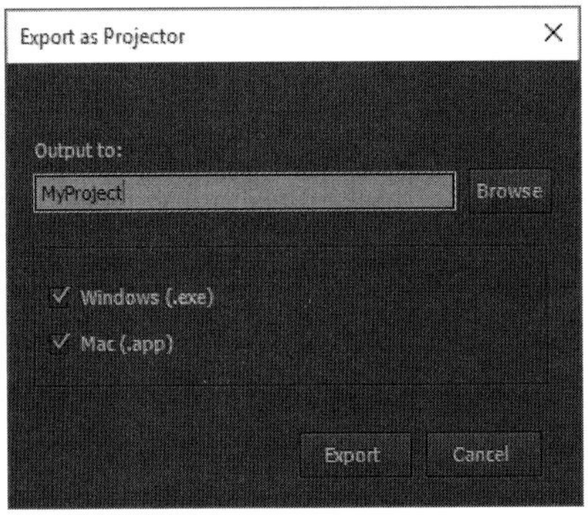

Figure 2.30 Generating a projector

NOTE

Unlike Adobe AIR applications, projectors do not even need to be installed–they just run.

Projectors don't require the use of a plug-in or browser, so they're easy to use and you don't have to install additional software. This format is a popular option for delivering Flash interactive media using USB drives, CDs, and hard drives.

Because it's so easy to install this format, it's a good option to consider when developing kiosks and presentations if you don't want or need the additional features or complexities of using Adobe AIR installers.

Challenge!

As we have designed the animation, it will continue to loop as long as the movie is running. It will never stop, and the ball itself will never adapt to forces like friction or inertia. However, when you're creating a simulation, it's important to consider every aspect of the system you're working in.

As a challenge, why not incorporate these other factors into the project? The bounce would decrease over time and the speed and height would lessen until the ball eventually just stops. Using what you've learned, you can use Animate CC to simulate this progression. Give it a go!

Conclusion

We covered a lot of content in this chapter! We looked at creating and preparing documents; creating shape assets; managing the timeline; animating through frames, keyframes, and tweening; making animation more natural and pleasant; and publishing your project.

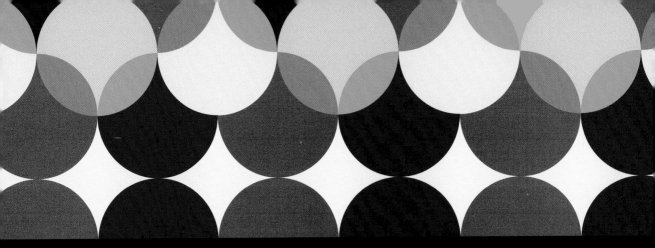

CHAPTER OBJECTIVES

Chapter Learning Objectives

- Manage layers in the timeline
- Import images to the Stage and Library
- Work with vectors
- Use masking to hide and reveal objects
- Create text elements
- Learn how to export a design in a variety of image formats

Chapter ACA Objectives

DOMAIN 3.0
UNDERSTANDING ADOBE FLASH PROFESSIONAL

3.2 Define the functions of commonly used tools, including selection tools, the Pen tool, other drawing tools, and shape tools.

3.4 Use design tools in the interface, such as rulers and guides.

3.6 Demonstrate knowledge of layers and masks.

3.7 Understand symbols and the Library.

DOMAIN 4.0
CREATING INTERACTIVE MEDIA CONTENT USING FLASH PROFESSIONAL

4.1 Create a new project.

4.2 Import and modify graphics.

4.3 Create static, dynamic, and input text and adjust text properties.

4.7 Create masks.

DOMAIN 5.0
TESTING, PUBLISHING, AND EVALUATING INTERACTIVE MEDIA ELEMENTS USING FLASH PROFESSIONAL

5.2 Understand Flash file types and file sizes.

5.4 Publish and export Flash documents.

CHAPTER 3

Construct an Internet Meme Image

You can use the basic tools in Adobe Animate CC to build a wide variety of projects. In this chapter, you'll use them to create a static **meme** image. Beyond the vector elements you used in Chapter 1, you'll work with imported bitmaps and text elements. In addition to these topics, you'll explore the Stage and timeline to see how to arrange and manage assets within your project.

> **NOTE** *Adobe has rebranded Flash Professional CC as Animate CC! They are essentially the exact same application—with absolutely no differences in capability aside from features introduced in the regular update schedule. All future updates to Flash Professional CC will be known by the name Animate CC. If desired, subscribers can run multiple versions of the product—branded as either Flash Professional or Animate—but I highly recommend using the latest available version of Animate CC to take advantage of all new features.*

This project is more of a graphic design project than anything else, using three core assets types: bitmap images, vector shapes, and text. You've been tasked by a client to create an Internet meme image (**Figure 3.1**). Apparently the client expects to get rich off these things—go figure. For an initial image, they've sent over a photo of their cat with some suggested text. The client does mention, however, that if you have anything you think is likely to "go more viral," you can use that instead.

▶ **Video 3.1** *Project Overview*

> **NOTE**
> *All of the videos for this book were recorded with a version of Animate CC branded as Flash Professional CC. It is important to note that everything that we demonstrate in the recordings can be applied to Animate CC—even if we refer to the application as Flash Professional. They are essentially the exact same application—with absolutely no differences in capability.*

Figure 3.1 The meme image you'll create in this chapter

Starting the Project

You'll begin by creating a new Animate document. The type of document you choose doesn't matter since any of the supported document types can be used to output a static image like the one we'll design here. However, if you choose an ActionScript 3.0 document type, you'll have access to all the tools and effects available within the software. So for this project, you'll use a standard ActionScript 3.0 document.

Don't worry about having to use the same document type for two projects in a row. You'll explore other document types throughout this book. But because the idea with this project is to start off simple and explore core functionality, it makes sense to employ the document type that Animate CC is most comfortable with. What's more, as mentioned previously, this allows you to use any tools you want.

Creating the project document

★ *ACA Objective 4.1*

▶ **Video 3.2** *Setting Up Our Project*

Let's begin.

1 Create a new ActionScript 3.0 document with a Stage resolution of 500px in width and height (**Figure 3.2**). The Stage color and fps are completely up to you. In fact, since we're producing a still image in this project, fps bears no consequence whatsoever.

CHOOSING A PROJECT TYPE

When choosing a new project document type, choosing ActionScript 3.0 doesn't mean you need to write any code for the project. It simply means that the target platform will be one of the Adobe runtimes, Flash Player or Adobe AIR. It also means that you'll be able to use all the tool options in Animate CC for any particular project.

2 Save the document as a new FLA file. Continue to save your project often.

NOTE *Animate CC now has the ability to autosave documents as well. This setting is on by default, but you can disable it or customize it by using the Preferences dialog box's General tab. Look for the Autorecovery option and you'll see it's a simple check box toggle. Also note that you can specify how many minutes you want the application to wait between automatic saves.*

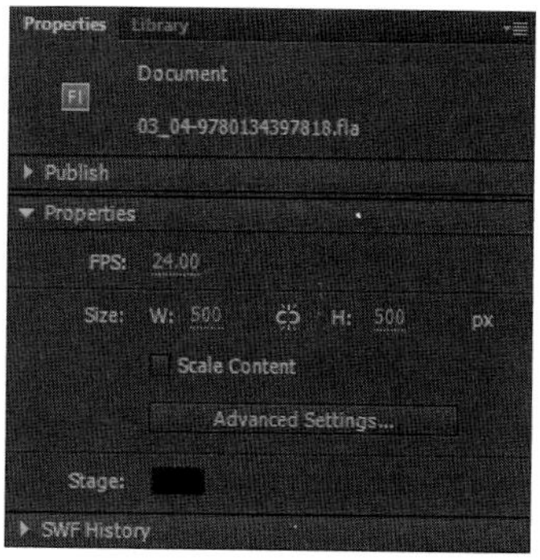

Figure 3.2 The Stage Properties panel

Setting up your project

★ *ACA Objective 3.4*

In the previous chapter, I went into some detail around snapping and how to modify the settings that go along with it. For this project, enabling rulers and guides will be of even greater importance when laying out the design. Let's have a look at these features before going any further into the project.

Guides and rulers help accurately place objects and identify specific areas of the visible project area. Interactive media applications are typically designed and created using pixels as a ruler unit, so create any preliminary artwork with this in mind.

ENABLING RULERS AND THE GRID

Rulers will not be visible by default. If the rulers are not currently visible in your project, you can enable them by selecting View > Rulers from the application menu to activate them (**Figure 3.3**).

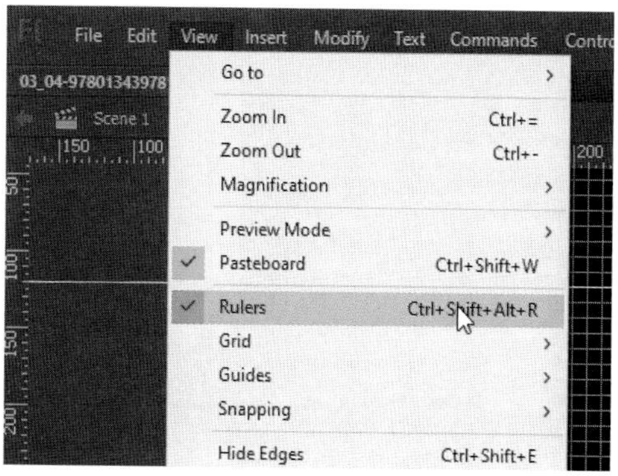

Figure 3.3 Activating rulers

▶ *Video 3.3 Rulers and Guides*

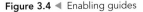

Similarly, you'll need to enable and modify the grid if you wish to use it in a project. The grid will not be enabled by default, but you can activate it by choosing View > Grid > Show Grid from the application menu. You can also edit grid spacing by choosing the Edit Grid option instead.

NOTE

Settings for rulers, the grid, and guides can (and should!) be managed in individual documents.

CREATING AND MANAGING GUIDES

Guides are the light blue lines that show up only while authoring, and they aren't visible in the final published file. Be sure to enable rulers first if you want to employ the use of guides within your project. To create a guide, place your cursor in the middle of either the horizontal ruler or the vertical ruler. Drag from the ruler to automatically create a new guide that you can place where needed. As you might imagine, the horizontal ruler produces horizontal guides; the vertical ruler produces vertical guides.

MODIFYING GUIDES AND GUIDE PROPERTIES

NOTE

With your rulers, grid, and guides properly configured, it will be much easier to draw and lay out all the elements of your project, no matter what the content is.

Existing guides can be modified using the View > Guides menu. This menu provides options to show or hide guides (**Figure 3.4**). Temporarily hiding the guides lets you view the layout without the light blue lines.

The Lock Guides option keeps important guides from being accidentally moved and can be used to lock down the design grid for an entire project. To unlock the guides, just toggle the selection in the menu.

The Edit Guides option (**Figure 3.5**) lets you customize the look and functionality of your guides by providing custom colors and the ability to adjust snapping, locking, and accuracy.

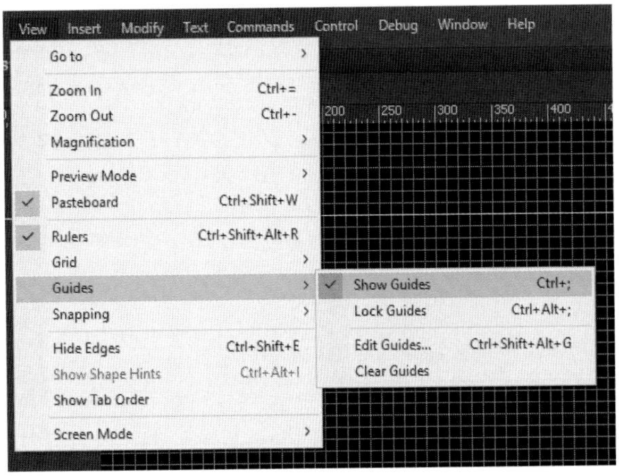

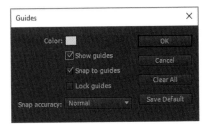

Figure 3.5 ▲ The Edit Guides dialog box

Figure 3.4 ◀ Enabling guides

Using External Graphics

Now that you've created your document and set up your project, the first thing you need to do in designing your meme image is to pull in an external bitmap file. Animate CC has support for many types of bitmap images, including **PNG**, **JPG**, and **GIF**. You can also import Photoshop, Illustrator, and even **SVG** files into your Animate CC project.

★ ACA Objective 4.2

Importing a bitmap image

The primary element in this project is the bitmap image being used as the subject of the project. Animate CC can use both **bitmap** and **vector** images in any project. For this project, you'll be using both types of graphics together, which is something that Animate CC excels at.

▶ Video 3.4
Importing a Bitmap Image

Take some time to choose the image you'd like to use, keeping in mind the message you'll use based on this image as the message of your meme. In the example files, I'm using a photograph of a cat provided by the client (**Figure 3.6**). It may not be the most original subject for a meme, but it's certainly time-tested!

1   To bring the image into your project, choose File > Import from the application menu.

2   Then do one of the following:

   ▪ Choose File > Import to Library to import the image to the Library.

   ▪ Choose File > Import to Stage to import the image to the Stage.

Figure 3.6 Cat photograph by Leslie Labrecque

Whichever decision you make, the image will be imported to the Library. If you do choose to import the image onto the Stage, however, in addition to being placed within the Library an instance of the image will be included on the Stage.

★ ACA Objective 3.7

THE PROJECT LIBRARY

The Project Library is an essential feature of Animate CC. Every project includes its own unique Library containing any imported assets used within the document, as well as any special objects created within Animate CC such as Movie Clip or Graphic symbols. The idea is that objects in the Library can have many instances created based off them and used within the project. In this project, you'll have a bitmap image in the Library and use an instance of it on the visual Stage.

TIP

You can also bring objects instances out of the Library at runtime via code by using the Library items Linkage ID. You can set the Linkage ID within the Library panel by double-clicking in that column for any object.

Video 3.5 *Using Photoshop and Illustrator Files*

If you choose to import to the Stage, your image will appear directly on the Stage at this point. If you decide to import to the Library only, you'll need to bring an instance of the image onto the Stage in order to use it within the project.

Importing from Photoshop or Illustrator

Importing files from Photoshop and Illustrator provides a valuable production tool when creating interactive media content. Animate CC recognizes PSD and AI files and launches a special Import window that lets you control how these files load their assets into your project (**Figure 3.7** and **Figure 3.8**).

With some good planning, you can build nearly all of your Animate CC artwork layers just by importing either of these formats. For instance, if your entire project uses bitmap images, you can use Photoshop to create and manage them all. If you prefer working with vector objects in Illustrator, then there's no reason you need to even touch the Animate CC drawing tools—just import everything!

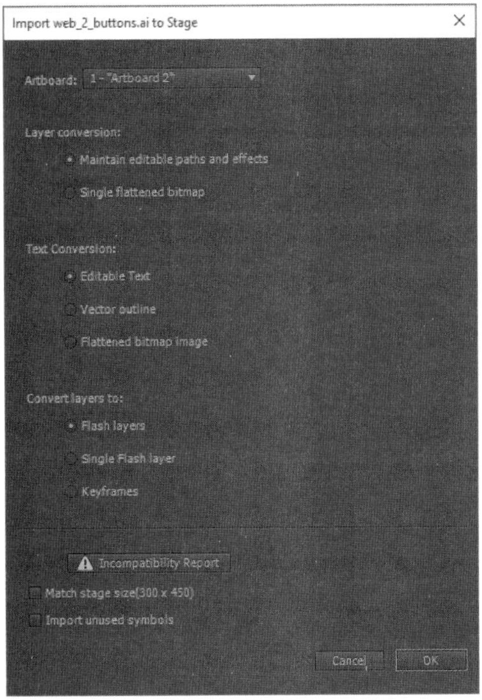

Figure 3.7 Illustrator import options

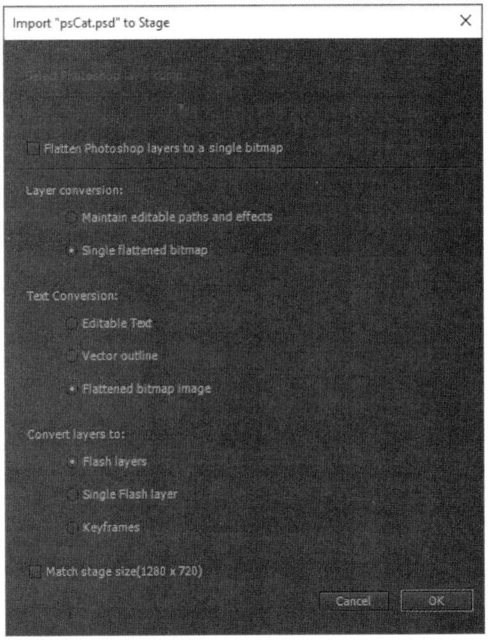

Figure 3.8 Photoshop import options

Here are some helpful options available to you when importing from AI and PSD files:

- Collapse all the layers of an Illustrator file to get a clearer view of the basic layer structure.

- Place objects at their original positions to preserve the relative positioning of the objects.

- Set the Stage size to the document size to automatically set the Animate document size to the size of the document being imported. (Just be careful—very few Illustrator documents are sized correctly.)

- Set each layer to be imported as a Movie Clip if you'll need to tween your layers or apply interactivity later.

To create an instance of an object in the Library (**Figure 3.9**), do the following:

1 Open the Library panel either by clicking the Library tab, if it is part of your current workspace, or by choosing Window > Library from the application menu.

2 Click the image object in the Library panel and drag it onto the Stage.

Releasing it onto the Stage will create an instance of the Library item. Notice that the Library still contains the original object. You can create as many instances as you like in this way.

Figure 3.9 The meme photo in the Library

Adjusting the image layout on the Stage

With the bitmap instance on the Stage selected, be sure to make any desired adjustments to the image so that it appears on the Stage as you like it to. Use the Selection and Transform tools to manage the position and scale of instances on the Stage.

Most Adobe creative software products use two main selection tools. This can be confusing because they look similar, but each serves a unique function. The Selection tool ( ) is used to select objects or shape elements like strokes and fills in their entirety. You can use this tool to move and position your imported image. The Subselection tool ( ) is used to manipulate the base points of a vector. When dealing with bitmap images, you'll find this tool fairly useless.

NOTE

With bitmap images especially, it's helpful to create the image in the exact resolution needed for your project. Unnecessary image data will make your project file size bigger than it needs to be.

Dealing with the timeline and layers

★ ACA Objective 3.6

Now that you have an instance of your imported bitmap image on the Stage, take note of the timeline. Notice how you have one **layer** within the timeline and one **frame** across time.

NOTE

You can also toggle layer visibility and out-line mode along with lock/unlock from this set of icons. Changing the visibility of layers can help you focus on the layers you're cur-rently working with. Viewing layer assets as outlines can help with fast rendering on old machines and, because nothing is obscured, can be useful when you're working with the size and positioning of objects in relation to one another. I sug-gest playing with these options to familiarize yourself with them.

If you were animating anything across time, you'd need to use a number of frames. Since you're not performing any animation in this project, you'll always be working in frame 1. However, you will be using a number of layers in the project, and taking care to name your layers is a good organizational effort to put forth.

The next step is to rename your present layer to something more descriptive.

1 Double-click the layer name and type in a new one, such as **Image**.

2 If the layer isn't locked already, you'll have to lock down the layer so you don't accidentally change anything in it (**Figure 3.10**). Do so by clicking the small Lock icon (🔒).

Figure 3.10 Image layer locked

Managing Bitmap Images

While you won't be dealing directly with any advanced bitmap management concepts in this project, you'll want to know the following commands and techniques. To get the most out of working with bitmap images in Animate CC, you should know what your options are. Go ahead and try some of these options on your imported image instance. Don't worry if you mess up; you can always delete the layer contents and simply drag a fresh instance from the Library.

Break apart an image

▶ **Video 3.6** Break Apart an Image

A bitmap image, the instance of a symbol, a drawing object, or a group can all be made of multiple individual parts. To see whether any object on the Stage is a com-plex element of this sort, double-click it. If it is composed of many different parts,

Figure 3.11 An image broken apart

you should be able to go within it to edit those pieces in isolation. You can access these parts by "breaking apart" the compound graphic using the Modify > Break Apart command (see **Figure 3.11**).

If the shape-based artwork or base bitmap is embedded several layers deep, you may need to run the command several times before you see the telltale small dots that indicate you are at the lowest level and can start using the shape tools. Breaking apart the imported image will create a simple vector shape with a bitmap fill.

> **TIP** *Try this technique on a block of text. It will first break the words into letters and then break the letters into vector shapes.*

Using Trace Bitmap

It's worth noting that you cannot edit individual pixels of a bitmap object in Animate CC. If you need to edit the image itself, you can import again or replace the image with a new version from its Properties panel.

To access an image's properties from the Library, right-click the image you'd like to replace and choose Properties (**Figure 3.12**).

Figure 3.12 Accessing the image's Properties panel

Figure 3.13 The Update Library Items dialog box

▶ *Video 3.7* Using Trace Bitmap

NOTE

It's also possible to swap one bitmap image for another by selecting the image and choosing Modify > Bitmap > Trace Bitmap from the application menu. This feature is great for creating templates, or even trying out a variety of images in the same project.

From here you can either update the existing image or import a replacement (**Figure 3.13**).

You can also transform an imported bitmap image into vector shapes. To do so, select the image on the Stage and choose Modify > Bitmap > Trace Bitmap from the application menu. This will display a small window that allows you to tweak how the image will be interpreted through a set of sliders. Click OK, and Animate CC will transform the bitmap image into a set of vector shapes based on the chosen selections.

To see this in action, select the photograph on the stage and choose File > Modify > Bitmap > Trace Bitmap. You can use the sliders and other options here to determine how Animate CC will translate the pixel data into vector assets. You have control over color threshold, curves, and more (**Figure 3.14**). Here you can see the original image as placed on the Stage. This is true pixel data and appears photographic.

After you perform a Trace Bitmap command, the image is noticeably changed. You're no longer dealing with pixel data but rather a set of vector shapes based on the interpretation of the original pixels. Just as with any vector shape data in Animate CC, you can easily modify the paths, change the colors that are applied, and more.

Tracing a bitmap involves converting a pixel-based image to a series of vectors. There are many possible reasons for doing this, but it's usually done just because it can look cool. A traced bitmap has an appearance similar to the photographic posterization that was popular in the late 1960s and early 1970s (**Figure 3.15**). Be careful, though, because this technique can dramatically increase your file size.

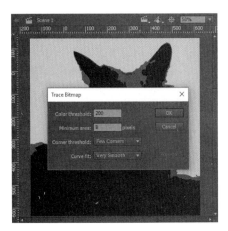

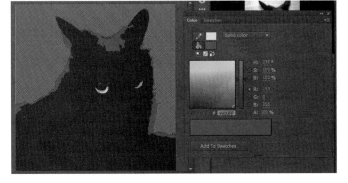

Figure 3.15 A vectorized photograph

Figure 3.14 Trace Bitmap options

Sharing Library items across projects

By saving an Animate document file that has assets only in the Library panel, you can create an external library that can be shared among several Animate CC projects. To access this external library, you can import it by choosing File > Import > Open External Library. The newly opened Library can be accessed from the Library selection drop-down in the Library panel (**Figure 3.16**).

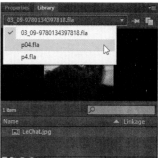

> **NOTE** *If you have several FLA documents open at once, you can also access all of the individual document libraries from the Library panel.*

Figure 3.16 Choosing a Library

If you're working with a group and anybody in that group changes an asset in the external shared library, the asset will be updated for everyone. Assets will not be updated for any FLA file already using the library, but the Library will be changed for any new FLA files created after the edit. Establishing good workflow rules can help minimize problems caused by sharing libraries.

Hiding content with a mask

★ *ACA Objective 4.7*

▶ *Video 3.8 Hiding Content with Masking*

Unless the image you imported was exactly the same size as your Stage, you'll probably notice that it makes things a little hard to handle. The photo obscures the boundaries of the Stage, leaving you guessing where visual elements end in relation to where the Stage and the pasteboard begin.

A good way to deal with this problem is to use a **mask** and a mask layer. To create a mask, you use one of the shape tools to draw a rectangle or ellipse, or the Pen tool or Brush tool to draw something unique.

Masking applies the shape of the mask layer to a single layer or even multiple layers beneath it (**Figure 3.17**). Setting up a mask is easy. Just put the vector element that will determine the mask shape in one layer and then place the artwork to be masked in a layer directly below that layer. Right-clicking the top layer will allow you to choose the Mask option.

Figure 3.17 The masked image

NOTE

You can mask just about anything. Try masking with videos and animation. You can even animate the mask layer content itself, if you like.

You'll notice in the timeline that the masking group is indicated with a special icon and a slight indent. You can add several masked layers to a single mask layer group. To see the mask effect in Animate CC, be sure to lock both the mask layer and the masked layers grouped beneath it.

Creating Black Vector Shapes

Next you'll create some thick black bars as part of the layout design for your image meme. To do this, you'll use the Rectangle tool and create some vector shapes. Vectors are described by equations represented by Bézier curves and rendered on the screen at runtime. Working with these curves can be challenging, but because of their mathematical nature, they can be scaled without any loss of quality. They're also usually much smaller in file size than imported bitmaps.

Creating shape elements

▶ ***Video 3.9*** *Drawing Vector Bars*

Next you'll create the upper and lower bars to place against your text. This will overlay the image file you've already imported and should help the text elements you have in mind to stand out in the design. First, you'll need to create a new layer on the timeline to hold your black bars. It's always preferable to place distinct objects within their own layers for organization and clarity.

1 To create the new layer, click the New Layer button beneath the timeline.

2 Double-click the layer name, and rename it **Bars** since it will contain both upper and lower bars (**Figure 3.18**).

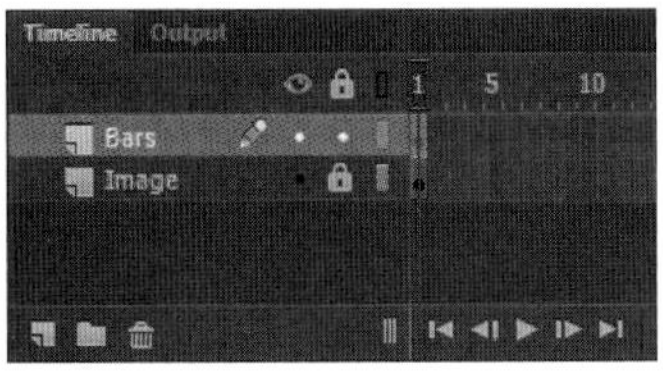

Figure 3.18 Creating the Bars layer

3 Choose the Rectangle tool ( ) from the Tools panel and change the fill color to pure black.

As you draw these elements, they'll automatically be colored black.

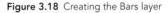

4 Draw two rectangle shapes, each 500px wide and 120px high. You may need to guess at first, but it's easy enough to modify the width and height after you create the shapes to match these specific settings.

5 Place the first rectangle at 0px on the x-axis and 0px on the y-axis.

This is the upper-left corner of the Stage; this element is now aligned perfectly to the top.

6 Place the second rectangle at 0px on the x-axis and 380px on the y-axis.

Because the rectangle is 120px high, it will align precisely at the bottom of the Stage. Now lock this layer so that you can't change anything by mistake (**Figure 3.19**).

Figure 3.19 The completed bars

NOTE *You could also use the Align panel with Align to Stage selected to easily align either vector shape to the top left or bottom left. There are a lot of different ways to accomplish the same task.*

Working with Text Elements

Now you'll add the text to your design as requested by the client. To create text elements in Animate CC, you'll use the Text tool and modify text properties like font, color, size, and so on.

★ *ACA Objective 4.3*

Creating text elements

▶ **Video 3.10**
*Creating Our
Meme Message*

Before you start working with the Text tool, you should lock all the currently existing layers to avoid making any unintended adjustments to content that you've already worked with.

1 Select each existing layer and click the Lock icon.

2 Create a new layer, double-click the layer name, and rename it **Text** (**Figure 3.20**).

Figure 3.20 The new Text layer

All of your text elements will exist within this single layer.

You can define the properties of a text element even before you lay out any text on the Stage. These properties include font and typographic information; color; anti-alias settings; superscript and subscript options; alignment; box behaviors, such as single line and multiline; link information; and the ability to apply filters to a text block.

For this project, you want the text to be big and white in contrast to the black bars already established.

3 Choose the Text tool from the Tools panel and take a look at the information and settings displayed in the Properties panel (**Figure 3.21**).

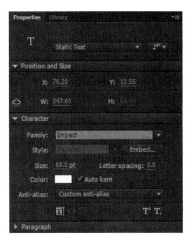

Figure 3.21 The Text Properties panel

4 You'll be using static text for this project (though it doesn't matter since you'll be rendering a flat image), so choose Static from the Text Type drop-down.

5 Select a big font such as Impact for your text and change the text size to 68 point.

6 Change the text color to white if it isn't already set to that value.

7 To create a text block, click and drag across the upper bar on top of the Stage.

8 Release the mouse; then type the text you want to display. Type in the first part of the text you saw in the final image shown at the beginning of the chapter: **WHATCHA**.

9 To create the second text block, click and drag across the lower bar. Release the mouse, and then type in the text **LOOKIN' AT?**.

10 Use the Selection tool or the Align panel to move your text blocks to the appropriate places in the design (**Figure 3.22**). Center each of them horizontally and vertically on their respective black bar shapes.

NOTE

Text blocks appear on the screen with anchor points on each corner. You use these points to adjust the height and width of the text block. You can resize the block, set margins and spacing, and choose the behavior type from the Properties panel.

Figure 3.22 Text completed

EXPANDING-WIDTH AND FIXED-WIDTH TEXT

A text block can be either an expanding-width or fixed-width element. By default, text blocks are expandable. Double-clicking the open circle on the right side of the text block will convert an expanding-width text block to a fixed-width text block. Double-clicking the open square on the right side of a fixed-width text block will convert that text block back to an expanding-width text block. Resizing the text box will convert the text block to the fixed-width setting

Additional information about text

Your text elements for this project are now set up, but there's a lot more to learn about text in Animate CC. Let's take a look at the various types of text elements you can create, the differences between them, and how to employ fonts, effects, and more.

TEXT TYPES

Available text types in Animate CC depend on your project's target platform. The different text types available can include Static, Dynamic, and Input text (**Figure 3.23**).

Figure 3.23 Text types

Static text is the simplest of all the text types—text that's created during authoring and that can't be changed at runtime. Even though it's the simplest text type, you can still choose numerous settings for static text through the Properties panel. One of the great things about static text is that you're not required to embed fonts for final publishing.

You can input dynamic text during authoring and change it with ActionScript or JavaScript during runtime. This makes dynamic text ideal for interactive projects where you need to provide user feedback in some way through textual data. Unlike the static text type, dynamic text has an option that lets you assign an instance name to the text element. This makes it possible to interact with the element through code. It's most always necessary to embed character sets from the font selected to properly display any characters that were not input during authoring when using dynamic text.

NOTE

You'll notice that subtle changes in options available appear as you change the text block type from Static to Dynamic to Input. These changes are necessary to let you properly set the properties of these various text types.

The input text type has all the functionality and configuration options of the dynamic text type but adds the ability for the end user to enter and edit text information. You can also specify a maximum number of input characters and select an option to apply a border around the Input text field to indicate that it's editable by the user.

EMBEDDING FONTS

Animate CC has the ability to embed fonts into an interactive media application, which expands a designer's type options.

Static text doesn't require font embedding, but creating dynamic text blocks for which the content or properties might be changed usually requires that at least a portion of the font character set be embedded into the file.

You can embed fonts by clicking the Embed button in the Properties panel. The Font Embedding dialog box provides options for the process (**Figure 3.24**). Notice the glyph count as you embed portions of a font. There's a huge difference in the glyph count when you embed the entire font, as opposed to just the Latin I subset and punctuation. The Latin I and punctuation subsets cover the characters needed for Western European languages. To keep file sizes small, embed only the glyphs or character sets required for the particular application.

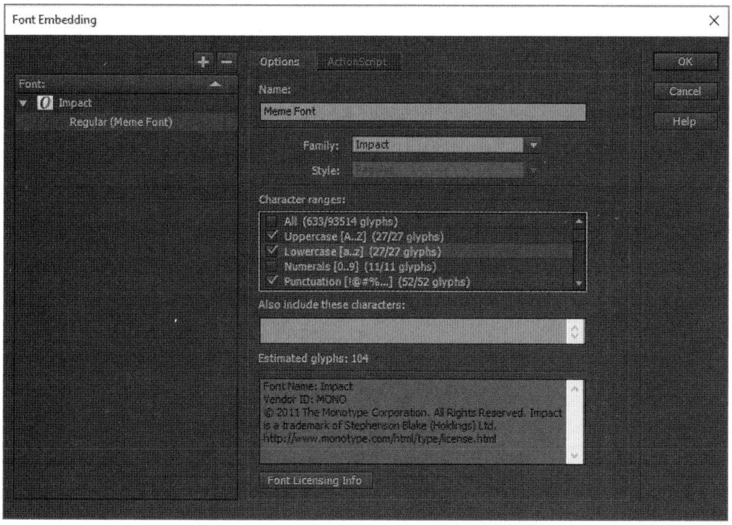

Figure 3.24 The Font Embedding dialog box

TIP

Once you've created an embedded font object, you can select that font to be used in individual text blocks and the font object itself will become available through the project Library.

TEXT ALIGNMENT

Most text-handling programs let you set the alignment or justification of text. In text blocks in Animate CC, text can be set flush left (ragged right), flush right (ragged left), centered, or justified (flush left and right). In addition to justification, line spacing and letter spacing can also be controlled through the Properties inspector.

ANTI-ALIAS PROPERTIES

Regardless of the type of text selected, you can select the anti-aliasing options for a text block from the Properties panel. **Anti-aliasing** refers to how the edges of the vector-based type characters will be rendered as pixels. This process involves feathering the edge of the type to create the appearance of a smooth edge even though it's created out of square screen pixels.

Video 3.11 *Using Text Effects*

You can specify how Animate CC anti-aliases these edges by selecting the options under the Anti-alias drop-down menu:

- **Use Device Fonts:** This option uses fonts on the end user's system.
- **Bitmap Text:** This option will not anti-alias at all and will produce rough, jagged type.
- **Anti-alias for Animation:** This option creates a smooth and rapidly rendered edge that will animate more smoothly with less processing.
- **Anti-alias for Readability:** This option creates a crisp anti-alias edge that enhances readability.
- **Custom Anti-alias:** This option lets you select the exact anti-alias parameters.

BREAKING TEXT APART

Text blocks can be broken apart using the Modify > Break Apart option. This provides some interesting animation possibilities. The Break Apart command splits words into individual letters. Choosing the command twice will break down the individual letters into shapes that can be edited using Animate CC's standard drawing tools.

Generating an Image

★ *ACA Objective 5.4*

Animate CC will generate any single frame of your project timeline as a static image file. This is useful for generating concept stills for a larger project or for generating fallback images for animated ads. To export our image, we don't need to select a frame at all, because we have only one frame to this project.

Video 3.12 *Exporting a Static Image*

To perform an export, choose File > Export > Export Image, and then you'll have to choose one of four image formats to render the output. Let's take a look at each of these and how they handle our design.

Export Image as JPEG

Video 3.13 *Additional Publish Options*

JPG (or JPEG) stands for Joint Photographic Experts Group. This is a great format for representing photographic content for the web. It is a highly compressed, lossy file format for image data.

The options when exporting a JPEG from a Animate CC project are as follows (**Figure 3.25**):

- **Width** and **Height** specify the image resolution. You can also select Minimum Image Area or Full Document Size from the drop-down to have these values populated based on your content.

- **Resolution** is the pixels per inch (ppi) for the JPEG. The default value for screens is 72.

- **Quality** deals with compression and is specified on a scale of 0–100.

- **Progressive** indicates whether the image is able to reveal portions of itself as it is being downloaded.

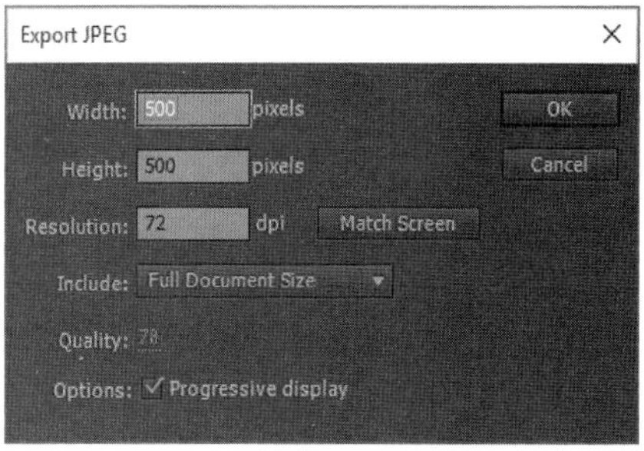

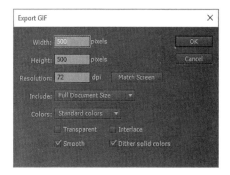

Figure 3.25 JPEG export options

Export Image as GIF

The Graphics Interchange Format (GIF) is a bitmap image format originally created by CompuServe way back in 1987. It's often used on the Internet today to display both static and animated content. Something important to keep in mind about the GIF format is that it is quite limited in the colors it can display and is best suited in representing solid vector content.

> **NOTE**
>
> *If you want to export an animated GIF, you can actually do so from the Publish Settings dialog box.*

The options when exporting a GIF are as follows (**Figure 3.26**):

- **Width** and **Height** specify the image resolution. You can also select Minimum Image Area or Full Document Size from the drop-down to have these values populated based on your content.

- **Resolution** is the ppi for the GIF. The default value for screens is 72.

- **Transparent** will allow transparency within the exported GIF image—though with GIF, transparency is quite limited.

- **Interlace** specifies whether the resulting image will be interlaced.

- **Smooth** will attempt to smooth the image.

- **Dither Solid Colors** specifies whether to dither the image.

- **256** or **Standard** refers to the color palette being used in the image.

Figure 3.26 GIF export options

Export Image as PNG

Portable Network Graphics (PNG) is a bitmap file format with lossless data compression, unlike JPEG. PNG was created as a non-patented replacement for GIF files. Although PNG is a great, lossless format, PNG files can be much larger than JPEGs or GIFs, depending on the settings you use.

The options when exporting a PNG are as follows (**Figure 3.27**):

- **Width** and **Height** specify the image resolution. You can also select Minimum Image Area or Full Document Size from the drop-down to have these values populated based on your content.
- **Resolution** is the ppi for the PNG. The default value for screens is 72.
- **Colors** will specify whether the resulting image is 8-bit, 24-bit, or 32-bit.
- **Smooth** will attempt to smooth the image.

Figure 3.27 PNG export options

Export Image as SVG

TIP

Learn more about Snap.svg at http:// snapsvg.io/ and download the Snap.svg Animator add-on for Animate CC at https://creative. adobe.com/addons/.

Scalable Vector Graphics (SVG) is an XML-based vector image format for two-dimensional graphics. An interesting side note is that this format includes support for interactivity and animation. Animate CC can both import and export static GIF files and, with custom platform support, can publish animated SVG through the Snap.svg JavaScript library.

The options when exporting an SVG are as follows (**Figure 3.28**):

- **Width** and **Height** specify the image resolution. You can also select Minimum Image Area or Full Document Size from the drop-down to have these values populated based on your content.
- **SVG Profiles** is grayed out and disabled, defaulting to SVG 1.1.

- **Include Hidden Layers** allows hidden layers in the timeline to be rendered in the final image.
- **Image Location** can be set to either Embed or Link. When you choose Link, you can also specify a folder to keep the images in.

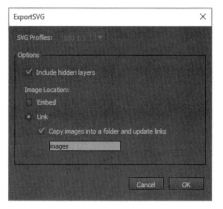

Figure 3.28 SVG export options

Challenge!

Import a number of bitmaps into the library and swap them out for a completely different message in the project. Change around the text as well—make this project your own!

Conclusion

This project and the last included a lot of the fundamental things you need to know when working in Animate CC regardless of project type. Here, you saw the interoperability of Animate CC between other applications in the Adobe Creative Cloud and how even though Animate CC was created as an animation program, you can also create static design content just as easily.

We've certainly covered quite a bit of ground with this project! We've managed layers in the timeline, imported images to both the Stage and Library, worked with vectors, used masking to hide and reveal objects, examined a variety of options when creating text elements, and finally had a solid look at exporting our design in a variety of image formats. Well done!

CHAPTER OBJECTIVES

Chapter Learning Objectives

- Work with HTML5 Canvas and WebGL publish targets
- Access the Brush Library
- Use the Paint Brush tool
- Create armatures with the Bone tool
- Work with Movie Clip symbols and instances
- Manage HTML5 Canvas publish settings

Chapter ACA Objectives

For more detail on ACA Objectives in this book, see the table on pages 212–215.

DOMAIN 2.0
UNDERSTANDING INTERACTIVE MEDIA DESIGN
2.4

DOMAIN 3.0
UNDERSTANDING ADOBE FLASH PROFESSIONAL
3.2, 3.6, 3.7

DOMAIN 4.0
CREATING INTERACTIVE MEDIA CONTENT USING FLASH PROFESSIONAL
4.1, 4.3, 4.4, 4.5

DOMAIN 5.0
TESTING, PUBLISHING, AND EVALUATING INTERACTIVE MEDIA ELEMENTS USING FLASH PROFESSIONAL
5.4

CHAPTER 4

Compose an Animated HTML5 Greeting

This chapter will build on everything you've learned so far, but we'll take things in a different direction from previous projects by authoring content that runs natively in the browser without the need for Flash Player. We'll also delve deeper into aspects of the Library and symbols while introducing some new tools.

> **NOTE** *Adobe has rebranded Flash Professional CC as Animate CC! They are essentially the exact same application—with absolutely no differences in capability aside from features introduced in the regular update schedule. All future updates to Flash Professional CC will be known by the name Animate CC. If desired, subscribers can run multiple versions of the product—branded as either Flash Professional or Animate—but I highly recommend using the latest available version of Animate CC to take advantage of all new features.*

This project involves the traditional web-based greeting card (**Figure 4.1**), but with a twist: the client wants you to design the card in such a way that it can be accessed via a web browser on a desktop, mobile device, or other similar means. In other words, since the browser-based Flash Player is widely available only on desktop browsers, in order to hit mobile targets we'll need to deploy using a native **HTML5** target. Luckily, Adobe Animate CC includes a number of target-platform document types suited specifically to this task.

▶ *Video 4.1* *Project Overview*

NOTE

All of the videos for this book were recorded with a version of Animate CC branded as Flash Professional CC. It is important to note that everything that we demonstrate in the recordings can be applied to Animate CC—even if we refer to the application as Flash Professional. They are essentially the exact same application—with absolutely no differences in capability.

Figure 4.1 The completed web-based greeting card that you'll produce with Animate CC in this chapter

Creating a New HTML5 Canvas Document

★ *ACA Objective 4.1*

▶ **Video 4.2** *Creating a New HTML5 Canvas Document*

Content created in Animate CC can now to be published directly to a number of modern HTML5 formats, including **Canvas** and **WebGL**. The primary document type that allows this publish target is HTML5 Canvas. When creating content using this publish target, Animate CC leverages the CreateJS JavaScript libraries to output an entire animation or interactive project for the HTML5 canvas element.

Setting up the project document

NOTE

The HTML5 canvas element is also used to display WebGL content.

The first thing you'll do is create a new document. On the Welcome screen, or via File > New in the application menu, choose HTML5 Canvas as your document type.

CREATEJS

CreateJS is a suite of modular JavaScript libraries and tools that work together or independently to enable rich interactive content on open web technologies via HTML5. See www.createjs.com to learn more.

Animate CC opens a new document, which initially will look exactly the same as the documents we've already worked with. You should note a number of differences, however:

■ First, notice that in the General tab of the New Document dialog box, the name of the file is appended with the (Canvas) qualifier (**Figure 4.2**). This lets you know that you're working in that particular document type. ActionScript-based projects have no such qualifier.

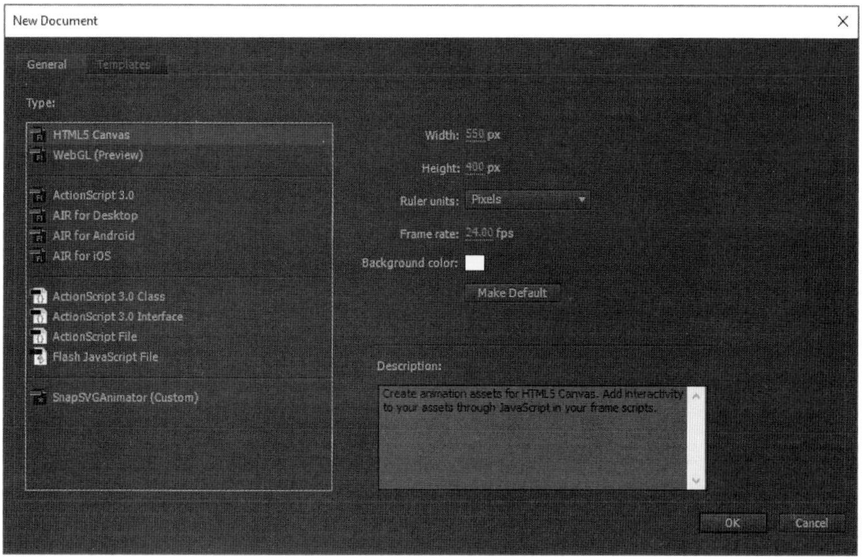

Figure 4.2 The New Document dialog box

■ There are a couple of tools in the Tools panel that are disabled, including the 3D Rotation tool ( ) and the 3D Translation tool ( ).

■ If you select the Text tool (T), you'll notice that you can only choose Dynamic Text. The other two text types are disabled.

■ When viewing Document Properties, you'll see that a lot of options under the Publish area are disabled because they pertain only to ActionScript-based projects.

Otherwise, creating and animating content targeting HTML5 Canvas should be nearly identical to what you have already encountered.

NOTE

The HTML5 canvas element is a structure through which bitmap data can be drawn and changed via JavaScript. It also includes the ability to process and respond to various modes of interactivity like mouse clicks and touch events.

Preparing the Stage and timeline

Before creating any assets in the greeting card project, you'll do some work on configuring the Stage and other project fundamentals.

1 In the Properties panel (**Figure 4.3**), set the Stage width to 550 pixels and the height to 400 pixels. This is the normal Animate CC default, so there may not be anything to change depending on your preferences.

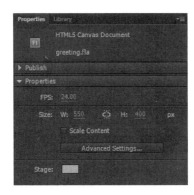

Figure 4.3 Configuring the Stage in the Properties panel

2 Make sure FPS is set to a value of 24 and choose a background color that suits you. I choose black most of the time, but in this project you'll be drawing a background anyhow, so it doesn't matter much.

3 Moving on to the timeline, rename the present layer **BG**. This is where you will draw your project background.

4 Use the New Layer button () to create an additional layer and name it **Frame** (**Figure 4.4**). This layer will contain assets that make up the basic background elements of your project.

Figure 4.4 Frame layer added

5 Save the document in a location that makes sense to you.

Even though you're using a different document type in this project, Animate CC treats the file the same way, even saving it in the same FLA file format.

Laying Out the Background Elements

Now that you have layers for your frame and background assets, you can create these elements using the shape and drawing tools in Animate CC. You'll be using some of the vector tools you're already familiar with, but you'll also be introduced to the concept of variable-width strokes and the super-cool Paint Brush tool.

★ ACA Objective 3.2

Drawing the background

To draw the background to the greeting card project, you'll use the new Brush Library and the Paint Brush tool in Animate CC.

▶ **Video 4.3** *Drawing the Background*

1 To begin, lock the Frame layer to ensure that you don't draw anything in it by mistake.

2 Select the BG layer within the timeline and choose either the Rectangle tool ( ) with Object Drawing Mode enabled or the Rectangle Primitive tool ( ).

   You're now ready to draw the background.

3 Click and drag from the top left of the Stage to the bottom right to draw a shape exactly the same size as the Stage: 550x400.

4 You may need to make some adjustments to the size and position of your shape, depending on your snap settings and how steady a hand you have. Do this from the Properties panel with the object selected.

5 If you haven't done so already, choose a background color for your shape. I'm using #FF9933 in the example shown in **Figure 4.5**, but you can choose whatever you like.

Figure 4.5 I'm using a black background for my shape.

NOTE *You can always turn off either Stroke or Color by choosing this option for either color value.*

6 You don't need any Stroke color for this project, so choose None for the Stroke color. It's represented in the color picker as the white block with the red diagonal line running through it (**Figure 4.6**).

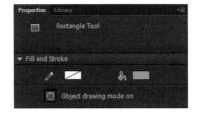

Figure 4.6 No stroke color as represented in the Properties panel

Decorating with the Paint Brush tool

Video 4.4 *Decorating with Art Brushes*

Now for some freeform fun! The Paint Brush tool ( ) is a new tool in Animate CC that lets you draw out strokes with vector art attached to them. This allows for massive creative possibilities, whether you're using built-in brushes from the Brush Library or using custom brushes you created with the Adobe Capture mobile app and shared with Animate CC via the CC Libraries panel.

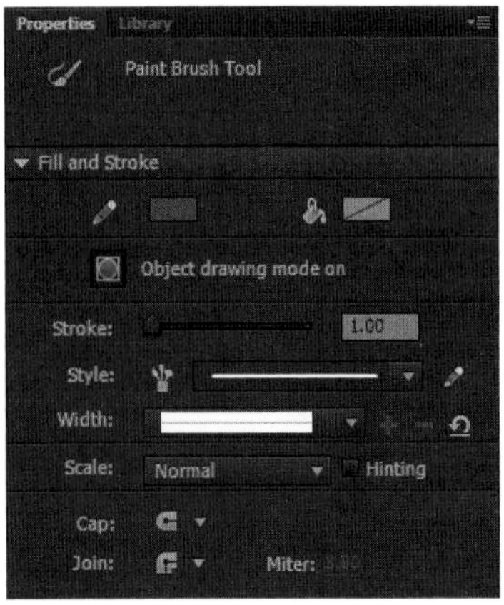

Figure 4.7 The Paint Brush tool Properties panel

1 To begin, choose the Paint Brush tool from the Tools panel.

   The Paint Brush tool Properties panel opens (**Figure 4.7**).

2 You'll be drawing these decorative assets in the BG layer, so be sure to enable Object Drawing Mode to prevent shape collisions.

3 Choose Window > Brush Library from the application menu to open the Brush Library.

   In the Brush Library you'll see a number of categories, which contain a wide variety of prebuilt vector art brushes.

4 Find one you'd like to use and select it.

   It should now show up in the Style area of your Properties panel. You can see in the next figure that I've chosen the brush named Chalk – Scribble from the Artistic > Chalk Charcoal category within the Brush Library (**Figure 4.8**).

   Now it's time to get creative!

NOTE *You can also access the Brush Library directly from the Properties panel by clicking its icon.*

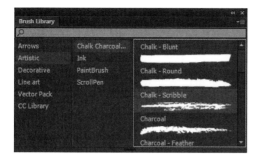

Figure 4.8 The Brush Library

5 Using the Paint Brush tool, click and drag around the Stage to generate free-form vector artwork. Don't make your art too busy…but don't hold back too much either. Make it interesting.

6 Select a Shape color. In **Figure 4.9**, I've chosen to use something a few steps darker than my background (#A35A12), but there's no reason you couldn't use a number of variations in color or even stroke width. You can control all these properties from the Properties panel with the Paint Brush tool selected.

Figure 4.9 The shape color I've chosen

7 Once you're happy with the results, lock the BG layer and unlock the Frame layer for the next step in this project.

EDITING VECTOR ART BRUSHES

You can also edit existing brushes by clicking the Edit Stroke Style icon (✎) from the Properties panel with the Paint Brush Tool selected. This allows even greater variation in how the vector art is mapped to your strokes.

Drawing the frame with variable-width strokes

▶ **Video 4.5** *Making a Frame*

Using variable-width strokes in your project is an easy way to impart a bit of controlled chaos to simple strokes. Animate CC will, in place of a linear stroke, impart a stroke whose width varies at certain points. The best way to grasp the concept is to use it. You'll create a nice frame for this project and apply a variable-width profile to the frame stroke.

Figure 4.10 Drawing Object Properties

1 Select the Frame layer so that you can draw the object. You may want to ensure all other layers are locked before proceeding.

2 Choose the Rectangle or Rectangle Primitive tool and draw a vector object the exact size of your Stage: 550px by 400px. Use whatever color you like for the stroke (in **Figure 4.10**, I'm using #336600), and choose a transparent fill.

3 With the object selected, choose a profile from the drop-down in the Properties panel. If something doesn't look right, select the Width tool from the Tools panel and tweak existing width points or even create new ones.

4 For an additional creative flourish, apply a vector art brush to the variable-width stroke as well. In **Figure 4.11**, I'm using Artistic > Chalk Charcoal > Chalk – Round from the Brush Library.

Figure 4.11 A little extra creative flourish added with a vector art brush

GROUPING THE LAYERS WITHIN A FOLDER

One of the best things you can do to keep things organized in your timeline is to group layers. You can accomplish this by creating a layer folder for specific sets of layers.

▶ **Video 4.6** *Grouping Layers*

1 Click the New Folder button below the layer stack on the bottom left of the timeline to create a folder to contain your static background elements.

2 Double-click the folder name and change it to **Background**.

3 Drag both the BG and Frame layers into the layer folder you just created (**Figure 4.12**).

Figure 4.12 BG and Frame layers added to the new layer folder

With the folder created, you can now control the lock status, visibility, and outline mode for all layers from the folder itself. You can also collapse and expand the folder by using the small triangle beside the folder icon.

Drawing the Flowerpot

Now that you've defined the static background elements for your greeting, you can begin work on the more complex, animated objects.

▶ **Video 4.7** *Drawing the Flowerpot*

Creating and modifying a vector rectangle shape

You'll begin by drawing a simple flowerpot.

1 Create a new layer and name it **Flower**.

2 With this layer selected, choose the Rectangle tool (▣). Don't select the Rectangle Primitive tool because in order for the shape to appear similar to the form of a flowerpot, you'll need to manipulate the shape.

Figure 4.13 The new square added on the Stage

Figure 4.14 Choose a dark brown for the inside of the flowerpot.

3 Draw a square about 120px by 120px (**Figure 4.13**). It doesn't have to be exact, and the color choices don't matter at this point. You don't have to include any stroke for this square.

4 Choose the Selection tool ( ).

5 With nothing selected, hover the cursor along the top edge of your rectangle shape. Notice how the cursor changes to include a small arc. This indicates that you can bend the paths that define your shape by pulling and pushing the edges.

6 Pull down slightly on the top of the square to form a nice dip. This is the top of your flowerpot.

7 You need to create the inside of the flowerpot as well. Choose the Oval tool ( ) and draw an oval that matches the arc and size of the flowerpot top. The color you use should be a dark brown (#4B2500) since this portion of the flowerpot will be in shadow (**Figure 4.14**). Don't apply any stroke to this object.

8 Using the Subselection tool ( ), select the bottom-left anchor point of your shape.

9 With the point selected, use the arrow keys on your keyboard to nudge the point over a few pixels, creating a taper in your flowerpot. Perform a similar action on the other side.

10 To finish the flowerpot shape, choose the Selection tool again and pull down the bottom of the shape slightly to give a little more perspective to the flowerpot, very similar to the modification you made to the top.

Applying colors and gradients

Gradients in Animate CC always start as either centered radial **gradients** or horizontal linear gradients. To adjust these gradients, you use the Gradient Transform tool ( ), which you can access by clicking and holding the Free Transform tool icon ( ) in the Tools panel.

The Gradient Transform tool lets you recenter, rotate, or stretch a gradient. It's very similar to the Free Transform tool, but it affects only how the gradient is displayed.

1 Use the Selection tool to select the flowerpot shape.

2 Open the Swatches panel and choose "Linear gradient" from the color type drop-down (**Figure 4.15**).

By default, you'll see a gradient that runs from pure white to complete black.

3 Change this to run from a slightly lighter brown (#824000) to a slightly darker brown (#582C00). Gradients often look best when there's a subtle change across the gradient.

As you adjust your linear gradient definition in the Color panel, your shape color will update to reflect the changes. If you want to preserve this color definition as a reusable swatch, click the Add to Swatches button to make it selectable from any Swatches panel within Animate CC.

If desired, you can use the Gradient Transform tool to adjust how the linear gradient is applied to the flowerpot shape. When an object with a gradient applied is selected using this tool, you can adjust the rotation, center point, width, and more.

Figure 4.15 The settings you choose in the Tagged Color Definition dialog box should match the ones shown here.

ABOUT TAGGED SWATCHES

A recent addition to Animate CC is the concept of tagged swatches. This allows you to choose a swatch from the Swatches panel and transform it into a tagged swatch by clicking the Convert to a Tagged Swatch icon (▣) below the swatches grid. Tagged swatches differ from other swatches in that a small white tag appears in the lower right of a tagged swatch.

When you have a number of shapes using the tagged swatch, you can easily update the swatch and the changes will automatically cascade across all objects using that tagged swatch.

Convert to a Graphic symbol

★ *ACA Objective 3.7*

▶ *Video 4.10*
Creating a Graphic Symbol

Symbols, at their most basic level, serve as containers for artwork. They come in three varieties, each with unique characteristics that allow them to be used for animation and interaction. Keep in mind that although Animate CC refers to "converting" elements to symbols, you're really wrapping the existing elements into symbols. Using symbols will allow nearly any graphical element to become a button, be animated in specific ways, or even be manipulated by code.

Creating a symbol from an existing set of elements is fairly simple. Here's how.

1   Select everything on the Flower layer of the timeline and choose Modify > Convert to Symbol from the application menu.

    Once the Convert to Symbol dialog box appears, you'll be given the option to type in a name for the symbol, select the symbol type, and specify a registration point alignment (**Figure 4.16**). There's also an area to access advanced options that are used primarily for linkage as a class within ActionScript.

Figure 4.16 The Convert to Symbol dialog box

TIP

It's a good practice to always name your symbols with no spaces and no special characters, and beginning with an uppercase letter. This has to do with how Animate CC views symbols, and it will simplify the process as you explore more advanced topics.

2   Name the new symbol **Flower** and choose Graphic from the Type selection box. Click OK.

    Once you click OK, the symbol is created and stored within the project Library. Additionally, an instance of that symbol remains on the Stage, exactly where the conversion occurred.

Types of symbols within Animate CC

You can to create three different types of symbols within a Animate CC project: Movie Clip, Graphic, and Button. In this project, you've created a Graphic symbol. The choice of which symbol type to use isn't always clear, but learning more about each of these symbol types can help you choose the one that will work within your interactive media application.

MOVIE CLIP SYMBOLS

A Movie Clip symbol has a timeline that behaves like—but is completely independent of—the main Stage and is the primary symbol for creating custom functionality within Flash. Movie Clip symbols can be controlled with ActionScript or JavaScript as well as through timeline manipulation, making them an extremely flexible tool for customizing an interface.

GRAPHIC SYMBOLS

Graphic symbols are fairly simple to create, and the operation of the symbol time-line is exactly the same as that of the main timeline. The main purpose of the Graphic symbol is to create reusable graphical elements and simple animations within an efficient package.

BUTTON SYMBOLS

Button symbols provide you with a quick and relatively simple way to create a stan-dard interactive media button. These buttons can be created out of nearly any type of artwork, including other symbol instances, and can support a static or normal state, a rollover state, a down state, and a hit state. You construct the artwork for these states using keyframes, but rather than relying on frame numbers, the inter-face for construction of a button symbol uses Up, Over, Down, and Hit to identify where the keyframes for these states should be placed (**Figure 4.17**).

Figure 4.17 Creating button symbols in the timeline

The hit state for a Button symbol is not visible, but the artwork in the keyframe defines the clickable area of the Button symbol. If a Button symbol has no hit state, the current keyframe artwork is used to determine the clickable or live area of the button.

NOTE

If a Button symbol has only a hit state, it is an invisible but-ton that will show up in light blue during author-time but will be invisible at runtime.

Editing the Flower Graphic Symbol

Symbols provide Animate CC projects with reusable elements that can be placed on the Stage as instances multiple times without re-creating artwork. This approach can drastically reduce file sizes and can also simplify editing a layout by minimizing the number of graphic elements required to produce an interactive media project.

Explaining symbols and instances

 Video 4.11
Editing Symbols
and Symbol
Instances

When a symbol is created, it resides in the project Library. The symbol acts as a blueprint to instruct Animate CC on how to construct an instance of that symbol.

Instances are representations of the symbol that exist on the Stage and timeline. When you drag a symbol from the Library to the Stage, you're creating an instance of that symbol. You can have multiple instances of a single symbol on the Stage (**Figure 4.18**). If you edit the symbol, all the instances will change as well.

Figure 4.18 You can have multiple instances of a symbol on the Stage.

This feature can be effective for making changes globally within a Animate CC project. However, it can also be frustrating if you want each instance to be slightly different.

Fortunately, symbol instances can be more than exact copies of the original symbol definition in the Library panel. You can modify the individual properties of each instance using the Properties panel or tools such as the Transformation tool. These property changes affect only the selected instance, not the original symbol definition.

Embedding additional symbols and elements within a symbol definition can also provide a means of customizing each instance using code. A common application is to include a dynamic text field within a symbol definition. With some simple programming, you can alter the content of this text field at the instance level. The nesting can get a bit complicated, but having only a single element in the Library can make it worth the trouble if you ever need to make global changes.

Differences between Movie Clip symbols and Graphic symbols

Movie Clip and Graphic symbols look very similar within the Animate CC authoring environment, but big differences between them exist. The first has to do with the synchronization between the symbol timeline and the main movie timeline.

A Graphic symbol is linked to the main timeline, whereas a Movie Clip symbol is an independent object whose timeline runs independently of the main timeline. If the main timeline is changing frames, so is the Graphic symbol. If the main timeline is paused, the Graphic symbol (which is linked frame by frame) is paused too. The Movie Clip timeline isn't bound to the main timeline and runs completely independently.

Another difference involves the use of ActionScript and JavaScript. Using code, you can access and control Movie Clip instances through the instance name assigned in the Properties panel (**Figure 4.19**). The Graphic symbol has no option to assign an instance name and is not accessible via code as an object.

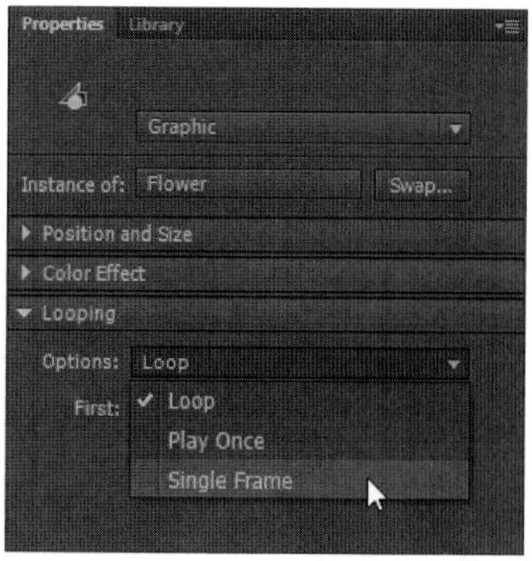

Figure 4.19 The Properties panel

A performance difference exists as well. Graphic symbols require less processing. Even with this advantage, many interactive media developers make nearly everything Movie Clips, just to increase the flexibility of the object, though animators often prefer Graphic symbols for the ability to specify the presented frame being shown at any time via the Properties panel.

Editing the flower symbol

You can edit symbols by double-clicking either any instance of the symbol on the Stage or the symbol within the Library panel.

> ▶ *Video 4.12*
> *Preparing the Symbol*

1   Double-click the symbol instance you created to edit it in place (**Figure 4.20**).

    When the symbol opens, notice that a breadcrumb trail showing the hierarchy of the object shows up in the top-left corner of the Stage. You can leave the editing mode by clicking the scene name in this breadcrumb trail.

Figure 4.20 Double-click to edit in place.

Now that you're operating within the symbol, notice that the symbol itself has its own timeline. In an Animate document, each symbol, no matter the type, has its own timeline. This allows for a great amount of creative possibilities.

The next thing you'll do is to manage this internal timeline a bit better. Because you already have a number of objects within this symbol, you can place each of them on its own layer.

NOTE *It doesn't matter if you double-click the symbol within the Library panel or use the edit-in-place option of double-clicking an instance on the Stage. You're still editing the base symbol—not the individual instance. This means that any changes you make will be made to all instances of that symbol. This doesn't matter much in this case, since you'll be using only one instance of this symbol.*

2 Select all the objects on the Stage either by dragging a selection rectangle around them with the Selection tool, or by giving the Stage focus and using the Select All shortcut, Cmd+A (Mac OS) or Ctrl+A (Windows).

3 With all of your elements selected, right-click them and choose Distribute to Layers from the drop-down menu that appears (**Figure 4.21**).

Transform	>
Arrange	>
Align	>
Break Apart	Ctrl+B
Distribute to Layers	Ctrl+Shift+D
Distribute to Keyframes	Ctrl+Shift+K

Figure 4.21 Choosing Distribute to Layers

This takes each object and creates a new layer for it and then empties the previous layer of all selected content. The original layer is empty, as indicated by a blank keyframe.

4 Delete the layer by clicking the Delete Layer icon (🗑) beneath the layer stack in the timeline.

Both the flowerpot shape and the darker, inner pot shape should now be on separate layers.

5 Rename main pot shape **pot**, and rename the layer representing the inner, backside of the flowerpot **potback**. Lock these layers before moving on.

Drawing a flower stalk

For the stalk of the flower, you'll create a simple shape with the Brush tool so that it isn't completely straight and appears a bit more natural. The Brush tool is a free-form tool that draws shapes composed of fill alone.

1 Create a new layer and name it **Stalk**.

2 Place this layer between the pot and potback layers by clicking and dragging the new layer into position (**Figure 4.22**).

   Now the order from top to bottom should be pot, Stalk, and potback.

3 Select the Brush tool ( ) and look at the Properties panel.

4 Choose a nice green color (#32CC32) for your fill and check the Brush Shape area of the panel to see the brush size and shape options. Select a round brush and bump the size way up for a thick stalk.

5 Draw a stalk beginning behind the pot and extending up. If you like, you can draw a straight shape by holding down the Shift key as you draw, though it may look more natural if you freehand it. The stalk, when complete, should measure about 230px in height (**Figure 4.23**).

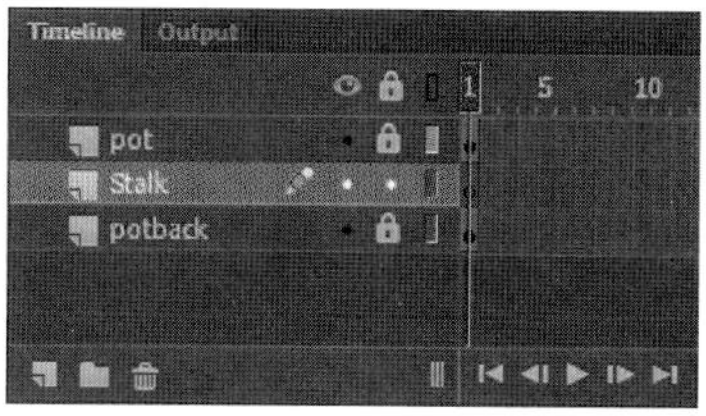

▶ *Video 4.13*
Drawing the Stalk

Figure 4.22 Place the Stalk layer in the middle of the layer stack.

Figure 4.23 Set stalk parameters in the Drawing object Properties

Animating the Flower Stalk with Inverse Kinematics

The Bone tool has been absent from Animate CC ever since the application was rewritten for 64-bit systems with the introduction of Animate CC CC. Today, however, the Bone tool, the Bind tool, **armature** layers, and everything else in the Animate CC inverse kinematics system are back.

★ *ACA Objective 4.5*

About inverse kinematics in Animate CC

Inverse kinematics allow you to animate objects in Animate CC using a series of bones chained into linear or branched armatures in parent-child relationships. This means that when one bone moves during an animation, that connected bones will also move in relation to it. Inverse kinematics is a unique way of animating content to create natural motion.

To animate using inverse kinematics, specify the start and end positions of bones on the timeline. These positions are known as "poses" within Animate CC. The armature will be automatically adjusted to tween positions of the bones in the armature between poses (**Figure 4.24**).

Figure 4.24 Animating using reverse kinematics

You can apply inverse kinematics within Animate CC in one of two ways: by drawing bones across a single shape or through the construction of an armature composed of multiple Movie Clip symbol instances. In this project, you'll create a shape-base armature from the flower stalk you just created.

Animating the flower stalk using an armature layer

▶ *Video 4.14* Using the Bone Tool

Your next step is to animate the stalk growing up and out of the flowerpot. To do this, you'll take advantage of the armature you've already created. You don't need to specify any sort of tween when working with armatures; Animate CC will handle all this automatically once different poses are defined.

1 First, you'll need to extend your frame span to frame 65. To do so, move the playhead to frame 65, select the frame, and choose Insert > Timeline > Frame from the application menu. These frames will provide enough time to nicely animate the growth of your stalk. Bring the playhead back to frame 1 when finished.

2   Select the Bone tool from the Tools panel. You'll use this tool to define the bones within your armature (**Figure 4.25**).

Figure 4.25 Defining the bones

3   To define a bone, click and drag a short way. Draw subsequent bones across the shape by clicking the end point of the previous bone and dragging out a new segment. Draw 3–5 bone segments across the stalk.

Notice how the layer color is now yellow and the icon for the layers is a small figure running? These changes indicate that this is now an armature layer (**Figure 4.26**).

Figure 4.26 The yellow layer color indicated that Stalk is now an armature layer.

Because you're using an armature, you need to use the Selection tool only to modify your pose. Try it out! Notice how everything naturally moves in relation to any portion of the stalk you click and drag? This is the power of inverse kinematics.

Once an armature is assembled, it has a default pose. When you modify a property on any particular frame, it's called a *pose*. Poses can be copied for easy modification and reuse. You want your ending frame to contain a pose with the stalk fully extended.

▶ *Video 4.15*
Managing Armature Poses

4   Select the small black diamond on frame 1 and right-click it.

5   Choose Copy Pose from the context menu and move the playhead to frame 65.

6   Select frame 65 and right-click again; this time choose Paste Pose.

     The duplicated pose is shown as a small black diamond. Now you need to define your additional poses across the frame span.

 **Video 4.16**
Animating the Stalk

7   Moving back to frame 1, modify the pose so that all segments of your stalk are collapsed down into the flower pot.

8   Move the playhead forward about 10 frames and create a new pose by guiding the growth of the stalk up and out of the flower pot.

9   Jump ahead about 10–15 more layers. Create as many poses and modifications to these poses as necessary to animate the snake-like motion of a plant growing up from the soil (**Figure 4.27**).

Figure 4.27 Keyframes set at 10-15 frame intervals, poses created

TIP *You can also use inverse kinematics to construct an armature out of multiple Movie Clip instances. This is useful when building an armature for a human form or something mechanical in nature. Shape-based armatures are more suited to plants with long swaying stalks or creatures like snakes.*

Designing and Animating the Flower Head

Now you'll create the head of the flower, which will bloom as the stalk grows. This process is pretty simple—you'll animate the flower head to follow the growth of the stalk and scale accordingly as the stalk rises until you have a fully matured flower.

Drawing the flower head

 **Video 4.17**
Drawing the Flower Head

To draw the head of your flower, you'll use the Oval or Oval Primitive tool. But you'll need to do a little setup before you start drawing.

1 Create a new layer directly above the pot layer and name it **Flower**.

2 Lock all the other layers and move the playhead to frame 45 (**Figure 4.28**). This is where your flower will first appear.

Figure 4.28 Playhead at frame 45

3 Choose Insert > Timeline > Blank Keyframe from the application menu to create a blank keyframe.

Now you'll use this new keyframe to contain the vector content that forms your flower head.

4 Choose the Oval Primitive tool and draw a small circle by holding Shift as you click and drag. The resulting circle shape should be about 40px to 44px in diameter.

5 Choose the same color for both the fill and stroke. I'm using #FF9900 in this example.

6 To roughen the stroke a bit, click the Brush Library icon with the object still selected and browse through the various brushes.

In this example I've selected Artistic > Chalk Charcoal > Charcoal - Tapered as my vector brush and adjusted the stroke width to a value of 8. This is the center of your flower.

7 To draw the petals, once again use the Oval Primitive tool and draw an oval that is roughly 25px wide and 65px tall. Change the color of the fill to something floral, like #FFFF99, and disable the stroke.

8 Duplicate this petal by making seven copies, resulting in eight complete petals.

9 Using the Free Transform tool, arrange each petal around the center circle shape created previously (**Figure 4.29**).

Figure 4.29 Petals arranged

10 Select all the petals and choose Modify > Group from the application menu.

All of the petals are now grouped together, making them easier to manage.

11 Right-click the new group and choose Arrange > Send to Back so that the center shape appears in front.

Animating the flower head along the stalk

Even though the flower head is made entirely out of shapes, you can't use a shape tween to animate it because it is too complex. Instead, you'll create a Movie Clip symbol and apply a motion tween to the instance that results.

1 Select all the parts of the flower head—the petal group and the center portion—and choose Modify > Convert to Symbol from the application menu.

2 In the dialog box that appears, name the symbol **Bud**. For the type, choose Movie Clip.

The Movie Clip Symbol itself will now be in your project Library, and an instance of that symbol is added to the Stage.

Now that you have your completed flower head as a Movie Clip symbol instance on the Stage, all you need to do is tween it along with the growth of your stalk to complete the flower animation (**Figure 4.30**). To do this, you'll adjust the scale and position of the instance with a motion tween.

Figure 4.30 Completed flower head on the stage

3   Select any frame or span of frames on the Flower layer between frames 45 and 65, right-click the frame(s), and choose Create Motion Tween from the menu.

The background of the entire frame span should turn blue, and the layer icon should change to a small box in motion, indicating the motion tween has been created.

Now all you need to do is adjust the scale and position of the Movie Clip instance on both keyframes.

4   On frame 65, the instance should be at full size and positioned at the top center of the fully extended stalk. On frame 45, scale it down using the Free Transform tool or the Properties panel so that it measures about the same width as the stalk.

5   Position it at the top of the stalk wherever it is at this point in the animation.

That should be it, although you may need to tweak the motion guide or even add an additional keyframe to help direct the tween.

NOTE

The motion guide is an overlay line that appears on the Stage when using a motion tween. The motion guide can be manipulated with the Selection tool to modify the tween path.

DETECTING PROBLEMS WITH TWEENS

Things may not always go as planned when tweening, and errors can occur. The most common tweening errors occur when you try to apply a tween on an incompatible element type.

An example is attempting to apply a motion tween to an object that doesn't support motion tweens. Animate CC tries to help you out by asking if you want to convert the object to a symbol to allow the tween. Although this works, you should have your instances properly converted before you apply the motion tween.

Another common error involves attempting to apply a shape tween to a pair of keyframes that don't contain shapes, in which case the option won't even be selectable. You can resolve this issue by using the Modify > Break Apart command to get the artwork to a basic vector level that a shape tween can be applied to.

Create a Personalized Text Message

★ *ACA Objective 4.3*

The final visual element to apply to your animated greeting is the message that the viewer sees after the animation has concluded. You might normally encounter problems working with text with HTML5 Canvas, since you can choose only Dynamic Text; you must be sure that the font used is a common font that everyone has installed. The old workaround is to break the text apart into shapes after it is created or to render the text elements to image data and then include those elements in place of editable text.

This is no longer necessary. Now Animate CC includes an option to render the text as outlines when publishing for HTML5 Canvas. So feel free to use any bizarre typeface you like in this greeting.

Building the text block

▶ *Video 4.19*
Creating a Text
Greeting

In this exercise you'll build a text message that you'll include on the main timeline.

1. If you're still within the Flower Graphic symbol instance, click the Scene 1 identifier in the location breadcrumbs above the Stage to return.

2. Extend the main timeline to 65 frames just like the Flower animation by moving the playhead to frame 65, selecting this frame, and choosing Insert > Timeline > Frame from the application menu (**Figure 4.31**).

Figure 4.31 Timeline extended

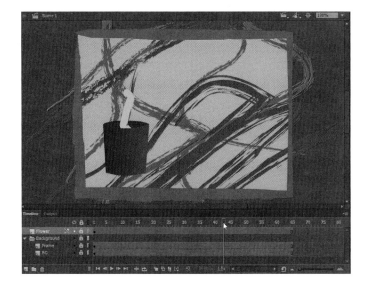

With the number of frames on the main timeline now matching those within the Graphic symbol instance, scrubbing the playhead will reveal one of the strengths of Graphic symbols. Notice that for every frame, the animation is completely synchronous. If you compare this with a Movie Clip symbol instance, you'll see only the first frame of that animation unless you test or publish. This is one reason Graphic symbols are great for animation.

NOTE *When you select the instance and check the Properties panel, you'll notice the Looping section. This section provides even greater control when using Graphic symbols; you can specify the starting frame, how many times the animation loops, and other options.*

3 Create a new layer above the Flower layer and rename it **Message**.

This layer will hold your text message content. The message won't display until the animation is complete, so you need to create an empty keyframe on frame 65 and create your message there.

4 To do so, choose Insert > Timeline > Keyframe from the application menu.

Notice that it created a blank keyframe even though you didn't choose that option. That's because there was no content in the previous keyframe, so inserting a keyframe simply duplicates the content of the previous keyframe—which, in this case, contained nothing.

5 Select frame 65 on the Message layer, lock every other layer, and then choose the Text tool.

6 Access the Properties panel and notice in the Text Type drop-down that only Dynamic Text is selectable because you're targeting HTML5 Canvas (**Figure 4.32**). Choose a font that looks nice to you and set the size value to roughly 60 pt.

7 For color, click the color swatch and then use the Eyedropper tool that appears to sample the color from the flower petals on Stage. You can, of course, color as you desire.

8 With your text properties in place and the Text tool selected, click and drag a text block in an empty area of the Stage. Feel free to move the Flower instance to the side if need be.

9 Type in a message. I'm using the generic greeting "A Flower for You!" but as with many choices in this project, it's really up to you.

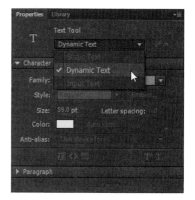

Figure 4.32 Choose Dynamic Text from the Text Type drop-down.

The text should display in the exact font, color, and size you have chosen
(**Figure 4.33**).

Figure 4.33 Text
displayed

10 Because the text is editable, select the text block to modify any of the properties within the Properties panel. You can also adjust the size of the text block
itself. Double-click anywhere in the text block to edit the text and change
your message, if needed.

Applying Text Effects

All text types accept filters, which can be applied from the bottom of the Properties
panel. You access these filters by selecting the text and then clicking the Add Filters
icon in the Filters area.

Available filters include Drop Shadow, Blur, Glow, Bevel, Gradient Glow, Gradient
Bevel, and Adjust Color.

Available filters for HTML5 Canvas are restricted to Drop Shadow, Blur, Glow, and
Adjust Color.

Next you'll add a Drop Shadow to your text.

1 Select the text block and then click the Add Filters icon in the Properties
panel.

2 Choose Drop Shadow and make the following adjustments: change Blur X
and Blur Y to a value of 6, keep Strength at 100%, and choose #000000 for a
color (**Figure 4.34**).

When you're using HTML5 Canvas as a publish target, many filters will work just fine on text. However, if you choose to render text to outlines in your publish settings, the filter will not be applied because a filter cannot be applied to simple shapes but only text blocks or Movie Clip content. As a workaround, you can always wrap the actual text within a Movie Clip symbol and then apply the filter to that instance on the Stage. You'll do this now.

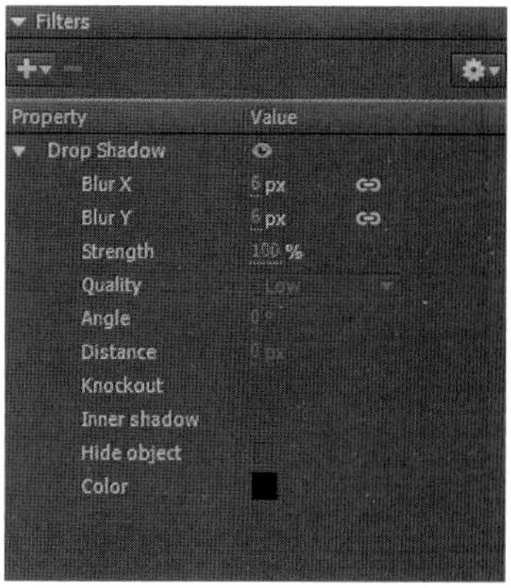

3 With the text block selected, click the Options icon in the Filters area of the Properties panel. Choose the "Copy all filters" option and then remove the Drop Shadow by selecting it and clicking the Delete Filter icon.

4 Choose Modify > Convert to Symbol from the application menu. When the Convert to Symbol dialog box opens, create a Movie Clip symbol named **Message**.

5 Select the instance on the Stage and access the Properties panel.

Movie Clip instances have a Filters area that's identical to what you've seen with text blocks.

6 Click the Options icon and choose "Paste filters." Watch as the Drop Shadow previously attributed to the text block becomes active on the Movie Clip instance.

Now, no matter how you choose to publish your text, it will render with the Drop Shadow applied in HTML5 Canvas (**Figure 4.35**).

Figure 4.34 Choosing Drop Shadow settings

Figure 4.35 Drop Shadow applied

Using JavaScript Code to Stop the Playhead

★ ACA Objective 2.4

If you test the project at this point by choosing Control > Test from the application menu, you'll see how well everything has come together. But the animation loops continuously and the actual text message blips by too quickly to digest as it exists on only one frame out of 65. You need to stop that playhead so the viewer can read the message.

Working with code in Animate CC

Whether you're working with ActionScript or **JavaScript** in Animate CC, the initial workflow is basically identical. Code can be placed on the timeline on specific frames to instruct the project to perform instructions in various ways. The two main panels you'll deal with when writing simple code are the Actions panel and the Code Snippets panel. You access both from the Window application menu item.

Figure 4.36 The Actions panel

ACTIONS PANEL

The Actions panel is a simple code editor where you write all your frame scripts (**Figure 4.36**). It doesn't matter what sort of code you're writing in the Actions panel—both JavaScript and ActionScript are completely supported.

Of course, you can use ActionScript only in an ActionScript-based project and JavaScript only in an HTML5-based project. Frame scripts are the pieces of code you bind to certain frames along the timeline. Additionally, you have a sidebar, which makes it easy to jump around to different pieces of code located on different objects and frames.

Figure 4.37 The Code Snippets panel

CODE SNIPPETS PANEL

Working in the Code Snippets panel (**Figure 4.37**) is a great way for those who are new to working with code to learn how to do some fundamental things within Animate CC projects. The snippets included are divided into three main categories: ActionScript, HTML5 Canvas, and WebGL. These correspond to whichever target platform you're working with.

Within these three main categories are a number of additional, functional categories. Every target platform represented has snippets to manipulate the playhead: either stopping the timeline from playing or jumping around to different frames. Take a look at the possibilities that snippets provide.

Using JavaScript to stop your animation

Now you'll stop that playhead and give your text more screen time with a little JavaScript. The first thing you need to do is decide where to place the code. You'll use frame 65 because that's the frame you need to stop the playhead upon—but which layer?

▶ *Video 4.21*
Stopping the
Playhead

It's best practice in Animate CC to create a layer called Actions where all your frame scripts will be placed. Not only does this make it easy to find any of your code, but it also keeps the code separate from your visual assets that exist in other layers.

1   Create a new layer and name it **Actions**.

2   Insert a blank keyframe on frame 65 by choosing Insert > Timeline > Blank Keyframe from the application menu.

    The only other thing you need to do is write some code within frame 65 on your Actions layer to stop the playhead.

3   With frame 65 of the Actions layer selected, open the Actions panel and place the cursor at line 1 (**Figure 4.38**). Type the following code within the panel:

```
this.stop();
```

Figure 4.38 Code entered in the Actions panel

It's important to understand what this does. In the code, **this** refers to the present Stage—the main Stage. The instruction **stop()** is a method that tells the playhead on that Stage to stop moving immediately and stay there, effectively stopping the animation. That's it! You could certainly use the Code Snippets panel to do this, but it is so simple that typing it in is the more direct route.

Notice on frame 65 that the keyframe has changed. In place of the empty circle, you now have a symbol that lets you know there is code on that keyframe.

> **NOTE** The syntax for stopping an animation in ActionScript is exactly the same as the syntax used here, in JavaScript. CreateJS was written to be as close to ActionScript as possible. Some major differences exist, however. Using JavaScript, frame numbers begin at 0 instead of 1 as they do when using ActionScript.

ANIMATING WITH CODE

All of the animation techniques discussed so far in this book involve working with the timeline. This is the easiest way for a new interactive media creator to get something to move on the screen. Using ActionScript or JavaScript code to animate your creations can be challenging, but it provides a level of control and interactivity that can't be achieved using the timeline alone.

Carefully analyze what you're trying to accomplish, and determine the best route to getting the results required for the project. Once you get past learning the syntax for whichever platform you're targeting, your animation will be much more flexible and easier to edit once created.

Publishing Your Project for HTML5 Canvas

★ ACA Objective 5.4

▶ Video 4.22
Publishing for
HTML5 Canvas

Publishing for HTML5 Canvas is a bit more straightforward than publishing for Flash Player, simply because you have fewer publish settings to set. When publishing for HTML5 Canvas, in place of a single SWF file, you'll have a number of different files that must all be kept together for the project to run. The number of files you have depends on the file types used in the project and your publish settings. The primary file among these is a JavaScript file (with the .js extension).

Publish Settings

You can access the Publish Settings for HTML5 Canvas in the same manner you do when targeting Flash Player. With nothing in your project selected, the Properties panel displays document properties.

1 Under the Publish area of the panel, click the Publish Settings button to open the Publish Settings dialog box (**Figure 4.39**).

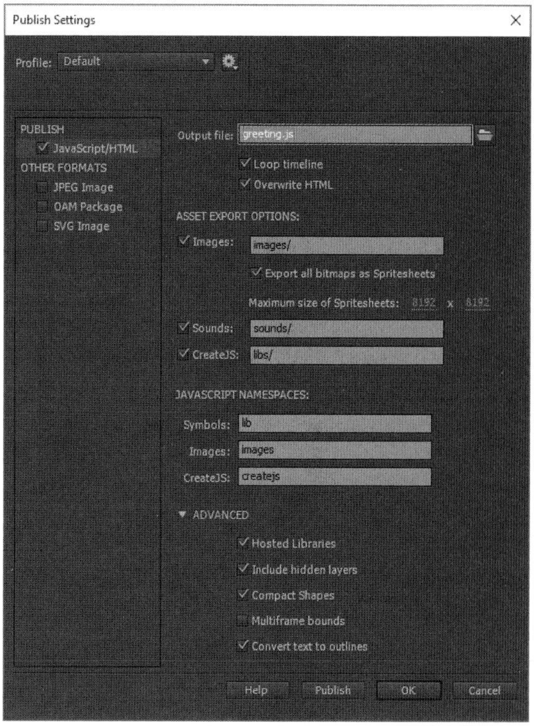

2 In the left-hand column in the Publish Settings dialog box, you'll see a column where you can select JavaScript/HTML under the Publish heading. Make sure this check box is selected. From here, you're able to choose a number of settings:

- The first section allows customization of the output file, asking you to specify the filename and directory for the output. You also have the options to loop the timeline or overwrite any existing HTML.

- Next are directories for your asset exports. If you use any images or sounds in your project, this is where they'll be published to. If you're including images, you can also export

Figure 4.39 The Publish Settings dialog box

them all to a single spritesheet using these settings. There is also a place to specify the directory for the published CreateJS files if you're not using the content delivery network (CDN).

- With the next option you can define JavaScript namespaces. This is useful when you're using a number of additional JavaScript libraries as part of your project to avoid conflicts.

HTML5 Canvas also has an Advanced section, which provides the following options:

- **Hosted Libraries:** Enabling this option means HTML5 Canvas will grab the CreateJS libraries from a remote CDN.

- **Include Hidden Layers: This** includes any layers hidden using layer control.

- **Compact Shapes:** Select this option if you want to make shapes as optimized as possible.

- **Multiframe bounds**: This includes frame bounds properties to objects.

- **Convert text to outlines:** Selecting this option means HTML5 Canvas will render dynamic text as shapes to preserve fonts.

3   When you're ready, click Publish.

WORKING WITH WEBGL

The secondary native HTML5 document type involves the use of WebGL (Web Graphics Library) technology. Interestingly enough, WebGL also makes use of the HTML5 canvas element, but in a different way. WebGL content is actually GPU-accelerated, meaning that it makes direct use of the hardware graphical processing unit (GPU) rather than sharing rendering tasks with everything else running on the central processing unit (CPU). This makes for a much more effective and powerful rendering target.

Although WebGL can be rendered in an accelerated way, it's more difficult to work with than HTML5 Canvas documents. Adobe has created a specialized WebGL runtime to make things easier, but it's still not as robust and direct in use as CreateJS. If you're considering WebGL, be sure that your project will benefit from being GPU-accelerated!

▶ *Video 4.23*
Converting to
WebGL

Challenge!

Right now, your message text just pops in. But it could transition into the message in a subtler way. Find a way to tween in the text as a fade, scale it in, or use some other mechanism for performing an advanced reveal. The next chapter will give you good ideas for accomplishing this.

Conclusion

So there you have it! You used a large variety of tools and techniques to build an animated greeting that can be run in your web browser without the need for Flash Player to be installed. That means your greeting will also run on mobile devices like Android phones and iPads. Of course, even if you do have Flash Player installed on your desktop, this project doesn't rely on or use it.

While working on this project, you've had a look at how easily some of the tools and concepts we already covered when targeting Flash Player are adapted to new publish targets. You've also explored new tools and techniques such as vector art brushes, the Paint Brush tool, variable-width strokes, the Width tool, armature layers, the Bones tool, Graphic and Movie Clip symbols and instances, text effects, and HTML5 Canvas and WebGL publish targets.

CHAPTER OBJECTIVES

Chapter Learning Objectives

- Import bitmap images
- Work with animated masks
- Use the PolyStar tool
- Design with 3D tools for animation
- Work with variable-width motion guides
- Use blend modes and filters
- Create animated text
- Perform raw video export and encoding with Adobe Media Encoder

Chapter ACA Objectives

For more detail on ACA Objectives in this book, see the table on pages 212–215.

DOMAIN 3.0
UNDERSTANDING ADOBE FLASH PROFESSIONAL
3.2, 3.5, 3.6, 3.7

DOMAIN 4.0
CREATING INTERACTIVE MEDIA CONTENT USING FLASH PROFESSIONAL
4.1, 4.2, 4.3, 4.4, 4.5, 4.7, 4.9

DOMAIN 5.0
TESTING, PUBLISHING, AND EVALUATING INTERACTIVE MEDIA ELEMENTS USING FLASH PROFESSIONAL

5.4

CHAPTER 5

Generate a Promotional Video

Animate CC, due to its rich and engaging history, is a great choice for producing flashy, animated content. This project will be a no-holds-barred example of this! You'll be targeting video for this project, so you don't have to worry about the limitations of certain platforms—you'll just make an awesome little video. One of the major uses of Animate CC is to animate and produce content for television and video, so you're in good company.

▶ **Video 5.1** *Project Overview*

> **NOTE** *Adobe has rebranded Flash Professional CC as Animate CC! They are essentially the exact same application—with absolutely no differences in capability aside from features introduced in the regular update schedule. All future updates to Flash Professional CC will be known by the name Animate CC. If desired, subscribers can run multiple versions of the product—branded as either Flash Professional or Animate—but I highly recommend using the latest available version of Animate CC to take advantage of all new features.*

In this project, you'll animate a **demo reel** intro video using imported images, animated masks, blend modes, and effects (**Figure 5.1**). You'll employ all sorts of tools like 3D Rotation and variable-width motion guides to build a real eye-catcher. Generating video content from Animate CC is easy, and it can be used in a variety of other applications.

Figure 5.1 A still from the animated demo you'll create

Video Project Setup

▶ **Video 5.2** *Video Project Setup*

NOTE

All of the videos for this book were recorded with a version of Animate CC branded as Flash Professional CC. It is important to note that everything that we demonstrate in the recordings can be applied to Animate CC—even if we refer to the application as Flash Professional. They are essentially the exact same application—with absolutely no differences in capability.

The first thing you'll need to do, as always, is to create a new document in Animate CC and prepare it for your project assets. At this point, you should know that if you're not targeting the web browser, an ActionScript based-document type is generally the best choice simply due to the amount of extra tools and filters available. In this project, you'll render a video from our animation, so you want to use as much of Animate CC as possible.

1 To begin, create a new ActionScript 3.0 document and save it to your machine.

2 In the Properties panel (**Figure 5.2**), set the Stage width to 1280px and the height to 720px.

This is a 16:9 aspect ratio, which is perfect for HD video. Leave the frames per second at a value of 24 as this is standard for film.

Figure 5.2 Setting properties for this project

3 Click frame 242 in the timeline (you'll have to scroll a bit) and fill this expanse with frames by choosing Insert > Timeline > Frame from the application menu (**Figure 5.3**). If you look down below all layers in the timeline, you'll see that 242 frames at 24fps will total 10 seconds of video. That's the target duration for your promo video.

Figure 5.3 Setting 242 frames as the target duration for this promo

Importing the backgrounds

For the background content, you'll animate between two static images. These images were created in Adobe Photoshop and measure 1280px in width by 720px in height—the same resolution as your project Stage.

★ ACA Objective 4.2

1 Create a new layer and name it **Background**.

2 Import a prepared background image by selecting File > Import > Import to Stage from the application menu.

▶ Video 5.3
Importing
Background Images

You're using the provided image bg.png (**Figure 5.4**). Since the image is the same size as the Stage, it should be placed automatically in the correct position.

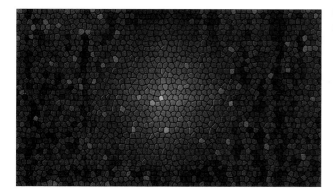

Figure 5.4 The provided background image

3 Lock the layer.

4 Create another new layer directly above the previous one and name it **Foreground**.

5 Import an additional background image, fg.png, into this layer.

This new image completely obscures the previous one.

6 Lock the layer to ensure the contents are not accidentally moved.

Both background layers are now in place and ready to be animated (**Figure 5.5**).

Figure 5.5 Background and Foreground layers in place

Creating Dynamic Backgrounds with Animated Shape Masking

★ *ACA Objective 4.7*

You saw a simple example of **masking** when creating your meme image in Chapter 3. Now you'll create a mask to animate your background content images. However, the images themselves won't be animated at all—the mask will be.

Drawing the mask shape

▶ **Video 5.4** *Create a Star Mask*

To draw the mask, you'll need a new layer.

1 Create an additional layer directly above the Foreground layer and name it **BGMask**.

   In this layer, you'll draw a shape to serve as your mask.

2 Select the PolyStar tool (▣).

   The PolyStar tool is a shape tool (not unlike Rectangle or Oval) that will create either a star or a polygon.

3 To set the number of sides your shape will have, click the Options button in the Properties panel with the PolyStar tool selected. The default is 5, and that should be fine for this mask.

4 Draw a star shape by clicking and dragging with the BGMask layer selected (**Figure 5.6**). The size doesn't matter much since you'll be scaling the shape across your animation, so just make it as large or as small as you want while still retaining manageability.

Figure 5.6 Star shape

5 To make this layer a mask layer, right-click the layer itself and choose Mask.

The layer icon changes its appearance to look like a rectangle with a circle punched out of it. This indicates a mask layer. The layer directly beneath the mask layer automatically becomes masked by this layer and changes its appearance as well. The layer icon changes to resemble the Mask Layer icon, but altered slightly in that it looks more like a turned-up page with a circle punched out of it (**Figure 5.7**). It also becomes nested and indented beneath the mask layer.

WARNING

You won't see the effects of the mask on any content layers in the authoring environment unless both the mask layer and the layers being masked are locked.

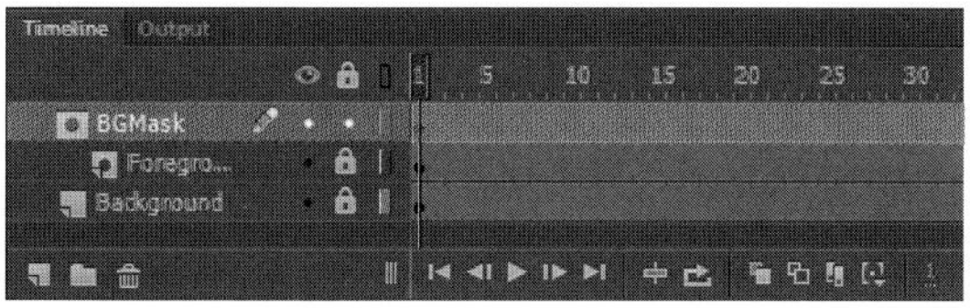

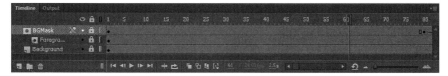

Figure 5.7 The BGMask layer is now easily recognizable as a mask layer by its layer icon.

Animating the mask

ACA Objective 4.5

Now you'll create a shape tween for the BGMask layer.

Video 5.5 Animating the Mask

1 Right-click the frame span and choose Create Shape Tween.

The frame span turns green, but you should also see a broken line across the frames. This happens because you have only a single keyframe at frame 1.

2 Move the playhead to the very end—frame 242—and choose Insert > Timeline > Keyframe from the application menu to insert an additional keyframe.

The broken line now appears solid, indicating a working shape tween (**Figure 5.8**).

Figure 5.8 Broken line now solid

3 Move the playhead to frame 80 and create an additional keyframe. This is where your animated mask will first appear.

4 Select the star shape and resize it to around 30px in width or height—you don't need to be exact.

5 You don't want your mask to appear until frame 80, so move the playhead to frame 1, select the star shape with the Selection tool, and in the Properties panel, make the width and height of this object both a value of 1.

6 Additionally, you don't want the star to animate from 1px to 30px from frame 1 to frame 80, so right-click anywhere along that frame span and choose Remove Tween from the menu that appears.

With your mask at 1px in total diameter across frames 1–79, you won't see any noticeable masking until you want to—at frame 80.

Here's the part where you can get really creative. What you need to do now is animate the shape, scale, position, or rotation of this shape using a number of additional keyframes between frame 80 and frame 242. The idea is to make it engaging and to provide constant motion. To accomplish this, you'll simply scale the star shape up and down between staggered keyframes along the timeline (**Figure 5.9**).

Figure 5.9 Animating the shape with additional keyframes in the timeline

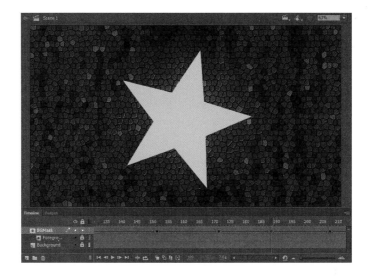

7 Next, preview the animated mask by locking both layers and scrubbing the playhead across the timeline (**Figure 5.10**). Alternatively, you can choose Control > Test from the application menu to compile and view the animation.

You should see the mask you've just created and animated revealing portions of the foreground image against the background image.

Figure 5.10 Previewing the animated mask

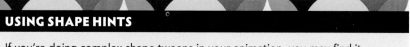

USING SHAPE HINTS

If you're doing complex shape tweens in your animation, you may find it helpful to employ *shape hints*. You can add shape hints to a tween by choosing Modify > Shape > Add Shape Hint from the application menu. You can add as many shape hints as you like (up to 26) to guide the shape tween more precisely between keyframes. Simply adjust the position of the hint circles from keyframe to keyframe on corresponding shape areas.

Design a 3D Rotating Headshot

The next step in your little promotional video is to import a nice **headshot** and then perform some **3D** transforms on it. Additionally, you'll employ some blend modes and effect filters to make things interesting. These are some great techniques that will make your content come to life.

Creating the headshot movie clip

The first thing you'll do is import your headshot image. If you don't have a nice headshot, you should go get one. At the very least, take a selfie with your mobile device and use that. This technique works best with a 1:1 ratio (a square), but if you don't have a square shot, just use what you have on hand.

ACA Objective 4.4

Video 5.6
*Importing the
Headshot*

1 Create a new layer in the timeline and name it **Headshot** (**Figure 5.11**). This
   layer should be positioned above every other layer, and those layers beneath
   it should be locked so that you do not mistakenly modify their contents.

Figure 5.11 The Headshot layer at the top of the
layer stack

Now you need to import the headshot image into your project.

2 Choose File > Import > Import to Stage from the application menu.

3 Browse to your headshot bitmap image and select it for import. Once it's on
   the Stage, depending on how large your image is, you may need to adjust its
   size. I've made mine measure 420px by 420px.

Video 5.7 *Stylize
the Headshot*

Now you'll stylize my image a bit by giving it a nice border (**Figure 5.12**).
The best way to do something like this in Animate CC is through the use of a
stroke, but how can you add a stroke to a bitmap image with no stroke or fill?
The solution is to break the image apart. Breaking apart a bitmap image will
render it as a simple shape object with a bitmap fill using the bitmap it previously was. Because it's a shape, you can easily apply a stroke using the Ink
Bottle tool.

Figure 5.12 Stylizing the
image with a border

4 Select the bitmap image on the Stage.

5 Choose Modify > Break Apart from the application menu and the bitmap will
   be converted to a shape.

6   Now select the Ink Bottle Tool ( ) and, using the Properties panel, choose a color for your stroke.

Clicking any of the four edges of your new shape will apply a stroke of that same color to the already present fill. Using the Properties panel, you can also change the stroke size, cap, and join properties. I'm using a size value of 20 with a square cap and join miter of 3 in order to simulate a nice, thick border.

Now that you've changed your image to represent the visual you desire, it's time to transform the shape into a Movie Clip symbol.

7   Choose Modify > Convert to Symbol from the application menu.

8   Choose Movie Clip as the symbol type and name it **Headshot** (**Figure 5.13**). Additionally, be sure that the registration point is at the center of the Movie Clip symbol.

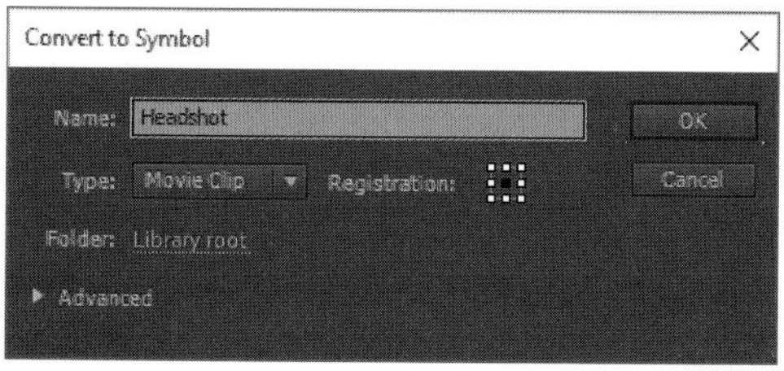

Figure 5.13 Customizing Movie Clip symbol settings in the Convert to Symbol dialog box

You now have a Movie Clip symbol instance on the Stage, but you'll want to perform 3D transformations on this instance yet still retain additional tween controls on the main timeline. To do this, you'll have to wrap this instance within yet another Movie Clip symbol.

▶ *Video 5.8 Prepare the Headshot for Animation*

9   Select the existing instance and choose Modify > Convert to Symbol from the application menu once again. This time, name it **RotatingHeadshot** (**Figure 5.14**).

This movie clip will contain within its timeline the actual 3D transformations and associated tweens.

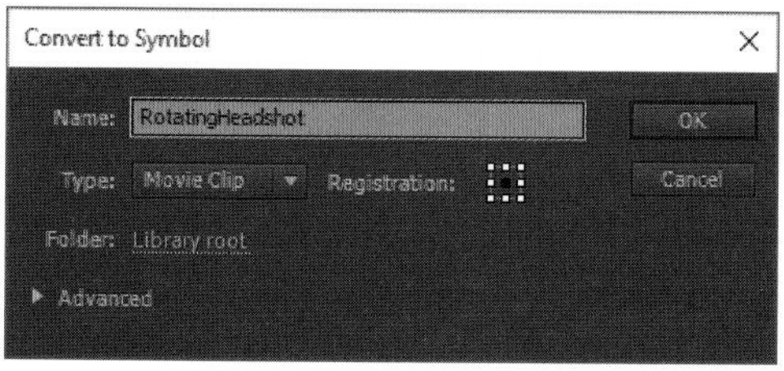

Figure 5.14 Naming the next Movie Clip symbol instance

Using the 3D Rotation Tool to rotate your Headshot movie clip

► **Video 5.9** *3D Tooling Introduction*

To focus this promotional introduction video on yourself, you'll have the headshot appear in the center of the Stage and begin rotating, keeping it constantly in motion while visible in the screen. You'll perform this effect by using the 3D tooling native to Animate CC CC. First, we'll go over some of the tools and concepts you'll use for this portion of the project.

THE 3D ROTATION AND 3D TRANSLATION TOOLS

★ *ACA Objective 3.2*

Animate CC offers two dedicated 3D transformation tools. The first is the 3D Rotation tool ( ) that allows you to rotate a 2D Movie Clip symbol instance around the x-, y-, or z-axis. When you use this tool to select the instance, a special graphical interface appears as an overlay.

NOTE

Notice the effect of the vanishing point, which is used to provide perspective to the artwork as it's moved through the simulated 3D environment.

To use this tool, just begin dragging on the outermost circle of the graphical overlay to rotate around either the x-axis or the y-axis. The inner circle lets you rotate around the z-axis (**Figure 5.15**). It takes some practice, but it's a quick way to simulate 3D using a 2D medium.

The 3D Translation tool ( ) lets you move a movie clip in simulated 3D space. The red horizontal arrow allows the element to be moved along the x-axis; the green vertical arrow moves the element about the y-axis (**Figure 5.16**). Dragging the blue dot will move the element along the z-axis.

Figure 5.15 Adding simulated 3D rotation

Figure 5.16 Adding movement along the x- and y-axes

CREATING THE ROTATION EFFECT FOR YOUR HEADSHOT

For this effect, make sure you're editing the RotatingHeadshot symbol timeline.

▶ *Video 5.10*
Creating the
Rotation Effect

1   To access the symbol timeline, either double-click the instance on the Stage to edit in place or double-click on the symbol in the project Library to edit in isolation (**Figure 5.17**).

Figure 5.17 Editing the symbol timeline

Whichever method you choose, the results will be the same.

To perform the rotation animation, we'll first extend the frames in your movie clip timeline to 40.

2   Select frame 40 within the RotatingHeadshot symbol and choose Insert > Timeline > Frame from the application menu to create a full-frame span across all 40 frames.

3   Right-click any of these frames and choose Create Motion Tween.

The background of the entire frame span turns blue, indicating a motion tween.

4   Rename the present layer Animation.

5   Select the3D Rotation tool (⬤).

You'll be rotating our headshot along the y-axis and have it flip vertically over and over again, making a continuous loop. The y-axis is indicated by the horizontal yellow line in the 3D overlay controls.

6 As you click and drag from this line, notice that a portion of the 360° circle overlay becomes shaded (**Figure 5.18**). This indicates the change in rotation from the present state.

Figure 5.18 The shaded area in the overlay indicates a change in rotation.

7 Move the playhead to frame 10 and click and drag along the y-axis until about a quarter of the circle is indicated through visual shading. This indicates that we will rotate this object 90 degrees along the y-axis. Now move the playhead up 10 additional frames to frame 20 and do the same thing, an additional 90 degrees; again at frame 30; and a final time at frame 40 to complete a 360-degree, complete rotation (**Figure 5.19**).

Figure 5.19 Adding more keyframes to complete the rotation

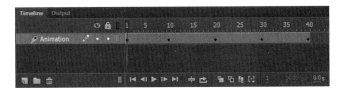

★ ACA Objective 3.5

A good way to visualize the rotation of our object is to open the Motion Editor by double-clicking the motion tween you've been working on. This will open within the timeline itself and allow you to adjust aspects of each property change across time. Here, you can see how the Transform > Rotation > Y value changes by a value of 90 across each keyframe, eventually ending as a complete 360-degree rotation (**Figure 5.20**). In addition to helping you visualize individual properties of an animation, the Motion Editor allows the use of advanced easing through manipulation of the adjustment curves and even automated easing through a set of presets.

NOTE

This is just one suggested approach to 3D rotation. You can choose to animate along any axis you wish, or even try out the 3D Translation tool as well to completely change perspective.

Testing the animation in the timelines should show a smooth rotation, consigned to the y-axis and moving in one direction only. If your animation is jerky or moves in the wrong direction, you can continue to tweak the rotation or even clear the keyframes and start again until everything animates exactly as you intend.

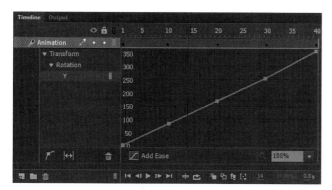

Figure 5.20 Visualizing the rotation in the timeline's Motion Editor

Applying filters and color effects

Filters can be applied to Movie Clip symbol instances and text blocks within your project, whereas Color Effects and Blend Modes are properties on only Movie Clip symbol instances. You'll use both of these effects to enhance perspective during the animation and to provide some interesting visual interaction between elements in your video.

USING BLUR FILTERS TO ADD PERSPECTIVE MOTION TO YOUR ROTATING HEADSHOT

All Movie Clip symbol instances accept filters, which can be applied from the bottom of the Properties panel. You access these filters by selecting the instance on the Stage and then clicking the Add Filters icon in the Filters area of the Properties panel. Available filters include Drop Shadow, Blur, Glow, Bevel, Gradient Glow, Gradient Bevel, and Adjust Color. You'll be using a Blur filter for this animation.

You'll apply the blur to those times when the headshot is rotated in such a way that you see only the thin-side view. Adding a blur to these frames will increase the perception of motion and perspective in 3D space.

1 Move the playhead to frame 15 and then select the object on the Stage with the Selection tool.

2 In the Filters area of the Properties panel, click the Add Filter icon and choose Blur as your filter.

3 Unlink the Blur X and Blur Y properties by clicking the linkage icon so that it appears broken. Now you can adjust each value independent of the other.

NOTE

Not all filters and blend modes are available for all project document types. One of the primary reasons you're using an ActionScript 3.0 document type for this project is so you have access to so many effects.

▶ *Video 5.11*
Employing Blur Filter Effects

4 Set the Blur X value to 200 and Blur Y to 0 and set Quality to High (**Figure 5.21**).

Figure 5.21 Setting blur properties

5 Move the playhead to frame 34 and right-click that frame.

6 Choose Insert Keyframe > Filter in the menu that appears.

This will duplicate the current filter properties on this frame. If you play back the animation or scrub through the timeline, you'll notice that far too many frames are blurred. You want to blur only a couple of frames before and after frames 15 and 34 (**Figure 5.22**). To do this, take your filter settings down to 0 values on certain frames.

Figure 5.22 Blurring additional frames in the timeline

7 Move the playhead to frame 12 and select the object on the Stage.

8 In the Properties panel, dial the Blur X value back down to 0. Do the same on frames 17, 32, and 37 (or whatever frames might look good to you).

9 Move the playhead back to frame 1 and select the object. Note that the default blur values are still present on this frame.

10 Take both Blur X and Blur Y down to a value of 0 and choose High for a Quality setting to match the rest of your filter settings.

If you open the Motion Editor now, you can see exactly how your Blur filter is plotted along the graph (**Figure 5.23**). Notice that you can select from all of the tweened properties in the left-hand column. You are blurring only along the x-axis, so you can select Blur X to highlight that line in the graph. You should see plainly through the spikes how your filter is applied to the instance and at which points it drops off completely.

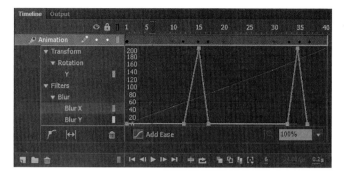

Figure 5.23 The Blur filter plotted in the Motion Editor

ANIMATING THE COMPLETED HEADSHOT WITH A FADE-IN

Now you'll go back out to your main timeline and focus on the Headshot layer. With all of the internal animation and effects properly designed, you can focus on creating a subtle **fade-in** for the complete headshot in your video. Since you're using a Movie Clip symbol instance and the timeline of a movie clip runs completely independent of the main timeline, you don't have to worry at all about syncing frames and can treat this instance independent of anything going on internally.

▶ *Video 5.12 Fade In the Headshot*

1 To achieve a fade-in effect, first right-click the Headshot layer and choose Create Motion Tween.

2 Move the playhead to frame 80 and use the Selection tool to select the object on the Stage.

3 In the Properties panel, go to the Color Effect area and choose Alpha from the selection menu (**Figure 5.24**).

   Since you have your playhead at frame 80, any changes you make to this value slider will be recorded as a new keyframe along the timeline.

   Notice how the object disappears completely if you pull the value slider down to 0? Pull it all the way back up to 100 to make your object completely visible again. The keyframe is preserved.

4 Move the playhead back to frame 30, select the object, and again pull the Alpha slider down to 0, keeping it there.

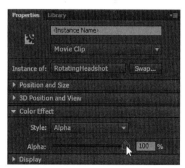

Figure 5.24 For Style, choose Alpha in the Properties panel.

5 Do the same thing on frame 1 to ensure the headshot never becomes visible until you hit frame 30 (**Figure 5.25**).

From frame 30 until frame 80, the Headshot object will fade in to a value of 100 and be completely visible for the remainder of the animation.

 Video 5.13 *Using Blend Modes*

ABOUT BLEND MODES

I've chosen not to use any blend modes on my animation, since it would be rather distracting. But it might enable some interesting effects between different layers in your animation, especially if you have different assets or have changed things up a bit. At the very least, take a look at the various blend modes available to you by selecting the Headshot Movie Clip symbol instance on the Stage and checking the Display area of the Properties panel. You'll find a number of blend modes there to choose from, including Normal, Layer, Darken, Multiply, Lighten, Screen, Overlay, Hard Light, Add, Subtract, Difference, Invert, Alpha, and Erase.

Blend modes cannot be animated from one to another, so whichever one you choose is applied to the entire animation.

Animating Your Name with Motion Presets

Since this is a personal promotional spot, your name is a pretty important part of it. Animate CC comes with a number of motion presets that enable some common animations through an easy-to-use mechanism. Now you'll create some text and then animate it using one of these presets.

Creating Your Name as a Movie Clip

★ ACA Objective 4.3

This part is pretty straightforward.

1. Create a new layer and name it **Name**.

2. Your animation will start at frame 40, so click frame 40 and choose Insert > Timeline > Blank Keyframe from the application menu. You could also choose Insert > Timeline > Keyframe, since there is no content in this layer yet.

3. Select the Text tool () and set some text properties in the Properties panel (**Figure 5.26**).

   I've chosen to use Static Text using a 96-point Futura typeface. Futura is a nice, thick font, so it will have some real presence at 96 points. I've also chosen pure white for my text color so that the name stands out against the darker background elements.

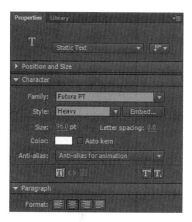

Figure 5.26 Setting text properties

4. Be sure frame 40 is selected on the Name layer, and create a new text block by clicking the Stage and typing in your name.

5. Open the Align panel. With Align to Stage selected, choose to align the text block to the Stage center (**Figure 5.27**).

   ▶ *Video 5.14*
   Creating the
   Headline Text

Figure 5.27 My name typed into the text block and aligned to Stage center

6. In the Properties panel, set the Y position to 120 pixels.

   With your text block created and positioned correctly, there's one more thing you need to do before applying a motion preset: you must convert the text into a Movie Clip symbol instance so that it can have a motion tween applied to it.

7. With the text selected, choose Modify > Convert to Symbol from the application menu.

8. Name it **Name** and be sure to set the registration point to the center. Click OK to create your Movie Clip symbol.

Animating with motion presets

▶ **Video 5.15**
*Animating with
Motion Presets*

Next you'll apply a motion preset to your Name Movie Clip symbol instance.

1 With the object on frame 40 of the Name layer selected, open the Motion Presets panel by choosing Window > Motion Presets.

   In the panel, check out the Default Presets category. You can choose among a number of existing motion presets, and the preview window above the selection area allows you to see how each preset will appear applied to a simple red ball object.

TIP

If you'd like to take a closer look at which properties are being tweened across the frame span, double-clicking the new motion tween that has been created along that frame span will open the Motion Editor.

2 Locate the zoom-in-2D preset and click the Apply button at the very bottom of this panel (**Figure 5.28**).

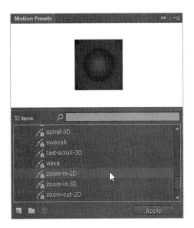

Figure 5.28 Applying the zoom-in-2D preset

TIP

You can also save your own motion presets, as well as load and export motion presets by clicking the Options icon in the upper right of the Motion Presets panel. This makes it easy to create animations that you can apply to many objects and even share with the community.

The motion preset is then applied directly to the instance selected, and a number of additional keyframes are produced (**Figure 5.29**).

You can adjust any of the properties here, and even further modify the motion tween by adjusting other properties if desired. You'll also want your name to remain on the screen for the duration of the entire animation, so you may need to extend the frames in this layer all the way to the end.

Figure 5.29 Additional keyframes created

Dynamic Animation with Variable-Width Motion Guides

One of the most creative enhancements to Animate CC in the past few years has been a rather nifty extension of the Classic motion guide. For this portion of the project, we'll put these enhancements to use when animating three descriptive, text-based movie clips across your animation.

Before moving on, you'll need to think of three words that best describe you or your work. You'll animate these words across the screen, and they'll be very prominent—so make them count!

Building the descriptor text movie clips

The approach you'll take with these objects is to build one of them completely and then duplicate and edit the copies as unique symbols.

▶ **Video 5.16**
Creating Descriptor Text

1 To begin, lock down all the current layers in your project.

2 Create a new layer and name it **Flying Text 1**.

3 Using the Text tool, create a text block using the first of your chosen words.

   I'm using the Impact font at 38 points, colored with a medium gray value of #999999. I recommend this gray color because, later on, you'll apply a color tint to these objects in your animation and they show up best on a neutral color like gray.

4 Choose the Selection tool and click the text you just created to select it. Convert it to a Movie Clip symbol by choosing Modify > Convert to Symbol from the application menu.

5 Choose Movie Clip as the symbol type, assign the registration point to the center, and name this symbol **Text1** (**Figure 5.30**).

   You now have a Movie Clip symbol that you can duplicate and edit to create the remaining two words for your animation.

Figure 5.30 Text named, registration point set

Video 5.17
Duplicate and Edit
Symbols

6 In the Library panel, right-click the Text1 symbol and choose Duplicate (**Figure 5.31**).

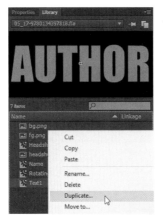

Figure 5.31 Duplicating the Text1 symbol

7 You'll be prompted to give the duplicated movie clip a new name, so name it **Text2**. Perform these same actions to create a third symbol, and name this one **Text3**.

8 With these two additional symbols created, double-click each one and edit the text blocks contained within to display your two additional words.

The words I've used for myself, and the corresponding movie clip names, are represented here. Note that I'm using all caps to give each word the maximum impact.

AUTHOR = "Text1" Movie Clip symbol

ARTIST = "Text2" Movie Clip symbol

ENGINEER = "Text3" Movie Clip symbol

Animating the descriptors with Classic motion guides

NOTE

A Classic motion guide layer is created to work alongside a Classic tween. You can't use a Classic motion guide on a motion tween. Motion tweens have their own motion guides built in.

With your Movie Clip symbols created and ready to go, you need to create some additional layers to contain their instances. Similar to how you created these symbols, the most efficient way to create additional layers, since the content is so very similar, is to duplicate them. But first, you'll create a parent layer, along with our Classic motion guide layer.

1   First, for the Classic motion guide layer, right-click the existing Flying Text 1 layer and choose Add Classic Motion Guide from the menu that appears (**Figure 5.32**).

    This automatically creates a new layer that will serve as your Classic motion guide and nests the selected layer within it, applying whatever guide you eventually draw on the Stage. Notice how the appearance of each layer changes to reflect all of this.

    Within your newly created guide layer, you need to create an element that will serve as your Classic motion guide.

Figure 5.32 Adding the Classic motion guide

2   Select the Line tool (); a stroke will serve the purpose of a Classic motion guide.

3   Draw a line that measures 2000 pixels across and is positioned 500 pixels along the y-axis and –360 pixels along the x-axis (**Figure 5.33**).

Figure 5.33 Line drawn across the Stage

This effectively centers the shape vertically across the Stage (**Figure 5.34**).

Figure 5.34 Text centered

4   Select the Flying Text 1 layer, and on frame 1, move the Text1 instance so that the transform point locks up with the line you just created.

    I've aligned it to a Y position of 500 and an X position of 1600. This places the text on the pasteboard, initially.

5   Move the playhead to frame 45 and select that frame. Choose Insert > Timeline > Keyframe from the application menu to create a keyframe.

6   Select the instance at frame 45 and modify the X position to –300 so that it appears on the opposite side of the Stage.

Since you're using a Classic motion guide, the instance will tween across this guide, even if the guide object is curved or similarly complicated in structure.

7   Right-click anywhere on that layer between these two keyframes and choose Create Classic Tween from the menu that appears.

The frame-span background turns purple, indicating a Classic tween has been created (**Figure 5.35**). Classic tweens are very similar to motion tweens but do certain things in slightly different ways.

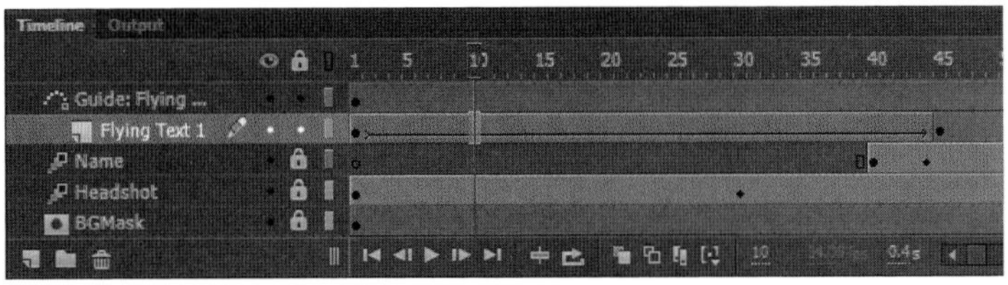

Figure 5.35 The purple frame span indicates a Classic tween has been created.

TIP

Since Classic motion guides require Classic tweens and Classic tweens require that keyframes be created in this way, you have to create additional keyframes like this manually.

▶ *Video 5.18*
Animating with Classic Motion Guides

▶ *Video 5.19*
Duplicating Layers and Swapping Symbols

8   Test the animation to be sure the Transform point of the Movie Clip symbol instance on both frame 1 and frame 45 are properly aligned and that the animation follows the guide we have established. If it doesn't, you'll need to adjust the positioning of these elements because the Transform point of the instance on each frame must come in contact with the guide element for it to be effective.

You've already created a Flying Text 1 layer tween that contains your Movie Clip symbol instance named Text1 and animates nicely in accordance with the established Classic motion guide. Why go through all that trouble two additional times when you can simply duplicate the layer and swap out symbols?

9   Right-click the Flying Text 1 layer and choose Duplicate Layers from the menu which appears.

Animate CC creates an exact copy of that layer.

10 Rename the layer to **Flying Text 2** and then swap out its Text1 instances on both frame 1 and frame 45 for Text2 instances (**Figure 5.36**). To do this, select the instance in question and, in the Properties panel, click the Swap button.

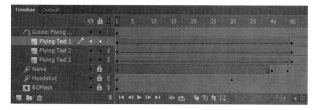

Figure 5.36 Flying Text layer duplicated in the timeline

11 In the Swap Symbol dialog box that appears, choose Text2 and click OK (**Figure 5.37**).

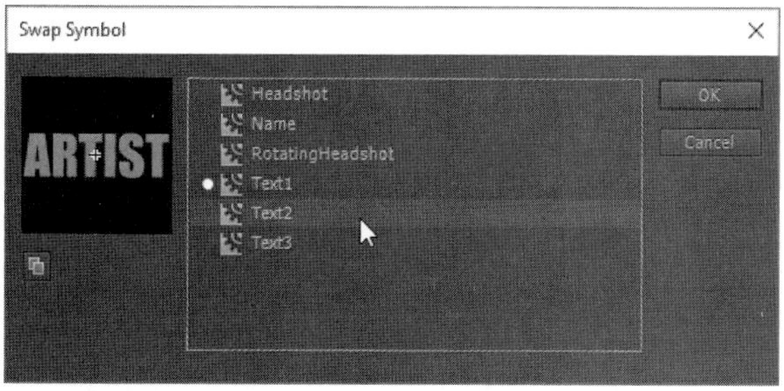

Figure 5.37 The Swap Symbol dialog box

12 Perform this same operation to create a third layer, naming it **Flying Text 3** and swapping its instances of frames 1 and 45 for Text3.

Now, you'll stagger your animated text instances to flow in one after the other accordingly.

13 Click and drag across all 45 frames of the Flying Text 1 layer, and then with that entire span of frames highlighted, click-drag it across the timeline so that the initial keyframe lands at frame 65 and the last keyframe at frame 110.

14 Perform the same action on the Flying Text 2 layer, but drag it so that the initial keyframe lands at frame 100 and the last keyframe at frame 145.

15 Finally, perform this same set of actions on the Flying Text 3 layer so that the initial keyframe lands at frame 135 and the last keyframe at frame 180.

All three layers should be nicely staggered (**Figure 5.38**).

> **NOTE**
>
> You can swap out any Movie Clip in the current project Library without having to change position, scale, color effects, or anything else applied to a symbol instance.

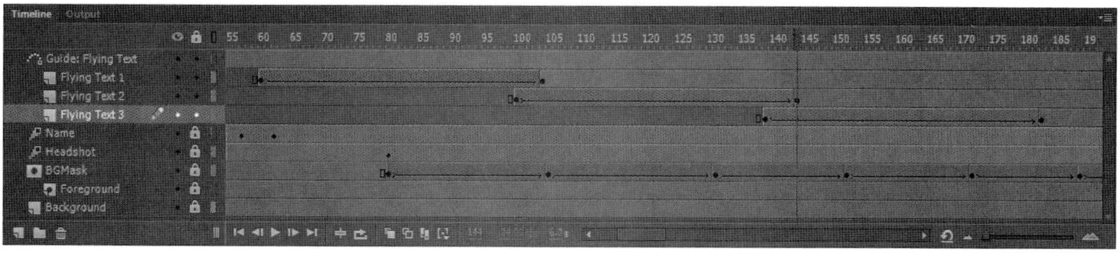

Figure 5.38 All Flying Text layers now staggered in the timeline

Employing variable-width stroke options

▶ **Video 5.20**
*Variable Width
Motion Guides*

Variable-width strokes can do more than simply adopt and adapt width profiles. When used as Classic motion guides, they can also influence the scale and color of the objects they are guiding. You'll convert your simple stroke guide to one that employs a variable width and use it to add more dynamic characteristics to our animation.

1 Select the stroke you have in your Classic Motion Guide layer and increase the stroke size in the Properties panel to a value of 77.

2 For the stroke color, choose the default rainbow-colored linear gradient swatch. Strokes can have gradients applied to them just like fills (**Figure 5.39**).

TIP

*Feel free to change
both the width profile
and color of your guide
stroke to adjust things
to your liking. Experi-
ment and have fun!*

Figure 5.39 Setting stroke properties in the Properties panel

3 Take a look at the variable width profiles in the Width selection box. Choose Width Profile 1.

Your guide stroke should now look sort of like a rainbow-colored flying saucer. You'll modify this with the Width tool.

4 Select the Width tool and then pinch down two new width points so that the stroke is thick in the center but thin everywhere else (**Figure 5.40**).

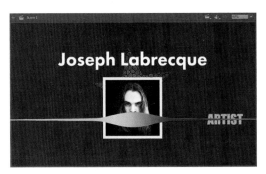

Figure 5.40 Shaping the guide stroke

5   Click the first text layer nested beneath the Classic Motion Guide layer.

This will select the Classic tween itself and allow you to manipulate some of its attributes in the Properties panel.

6   In the Tweening section, enable both Color Along Path and Scale Along Path (**Figure 5.41**).

These options are peculiar to Classic tweens and work only in conjunction with a Classic motion guide like the one you created here. Test your project and watch as the scale and color shifts across the entire tween.

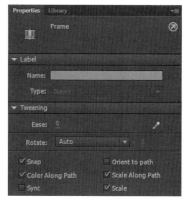

Figure 5.41 Setting Tweening properties

Rendering and Converting the RAW Video

Now that you have completed the animation for your video, it's time to convert it to actual video data. Right now, the project is just data wrapped in an FLA. If you publish this project, it will be compiled to SWF for playback in Flash Player. You're going to do something different, though: render this project to a **raw** HD video file.

★ *ACA Objective 5.4*

Exporting video from Animate CC

When your animation is complete and you're ready to render it all to a video file, select File > Export > Export Video from the application menu. The Export Video dialog box appears, allowing you to specify a number of settings before rendering the video file to disk (**Figure 5.42**).

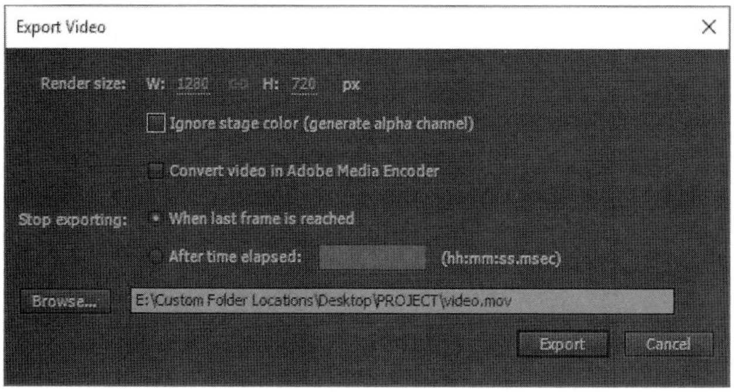

▶ *Video 5.21 Rendering the Video*

Figure 5.42 The Export Video dialog box

Among these settings are the render width and height, the path you want to export to, and whether to open the resulting video in Adobe Media Encoder for further transcoding. Once the file is in Adobe Media Encoder, you can apply a wide variety of settings to create as many derivative video files as needed.

Adobe Media Encoder

Even without considering digital rights management (**DRM**) issues, the sheer variety of file formats can be overwhelming. Adobe Media Encoder is a dedicated video transcoding application that is part of Adobe Creative Cloud and provides an efficient interface for converting media file formats for all sorts of purposes (**Figure 5.43**).

▶ *Video 5.22* Using Adobe Media Encoder

The software has an elegant interface that lets you convert one file at a time using presets. You can even set up a drop folder to process your media automatically using a custom compression setting as soon as it is copied into that directory.

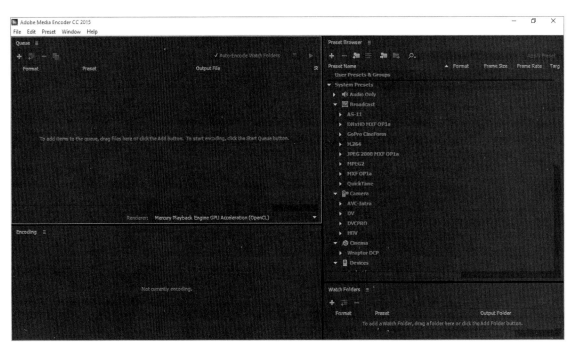

Figure 5.43 Adobe Media Encoder

TRANSCODING THE VIDEO

Before using the video you just rendered on the web, you'll need to **transcode** the raw render to a compatible format for your target. You'll use Adobe Media Encoder to convert this video for the web using presets.

1   Start Adobe Media Encoder and drag and drop your rendered video into the Queue panel of the interface. (You'll see a message in the middle of the panel that reads "To add items to the queue, drag files here," so it's pretty hard to miss.)

2   Once the video has been added to the queue, select a preset from the Preset Browser panel (**Figure 5.44**). You could also use the drop-down list under the Format and Preset columns. For this project, select H.264 for Format and YouTube 720p HD for Preset.

These selections will produce a video file that is playable on the vast majority of web browsers and is optimized for upload to YouTube.

Figure 5.44 Adobe Media Encoder's Preset Browser

3   When ready, click the Start Queue button that appears as a small green arrow.

Any items within the queue will then be transcoded and output to their specified destinations.

Using the video

TIP

You can also use an MP4 file with additional playback options— both HTML5 and JavaScript players and those based on Adobe Flash Player. It's a truly versatile video format.

With a standard **H.264**-encoded MP4 file in your possession, you can now distribute your video to the world! It's simple enough to upload your video to a service like YouTube or Vimeo, and if you've chosen to export an MP4 file, you can integrate it into a web page and deliver the video yourself.

To embed the video for playback in a web browser, you can use the native HTML5 video element. Here's a simple example:

```
<video width="1280" height="720" controls
src="myRenderedVideo.mp4"></video>
```

Video in Animate CC

★ *ACA Objective 4.9*

Animate CC and video playback have been closely related for many years. For years, web browsers had no way of implementing video playback natively. Instead, browsers needed to leverage some sort of plug-in to play back video. Before Flash Player became the de facto standard for web video, an assortment of additional plug-ins were used, including Real Player, Windows Media Player, and QuickTime.

With the advent of YouTube in 2007 and thanks to a number of video playback and streaming advancements in the Flash Player runtime, Flash Player took over the video scene very quickly, becoming the primary method of video playback on the web for years. Recently, web browsers have begun to support native video playback using the HTML5 video element. However, this format is widely supported only for progressive video playback; the majority of browsers have no native solution for streamed video content.

Supported video file types

Animate CC projects targeting ActionScript 3.0 support a number of video file types. These range from those file types with unique, specific qualities that can be used only in ActionScript-based projects to the most widely used video file type on the web today: MP4.

- **FLV:** The FLV format is usually presented in a smaller, standard-definition resolution and can be embedded directly into a Animate CC FLA project. However, you probably don't want to do that unless the video is very small; streaming video is much more efficient. FLV can be streamed as well using Adobe Media Server or other rich media services. One unique feature of an

FLV is that it can include a full alpha channel, meaning that you can use video with transparent backgrounds in your Animate CC project. No other video format on the web today can do this. Note that this format can no longer be output using Adobe Media Encoder.

- **MP4:** The MP4 file format, or H.264, is the standard for web video and is supported by many mobile devices. It allows for high-resolution video delivery and includes a number of different profiles, nearly all of which are supported by the Adobe Flash runtimes. This allows the Flash Player or Adobe AIR–based playback to play videos that are also compatible with tablet devices and smartphones that don't support the Adobe Flash runtimes through alternate means, such as the HTML5 video element.

- **F4V:** The F4V format also supports high-definition resolution and has much more metadata associated with the file. F4V is based on the MP4 specification, but it includes additional metadata to work specifically with Animate CC projects.

Embedding video files

Video can be added to an ActionScript 3.0 Animate CC project either by placing an FLVPlayback component on the Stage and configuring the properties through the Properties panel or by using the File > Import > Import Video command. The latter will take you to a wizard that will walk you through the steps to configure the FLV-Playback component to play the selected FLV, F4V, or MP4 file (**Figure 5.45**). When you have finished those steps, you'll be set up with the very same components that you would have had if you had done it manually.

NOTE

As mentioned, video embedding is available only for use in the ActionScript 3.0 document type. Embedded video works best for smaller video clips, with a playback time of less than 10 seconds. If you're using video clips with longer playback times, consider using progressively downloaded video or streaming video using Flash Media Server.

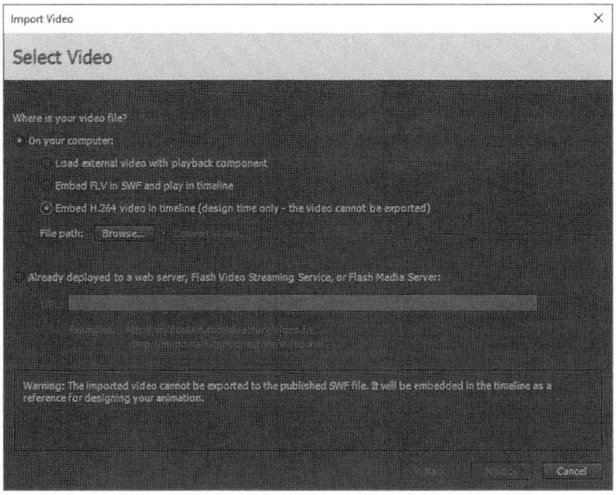

Figure 5.45 The Import Video wizard

ADDING MP4 VIDEO AS A GUIDE

With the most recent releases of Animate CC, you can also import video to be used as a guide for your animated content. To do this, choose the File > Import > Import Video command from the application menu and select "Embed H.264 video in the timeline." When an MP4 video is embedded, the frames of the video are rendered on the Stage as you scrub along the timeline. This feature enables you to use videos as a guide to synchronize your animation on the Stage.

Working with published video

Whether the video content originates from a Animate CC project—as is the case with the project you produced in this chapter—or from some other source, you have a few options for playing back that video either through the Adobe Flash runtimes or through the native HTML5 video element in the browser. Whatever your source, be sure to encode the video file as an H.264-compliant MP4 file to ensure the broadest amount of compatible playback options.

PLAYBACK USING PROGRESSIVE DOWNLOAD

Progressive download is a simple form of video playback that involves the download of an entire MP4 file for playback through either Flash Player or the HTML5 video element. All it takes to enable this sort of playback is for the video files to be served via HTTP from a web server. This is the only widely supported delivery mechanism for the HTML5 video element.

The positive aspect of progressive download delivery is that it's easy to implement. Just place the video file on a web server and point your playback to the file.

The downsides of this method of video delivery are that the user can't skip around to various parts of the video until those portions have been downloaded. This is quite problematic for long videos as the entire video must be downloaded before the user can view later portions. What's more, with progressive download, there is generally no security or DRM protection enabled on the video. Because this is basically a direct download, the entire video is copied from the web server to the client machine.

PLAYBACK USING VIDEO STREAMING

Deploying the videos through use of Adobe Media Server or through some other video streaming service will not only allow true streaming but also can automatically adapt the quality of the video based on the end user's bandwidth. All of this happens on the fly, meaning the quality can be throttled even as the video is playing.

The positive aspects of streaming delivery are that the user can easily skip around to various parts of the video as soon as a connection to the server is made and the stream is initiated. They never have to wait for the video to download—just for the stream to buffer a little.

Streaming a video is the most secure method of delivery since the actual video file never touches the client machines. Instead, small chunks of video content are delivered in a stream and removed from memory as soon as they are consumed.

The downsides of this method of video delivery are that streaming is complicated, and it involves an additional, specialized streaming server. You must also take into account the streaming protocols you want to use and whether a specific playback mechanism supports those protocols.

TYPES OF STREAMING

The Adobe Media Server software is a system that streams audio and video files from a server to an end user's system. It can assess the end user's bandwidth and automatically throttle quality up and down in real time to make the most of the connection. It also allows videos to be scrubbed backward and forward, even allowing forward scrubbing to parts of the video that have yet to download. It will simply start downloading from the point the playhead is released. Adobe Media Server (**Figure 5.46**) supports three main streaming protocols: RTMP, HLS, and HDS.

- **RTMP** stands for Real Time Messaging Protocol and originally began as a basic communications protocol in Macromedia Flash Communication Server, which was later renamed Adobe Flash Media Server (once the video streaming capabilities became popular) and finally Adobe Media Server (now that it can deliver video content over a variety of protocols). RTMP is used to deliver content to Flash Player and Adobe AIR over port 1935.

- **HLS** stands for HTTP Live Streaming and was created by Apple. It delivers content over HTTP (port 80) by way of a set of chunked file fragments tied together with an index manifest file instructing the playback how to assemble the stream. This format can be generally consumed with the OS X and iOS Safari browser, some Android browsers, and Flash Player and Adobe AIR via an HLS transcode library. It's important to note that even though this protocol is delivered over HTTP, nearly every desktop browser is incapable of playing it natively.

Figure 5.46 Adobe
Media Server

- **HDS** stands for HTTP Dynamic Streaming. It works in a similar way to HLS, though it's used only to deliver content to Flash Player and Adobe AIR. HDS can be seen as a competitor to HLS, though isn't used much outside of Adobe solutions.

PROTECTING VIDEO WITH DRM

DRM is encoded data within a video or audio file that is meant to prevent you from accessing, copying, and converting that data. To prepare audio and video for use with Animate CC content, you often need to run the media through a conversion process that can enable DRM on the video. If the file has DRM, most encoding software will not be able to process the file properly.

Although it may be possible to "crack" the DRM, it's probably there to protect intellectual property. Always request a non-DRM version if the copyright and intellectual property information has already been cleared.

Challenge!

What good is video if you can't play it back? Try taking the video file you've created and working with it in some other capacity. Take it into an Adobe Premiere Pro or Adobe After Effects project, build a simple player in Animate CC, or even just try for simple playback through the HTML5 video element by using Adobe Dreamweaver.

Conclusion

You should come away from this chapter thinking primarily about the various ways of working with video in relation to Animate CC—whether through content creation, ingest, or playback. Video is such a huge part of Animate CC and the wider Adobe Flash platform story that it deserves much attention.

We've covered a lot of great visual effects and techniques in this chapter: image import, animated masks, the PolyStar tool, 3D animation tools, variable-width motion guides, blend modes, effects and filters, animated text, raw video export, and the use of Adobe Media Encoder. Additionally, we've explored other video playback and streaming concepts that should provide a solid base for determining playback methodologies.

CHAPTER OBJECTIVES

Chapter Learning Objectives

- A brief introduction to ActionScript
- Work with Adobe AIR for Desktop
- Build nested, interactive Movie Clip symbols
- Manipulate visual assets through code
- Implement basic ActionScript concepts like variables, functions, and event listeners
- Import sound files and using them on the timeline
- Control sound from ActionScript code
- Publish an Adobe AIR for Desktop project

Chapter ACA Objectives

For more detail on ACA Objectives in this book, see the table on pages 212–215.

DOMAIN 3.0
UNDERSTANDING ADOBE FLASH PROFESSIONAL
3.2, 3.6, 3.7

DOMAIN 4.0
CREATING INTERACTIVE MEDIA CONTENT USING FLASH PROFESSIONAL
4.1, 4.2, 4.3, 4.4, 4.6, 4.8

DOMAIN 5.0
TESTING, PUBLISHING, AND EVALUATING INTERACTIVE MEDIA ELEMENTS USING FLASH PROFESSIONAL
5.1, 5.4

CHAPTER 6

Tick-Tock…
Build a Virtual Clock

In previous chapters, you've seen how you can use Adobe Animate CC
to create static and animated content for various target platforms. In this
chapter, you'll break free from the web browser and move into the realm
of merging design and development in order to target publication to the
desktop operating system.

> **NOTE** *Adobe has rebranded Flash Professional CC as Animate CC!
> They are essentially the exact same application—with absolutely no
> differences in capability aside from features introduced in the regu-
> lar update schedule. All future updates to Flash Professional CC will
> be known by the name Animate CC. If desired, subscribers can run
> multiple versions of the product—branded as either Animate CC or
> Animate—but I highly recommend using the latest available version
> of Animate CC to take advantage of all new features.*

Figure 6.1 Our virtual clock

In this project, you'll build a functional, animated clock application (**Figure 6.1**) that can be installed on either the Windows or
OS X desktop. To do this, you'll employ Adobe AIR and a nice
bit of ActionScript code to get everything wired up. Don't think
you won't be designing and animating, though! One of the strengths of
Animate CC is the tight integration between design and development.
This project aims to be a true showcase of this fact.

> **NOTE** *All of the videos for this book were recorded with a version of
> Animate CC branded as Flash Professional CC. It is important to note
> that everything that we demonstrate in the recordings can be applied to
> Animate CC—even if we refer to the application as Animate CC. They are
> essentially the exact same application—with absolutely no differences in
> capability.*

▶ **Video 6.1** *Project
Overview*

Working with ActionScript 3.0

ACA Objective 2.4 **ActionScript** is a programming language originally developed for the manipulation of 2D graphics. It has gone through many iterations and has evolved into a powerful interactive media development environment. It can control and create a wide variety of interactive media objects, including images, type, sound, and video.

ActionScript uses standard syntax, making it accessible to programmers familiar with JavaScript. The included libraries simplify the control of many advanced interactive media interactions.

Versions of ActionScript

ActionScript has been through three major revisions. Previous versions of Animate CC allowed authors to select which version of ActionScript they wanted to use for authoring. Flash Professional CC now requires all documents to be authored in ActionScript 3.0 if an ActionScript-based target platform is selected. ActionScript 3.0 is much more powerful, flexible, and efficient than previous versions.

The only downside to the **deprecation** of previous ActionScript versions is the maintenance of older code that should have been updated long ago for security and performance reasons. If you need to update or publish ActionScript 2.0 projects, you'll have to use Animate CC CS6 to do so.

ActionScript vs. JavaScript

Although ActionScript may seem quite different from JavaScript, the truth is that both languages have a lot more in common than is readily apparent. Both are based on the **ECMAScript** specification—or, rather, different versions of that specification. When Adobe (and ActionScript's originator Macromedia) was developing ActionScript 3.0, developers made a great deal of effort to align the language with the upcoming ECMAScript 4 specification, which would form the basis of the next version of JavaScript. The idea was that ActionScript and JavaScript—being nearly identical in their implementation of the ECMAScript specification—would be the best thing for everyone.

This plan would've worked out wonderfully if ECMAScript 4 hadn't been declared dead before it could be implemented in JavaScript. Unfortunately, JavaScript would never see all the goodies in ECMAScript 4 like packages, classes, strong typing, and the rest. But ActionScript 3.0 would see these things since it was (and remains) based on this abandoned specification. Not only can you use the advanced programming concepts described here, but you've been able to do so for nearly a decade while these capabilities remain unavailable in JavaScript.

So although ActionScript and JavaScript do share a lot of syntax—they are based on similar specifications—just enough differences exist to make the relationship confusing to newcomers. In this project, you'll be using ActionScript, so you can use all the extra features you want!

ACTIONSCRIPT 4.0

A few years ago, Adobe began researching what it referred to as "Action-Script Next" (**Figure 6.2**), which was intended to be the next iteration of the ActionScript programming language. Adobe eventually decided that the direction the new version was taking would be too drastic a difference—especially considering the number of frameworks and libraries being written for ActionScript 3.0 that would be rendered unusable in this new version.

Adobe announced in January 2013 that the company would abandon further research into this new version of ActionScript and instead focus on adding planned features (such as workers) into the current version of the language.

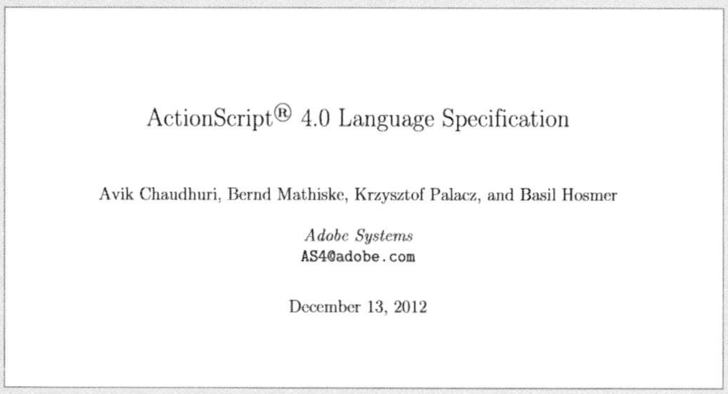

NOTE

If you're interested, you can review the work Adobe has completed in this effort by viewing the Action-Script 4 Language Reference, Virtual Machine Specification and White Paper archive at https:// github.com/ adobe-research/ ActionScript4.

ActionScript® 4.0 Language Specification

Avik Chaudhuri, Bernd Mathiske, Krzysztof Palacz, and Basil Hosmer

Adobe Systems
AS4@adobe.com

December 13, 2012

Figure 6.2 ActionScript 4.0

Actions panel

You encountered the Actions panel (**Figure 6.3**) earlier in this book, and you'll spend quite a bit of time there in this project. To open the Actions panel, choose Window > Actions, or press F9. The code you write can be stored externally or attached to a frame—known as a frame script—and be completely contained along with all assets and animations with a single FLA file.

Figure 6.3 The Actions panel

When you're working with frame scripts, it is best practice to start by creating a dedicated layer for your code on the timeline named **Actions**. Any code that is bound to a specific frame in that layer will be executed when the playhead reaches it. You'll write a good amount of ActionScript in this panel as you work through this chapter.

Creating an Adobe AIR for Desktop Document

As with most projects designed using Animate CC, the first thing to do is create a new document and prepare for the work ahead. For this project, forget the web—you're building a desktop application with Adobe AIR.

About Adobe AIR for Desktop

If Flash Player can be considered the primary Adobe runtime, then the secondary Adobe runtime is Adobe AIR (**Figure 6.4**). AIR is an acronym for Adobe Integrated Runtime and allows programs written in ActionScript to run directly on the operating system as an installable application, completely bypassing the browser environment. Depending on the version of Adobe AIR in use, you can target Windows, OS X, and certain Linux-based operating systems.

Figure 6.4 Adobe AIR

Adobe AIR programs can be packaged in two different ways. The primary method of program distribution is to package the program as an AIR file and install it on a system that already has the Adobe AIR **runtime** installed separately. The drawback of this approach is that the user must install both your program and the runtime on which it relies. The benefit is that you're choosing a completely cross-platform method of distribution: both Windows and OS X users can share and install the same AIR file.

The second (and recommended) way of distributing Adobe AIR programs on desktop operating systems involves packaging the actual AIR runtime itself along with your program within a single-installer package. Not only does this strategy remove the reliance on a separate runtime install, it also ties your program to a specific, tested version of Adobe AIR. It allows for extended native desktop capabilities such as the powerful Native Process **API**, enabling you to tap into additional executable code and processes that are either bundled along with your application or native to the operating system. The downside is that you must produce separate packages for each operating system you're targeting. What's more, it will result in a much larger package of files.

NOTE

Linux is supported only for Adobe AIR versions up to and including 2.5. Later versions are no longer supported due to the small user base on Linux systems.

Setting up the Adobe AIR project document

To create an Animate document that targets Adobe AIR for Desktop, you'll make choices similar to those you've made when beginning other projects in this book.

1 From the Welcome Screen, choose Create New > AIR for Desktop (**Figure 6.5**). Alternatively, choose File > New > AIR for Desktop from the application menu.

However you've gone about creating your document, it should now be open and ready for you to start working.

★ *ACA Objective 4.1*

▶ *Video 6.2 Creating a New AIR for Desktop Document*

Figure 6.5 The New
Document dialog box

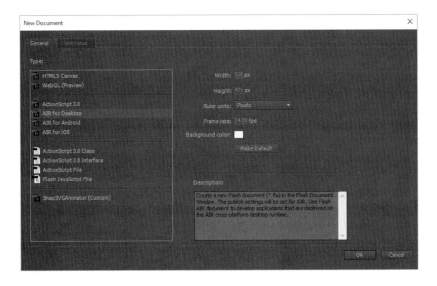

For this project, you'll be building a small clock application that can tell time in both analog and digital formats. The application Stage does not need to be very large for this, but neither do you want it to be too small.

2 Choose a width and height of 500 pixels to form a completely square Stage.

3 Set the background to whatever color you want. (I'm choosing black again.) Set the fps to 12.

You won't have a lot of animated content on the timeline for this project, so keeping the fps down a bit will save resources for the end user.

4 Choose AIR 19 for Desktop from the Target drop-down (**Figure 6.6**).

Figure 6.6 Adobe AIR document properties

UPDATING ADOBE AIR

Animate CC includes a simple mechanism to update Adobe AIR to the latest version, in case your software is a version or two behind. Adobe delivers major, numbered releases of AIR every quarter, and security and bug updates as needed between quarters. Animate CC generally has only a couple of updates a year and so it may be necessary to update your internal AIR SDK more frequently than you update Animate CC.

1   To update or add versions of Adobe AIR to Animate CC, choose Help > Manage Adobe AIR **SDK** from the application menu.

The Manage Adobe AIR SDK dialog box (**Figure 6.7**) appears, prompting you to locate a downloaded AIR SDK via your system file browser.

Manage Adobe AIR SDK ✕

Version	Path
17.0	C:\Program Files\Adobe\Adobe Flash CC Prerelease\AIR17.0
19.0	C:\Program Files\Adobe\Adobe Flash CC Prerelease\AIR19.0

OK   Cancel

Figure 6.7 The Manage Adobe AIR SDK dialog box

TIP

There are a number of places where you can download AIR SDK versions, but the safest is directly from Adobe: http://www.adobe.com/ devnet/air/ air-sdk-download.html.

2   Locate the SDK you have downloaded.

Animate CC will add it to the list of available AIR versions in both the Manage Adobe AIR SDK dialog box and the Publish Target drop-down.

Creating the application background

Now you'll add a background to the Stage using an image I've prepared that looks very much like an old wall texture.

1   Rename the Layer 1 layer that is created by default to **Background** by double-clicking the current name and typing in the new one.

2   Choose File > Import > Import to Stage from the application menu and choose the wall.png image, or use your own background image if you like.

The bitmap image is imported into the project Library, and an instance of the bitmap is placed perfectly on the Stage (**Figure 6.8**).

★ *ACA Objective 4.2*

▶ *Video 6.3 Import the Background Texture*

NOTE

When using Adobe AIR as a publish target, you can create an application with a transparent background, if you wish. You can even completely disable all visual elements of the application window system chrome (through the Application Descriptor file). You'll learn more about this topic later in this chapter.

Figure 6.8 The time-line and Stage with Background

3   Be sure to lock down this layer and save your document when finished.

Building the Basic Clock Visual Elements

⭐ *ACA Objective 3.2*

Before you get into any sort of development for this project, you'll want to design a number of visual elements. Some of these elements will remain static, whereas others will have their properties manipulated through the ActionScript code you will write.

Building the clock body

▶ **Video 6.4** *Build the Clock Body*

You have your application background already established, so now you'll build the main body of your clock. The body will consist of a main cabinet, and you can also create the visual effect of having a recessed space to house the clock pendulum.

1   Create a new layer to hold the clock body visual assets and name it **ClockBody**.

2   With that done, choose the Rectangle tool (▢) and draw a shape that measures 340px in width and 500px in height.

3   Be sure that Object Drawing Mode is enabled, or choose the Rectangle Primitive tool (▢) instead.

4 For the visual properties to your shape, use the Selection tool () to select it and then have a peek at the Properties panel.

5 The shape should have no stroke whatsoever, so get rid of the stroke if your shape currently includes one.

For the fill, you'll be using a bitmap fill, which is generated from an imported bitmap image file. You can select this special fill type from the Color panel, but first you need to import the bitmap image to the project Library.

6 Choose File > Import > Import to Library (**Figure 6.9**) and find the woodgrain.png image. Click OK to import it.

Figure 6.9 Locating the image in the Library

7 Now, with the shape selected, open the Color panel and choose Bitmap Fill, specifying the image just imported as the fill.

8 Use the Align panel to center this shape both vertically and horizontally to the Stage.

This comprises the main clock body (**Figure 6.10**), but you still need to create a nook (**Figure 6.11**) for the pendulum to reside in.

9 Within that same layer, with the Rectangle tool selected, modify the fill so that you're using black with a 40% transparency through the Color Picker.

10 Draw a rectangle measuring 140px wide and 290px tall using these settings. Using the Align panel, center this object vertically on the Stage and align it horizontally to the Stage bottom.

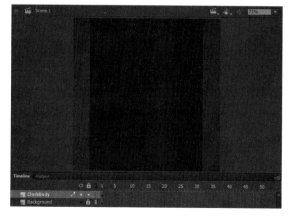

Figure 6.10 The clock body

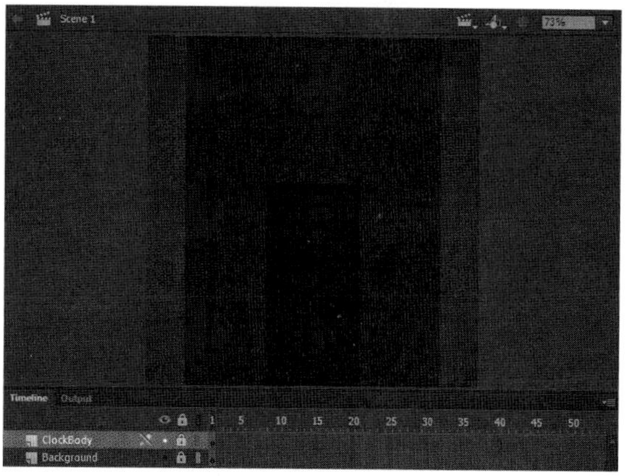

Figure 6.11 The clock body with a nook

Drawing the clock face

▶ *Video 6.5* Build the Clock Face

The clock face is probably the most recognizable portion of the application; this visual asset contains numerals that indicate the current time in hours, minutes, and seconds. It also serves as the main interactive element of our application. Before you begin, be sure all additional layers have been locked down.

1 Create a new layer and name it **ClockFace** (**Figure 6.12**). Choose the Oval tool () with Object Drawing Mode enabled, or choose the Oval Primitive tool (   ).

Figure 6.12 The ClockFace layer

2 In the Properties panel, set the stroke to black and the fill to #E0CDB0. Draw a circle measuring 266px in diameter by clicking and dragging across the Stage with the Shift key held down (**Figure 6.13**).

With this shape created, you'll position it on the Stage with help from the Align panel.

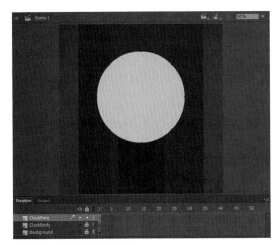

Figure 6.13 The ClockFace shape on the Stage

3 Center the object to the Stage along the x-axis and shift the object to 80px along the y-axis. This is the proper positioning for the clock face; it allows a bit of room for the digital display above and for the pendulum below.

LAYING OUT THE CLOCK FACE NUMERALS

★ ACA Objective 4.3

The numerals on the clock face will range from 1 to 12. They'll be arranged in a traditional way around the entire clock face, using the round portion you've already created as a guide and a backdrop.

1   Select the Text tool (**T**). In the Properties panel, select Static Text from the text drop-down list and choose your font (I chose Trajan Pro 3 at 44pt.). The font color will be a nice, dark brown such as #663300 (**Figure 6.14**).

2   Create 12 separate text blocks, each displaying numerals 1–12 using these same settings. Position all of these numerals as they would appear on a traditional clock face.

3   When you're done positioning the numerals, select all the individual text blocks with the Selection tool ( ) and group them together by choosing Modify > Group command from the application menu.

You can now move all the numerals around as a single group (**Figure 6.15**).

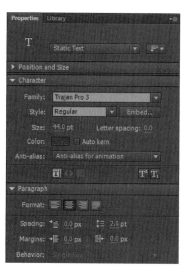

Figure 6.14 Numeral text properties

Figure 6.15 The numeral group

▶ **Video 6.6** *Creating Clock Face Numerals*

Working with dynamic text

Next you'll create a dynamic text block that will display the current time in a digital format directly above the analog clock face. This portion of your clock doesn't work directly with any of the other visual assets you've built so far. It's only a supplementary addition through which you'll output a digital readout of the current time.

1   Create a new layer for your dynamic text block and name it **Digital**.

2   Select the Text tool (**T**) once again and change the text type to Dynamic Text.

▶ **Video 6.7** *Create a Digital Readout*

3   For your font selection, choose a monospaced font so that the shifting digits don't cause any visual aberration. I've chosen Source Code Pro as my typeface at 44pt size.

4   Using the Text tool, create a text block on the Stage directly between the top of the clock face and the top of the Stage itself (**Figure 6.16**). It's a good idea to put some placeholder text in the text block so that you can see how it will appear when you run the application. I've entered **12:00**.

Figure 6.16 Dynamic Text object

5   Select the newly created text block using the Selection tool and take a look at the Properties panel. Notice that since you're using the dynamic text type, you can enter an instance name in the panel. This instance name is what allows you to target the specific dynamic text block for manipulation through ActionScript code.

6   Click within the empty input field and provide the instance name of **timeDisplay** (**Figure 6.17**). You'll use this later to change the text that's displayed in our text field to the current time.

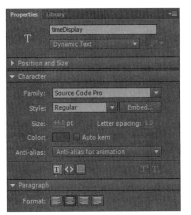

Figure 6.17 `timeDisplay` properties

Designing the Clock's Animated Movie Clip Assets

You'll be using two different methods of animation for this application. You're already familiar with one of them: timeline animation through the Animate CC tweening engine. The other is something we haven't touched on yet: dynamic animation through the manipulation of visual assets with code.

Building the clock face movie clip

One of the most powerful structures used in Animate CC is the concept of a nested Movie Clip symbol. Not only can you achieve multiple layers of independent animation in this way, but when working in ActionScript, you also have full control over the nested hierarchy of instances, as long as you provide appropriate identifiers.

★ *ACA Objective 4.4*

1   Using the Selection tool, select both the round clock face and the group of numerals you've established.

2   From the application menu, choose Modify > Convert to Symbol to open the Convert to Symbol dialog box.

3   Create a Movie Clip symbol and name it **ClockFace**.

▶ **Video 6.8** *Create a Clock Face Movie Clip Symbol*

Before you edit the ClockFace symbol, you need to provide the instance you now have on the Stage with an instance name just as you did with the dynamic text block.

4   Select the instance on the Stage and locate the Instance Name field in the Properties panel. Click in the empty input field and type the instance name **clockFace** (**Figure 6.18**).

Now you'll be able to directly target this symbol instance through use of ActionScript code.

Figure 6.18 The clockFace instance name

> **NOTE** *Instance names are case-sensitive, so be sure you remember both spelling and case as you continue.*

5   Double-click the symbol instance on the Stage to enter it.

6   In the clockFace symbol timeline, select both the clock face shape and the group of numerals. Right-click and choose Distribute to Layers from the context menu.

7   Don't delete the empty layer yet; you'll use this in the next step. But do rename the two new layers to **Face** and **Numbers** accordingly (**Figure 6.19**).

Figure 6.19 clockFace symbol layers

Creating the clock hands

▶ **Video 6.9** *Building Vector Art Clock Hands*

You will be using three rotating clock hands in order to display the current hours, minutes, and seconds based on the time gathered through ActionScript. You must build each one to be visually unique so that the user can easily distinguish between the three different values indicated.

The first thing you'll do is create the hour hand of the clock in the empty layer left over from the last step in the previous exercise. The new Brush Library contains some neat arrow brushes that are perfect for building clocks.

1   Choose the Line tool (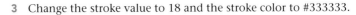) and click the Brush Library button to access that panel.

2   Choose Arrows > Arrows Standard and select Arrow 1.29 by double-clicking it.

    This brush will now appear in the Properties panel as your selected Stroke style.

Figure 6.20 HourHand properties

3   Change the stroke value to 18 and the stroke color to #333333.

4   With that set, draw out a straight vertical stroke on the Stage measuring 80px tall. Select this new shape object with the Selection tool and choose Modify > Convert to Symbol.

    You'll make this a Movie Clip symbol with its registration point anchored to the bottom of the symbol.

5   Name this symbol **HourHand**. With the instance of this symbol selected on the Stage, go to the Properties panel and assign it an instance name of **hourHand** (**Figure 6.20**).

    You'll now do something very similar for the creation of the minute hand.

6 Select a different brush located within the same category: Arrows > Arrows Standard. This one is called Arrow 1.09. With this new brush assigned to the Line tool stroke style, change the stroke value to 12 and the stroke color to #333333 as before.

7 Draw a straight vertical stroke on the Stage measuring 126px tall. Convert this shape to a Movie Clip symbol with its registration point anchored to the bottom.

8 Name this symbol **MinuteHand**, and with the symbol instance selected on the Stage, in the Properties panel assign it an instance name of **minuteHand** (**Figure 6.21**).

Now for the final Movie Clip symbol of the whole set: the seconds hand.

Figure 6.21 MinuteHand properties

9 With the Line tool chosen and the Brush Library open, select the Arrow 1.11 brush located from the Arrows > Arrows Standard category. This one is nice and thin—perfect for a seconds hand.

10 In the Properties panel, change the stroke value to 8 and the stroke color to #990000

11 Draw a straight vertical stroke on the Stage measuring 120px tall. Convert this shape to a third Movie Clip symbol with its registration point anchored to the bottom in the same way as before.

12 Name this symbol **SecondHand**, and with the symbol instance selected on the Stage, in the Properties panel assign it an instance name of **secondHand** (**Figure 6.22**).

You could just leave all three of these instances in the same layer; changing object properties through ActionScript does not require everything to be in single, unique layers like motion tween and shape tween animation. But to be as organized as possible, you'll place each on a new layer.

Figure 6.22 SecondHand properties

13 To automate this process, select all three instances, right-click, and choose Distribute to Layers.

Animate CC creates a new layer for each instance, and even names them properly for you.

14 Delete the empty layer (**Figure 6.23**).

Figure 6.23 The completed ClockFace symbol

▶ Video 6.10 *Modify Art Brushes*

Having assigned each of your clock hand instances specific instance names, you can now target them in your clockFace instance in order to manipulate various properties such as rotation. With the clock hands registration points all aligned to the bottom, they will all rotate around this point—just like a real clock!

Building the clock pendulum

▶ Video 6.11 *Construct a Pendulum*

This portion of your project is the only piece that is animated along the timeline; everything else is driven by ActionScript code. Now you'll create a perpetual swinging motion for your clock pendulum to show that time is indeed flowing.

1   If you're not there already, go back out to the main timeline and create a new layer named **Pendulum**.

2   Lock all other layers so you don't mistakenly draw assets where they don't belong (**Figure 6.24**).

Figure 6.24 Pendulum layer

3   Choose the Rectangle tool and set the fill color to #B0A795 and the stroke color to transparent.

4   Enable Object Drawing Mode so that you do not create destructive shapes. Draw a rectangle on the Stage that measures 200px high and 9px in width.

This will serve as the rod of your pendulum.

5   To build the weight, choose the Oval tool with Object Drawing Mode enabled. Holding down the Shift key, click and drag a circle measuring 44px in diameter. The stroke should be disabled with a fill color of #B0A795, just as you did when drawing the rod.

6   Move the weight shape to the bottom of the rod shape until both are vertically centered (**Figure 6.25**). Optionally, you can use the Align panel to perform this action.

Now you have a set of pendulum assets that you can animate, but you'll want to animate them as a unified whole.

Figure 6.25 Centered pendulum assets

7   Select both the rod and weight shapes and choose Modify > Convert to Symbol from the application menu.

8   Name the new Movie Clip symbol **Pendulum** and set the registration point to the top center, which should be the top end of the rod opposite the weight (**Figure 6.26**).

Figure 6.26 Pendulum Movie Clip symbol

9   With this Movie Clip symbol created and an instance sitting on the Stage, select the instance and once again choose to convert that instance to a Movie Clip symbol, this time named **SwingingPendulum**.

Doing this effectively nests an instance of the symbol you just created within an additional symbol. This new symbol is where the repeating pendulum animation will take place since the timeline of a Movie Clip symbol will continue playing and looping, regardless of how many frames it occupies within a parent timeline.

10 On the main timeline, create a new layer group and name it **Analog**.

All of the elements of your analog clock face will be nested in this new layer group.

11 Click and drag the ClockBody, Pendulum, and ClockFace layers in the Analog layer group (**Figure 6.27**). Lock everything but the Pendulum layer before moving on.

Figure 6.27 The Analog timeline folder

ANIMATING THE CLOCK PENDULUM

★ *ACA Objective 4.5*

▶ *Video 6.12*
Animating the
Pendulum

Figure 6.28 Movie clip nesting navigation

Now that you have the assets for the pendulum created and formed as a single Movie Clip symbol, you need to animate it swinging back and forth in the body of the clock. You'll use a motion tween to accomplish this.

1 Double-click the SwingingPendulum instance in the Pendulum layer on your main timeline to edit the symbol in place.

You should now be in the symbol itself and able to modify the symbol timeline (**Figure 6.28**).

2 Extend the frame span to 20 frames by selecting frame 20 in this layer and choosing Insert > Timeline > Frame from the application menu.

3 Right-click the frame span and choose Create Motion Tween from the context menu.

Now you're almost ready to animate the clock pendulum.

4 Before you begin animating, choose the Free Transform tool and select the instance of the pendulum on the Stage in order to shift the transform point to the top center of the object (**Figure 6.29**).

Figure 6.29 Transform point

5   On frame 1, hover the cursor just outside any of the bounding box corners until the cursor appears as a circle of arrows. Click and drag to rotate to the left and stop the rotation when the weight of the pendulum touches the side of the indentation you created earlier.

6   On frame 11, perform the same rotation action, but rotate to the right until the weight again touches the indentation asset edge. Finally, on frame 20 duplicate the rotation that exists on frame 1. It doesn't have to be exact, but it should be close (**Figure 6.30**).

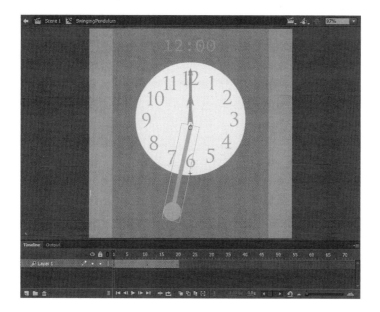

Figure 6.30 Keyframed pendulum animation

TIP

This might be a good chance to play with easing when animating the pendulum swinging back and forth. Think of the way a pendulum moves in space and try to replicate that movement through easing controls or even in the Motion Editor.

Using Imported Audio in an ActionScript Project

Audio has numerous uses within interactive media, and those uses are growing every day. In Animate CC, you can use ActionScript to bring audio into the timeline, bind sounds to specific keyframes, or even play audio from the project Library. It's also possible to play external audio files with a little ActionScript.

★ *ACA Objective 4.8*

Audio file types

Before importing a sound file into your project, you need to make sure it is in a compatible format. Animate CC currently supports the following audio file types when working in an ActionScript-based project:

- AIFF
- WAV
- **MP3**
- Adobe Sound Document
- Sun AU
- Sound Designer II
- Ogg Vorbis
- FLACC

NOTE
You can convert only media that doesn't have DRM encoded into the file.

Fortunately, Animate CC installations include another Creative Cloud application called Adobe Media Encoder, a software package that converts other file formats to those compatible with Animate CC and other applications. If you need to deliver the audio files in both an ActionScript and an HTML5-compatible format, you'll most likely want to stick with MP3. Animate CC will automatically convert any audio format to MPEG Audio Layer III (MP3) for playback in the Flash Player or Adobe AIR on project compilation.

Audio file import

▶ *Video 6.13*
Inserting Audio

An audio file is imported just like a bitmap file, using the File > Import > Import to Library command. Once the sound file is in the project Library, you can set it up to be called by ActionScript or place it manually on the timeline.

NOTE
It doesn't matter if you choose Import to Stage or Import to Library; Animate CC imports all audio to the project Library regardless of the command.

Placing audio on the timeline isn't quite the same as it is with a graphic or an image. It's usually done through selecting a frame on the timeline and choosing an audio file from the Properties panel. The sound will be attached to the keyframe and is not visible on the Stage; however, you should see a waveform displayed in the layer itself on those frames that are affected.

We've prepared three audio files for use in this project:

- **tick.mp3**: You'll use this file as part of the swinging pendulum.
- **tock.mp3**: You'll also use this file as part of the swinging pendulum.
- **mechanical.mp3**: You'll use this file as a constant, looping background sound.

1   To import these files to the project Library, choose File > Import > Import to Library from the application menu. In the file browser that appears, select all three MP3 files and choose Open.

Animate CC will bring the MP3s into the Library as audio files.

2   In the Library panel, take a look at the files you've just imported (**Figure 6.31**).

You'll use the files tick.mp3 and tock.mp3 in the Pendulum Movie Clip symbol timeline as sound effects in synchronization with the pendulum animation. You'll invoke the other file, mechanical.mp3, from the project Library with ActionScript code when your application is running.

To make an audio file in the Library available through ActionScript, you need to provide a linkage ID.

3   Notice that the Library panel has two columns: Name and Linkage. Find the mechanical.mp3 asset in the project Library and double-click the Linkage column directly next to it.

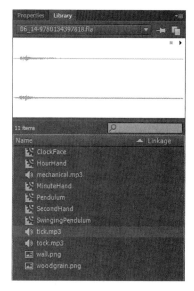

Figure 6.31 Audio in the Library

4   You can now input a linkage ID (**Figure 6.32**) specific to this object. Type **Mech**. Remember this identifier for later when you are writing your ActionScript code!

> **NOTE** *What you input as a linkage ID basically becomes a Class reference in ActionScript. You'll see how this works later in this chapter.*

Figure 6.32 Your Mech linkage ID

Using audio on the timeline

Keep in mind that when you place audio on the timeline, you're placing it inside a keyframe. It is a good idea to have a separate layer just for audio, because the keyframe will show the waveform of the audio, which can be helpful for synchronization tasks.

Now you'll add some audio in your SwingingPendulum Movie Clip symbol.

1   First, enter the symbol edit mode by double-clicking either the symbol in the Library panel or an instance on the Stage.

2 To attach the audio to a keyframe in the timeline, select the keyframe and then, from the Properties panel, choose the audio file from the Name drop-down menu within the Sound subpanel (**Figure 6.33**).

Figure 6.33 Frame sound properties

This attaches the sound to the keyframe; it will begin playing as soon as the playhead reaches that keyframe.

3 With frame 1 selected, choose the tick.mp3 sound from the Properties panel and set the sync type to Stream.

4 On frame 11, choose the tock.mp3 sound, and set the sync type once again to Stream (**Figure 6.34**).

Figure 6.34 Audio on the timeline

STREAM VS. START OR EVENT SOUND

While you're in the Properties panel, you'll notice another drop-down menu called Sync. It has three important options: Start, Event, and Stream.

- The Start and Event settings trigger the sound as soon as the playhead hits the keyframe and play that sound completely.

- The Stream setting also triggers the sound as soon as the playback head hits the keyframe, but it synchronizes the sound to the timeline. If the timeline stops, the sound stops. This option is best used for narration but is pretty good for clocks as well!

Using the Stream setting, you can place animated events on the timeline at the same time the sound occurs. Animate CC will keep these in sync no matter what happens. If you choose the Start or Event setting for an application like this, there will be no synchronization between the timeline animation and audio track.

SOUND EFFECTS

Animate CC also has options you can set in the Properties panel to determine how the audio plays. You can access these settings using the Effect drop-down menu in the Sound subpanel. In this menu you'll find prebuilt options for fading in and across channels.

Also, next to the Effect menu you'll see a small pencil icon, which is the Edit button. Clicking this button brings up a much more capable editing dialog box that lets you trim the audio as well as control volume and panning by placing anchor points along a control line for each channel.

▶ **Video 6.14** *Audio Effects*

TIP
You should perform any heavy audio editing your tracks require before importing them into Animate CC, using a more full-featured audio-editing software package such as Adobe Audition CC.

A Primer on ActionScript

ActionScript and Animate CC have a deep history together, and using the language to get the most out of your ActionScript-based project requires background knowledge. Let's go over some fundamentals of writing ActionScript in Animate CC projects.

Symbols and interactivity

Combining symbols with ActionScript is where things start to get interesting in Animate CC development projects. You can access both Button symbol and Movie Clip symbol instances, and even dynamic text blocks via an instance name that you assign using the Properties panel. In this project, you've provided instance names to a number of objects on the Stage.

You can use ActionScript to directly manipulate the properties of these instances, such as text, rotation, width, height, and position. Another common interaction is using ActionScript to assign a specific event listener to a symbol instance. This allows your project to react to events that occur involving those instances. Mouse clicks, playhead movement, and even asset and data loading are examples of events that can be used as triggers for other operations.

Movie Clip symbols provide self-contained, reusable elements that are essential to interactive media development. Newcomers often find it difficult to decide which type of symbol to use and how to implement that symbol. But with practice you can master the art of nesting symbols and combining different types to get exactly what you want. In this project, the clock face is a complex, nested symbol.

TIMELINE FRAME LABELS

Figure 6.35 Frame labels

Individual keyframes can be identified by their frame number, but a better way of referencing them is to label these keyframes using the Name option in the Properties panel. The label will show up as a flag on the timeline. You can use it as a visual reference to help you better understand the organization of your project.

The label (**Figure 6.35**) can also be used as a reference for navigating a timeline when using ActionScript or JavaScript, depending on your target platform. It's usually better to navigate a timeline using frame labels instead of frame numbers, because edits to the project may cause the frame numbers to change as content is added or removed from the timeline.

ActionScript essentials

Whether writing ActionScript in Animate CC or using a code-only editor like Adobe Flash Builder, you'll need to grasp some essential concepts if you want to start writing effective code.

VARIABLES

Variables in ActionScript are objects that hold a particular type of value that can be changed across the lifetime of the application. Variables can be just about any class type, but the most common variables in basic Animate CC projects are numbers and strings.

A **number** is a variable that holds a numeric value. The syntax for creating a numeric variable looks like this:

```
var myNum:Number = 7;
```

First, you define a variable with the `var` keyword, and then you give the variable the identifier `myNum`. The type of `Number` tells Animate CC what type of variable you are defining, and `= 7` sets the initial value of that variable. The semicolon simply declares the end of an instruction.

Another common variable is a **string**. Variables typed as strings are basically blocks of text. This is generally noted by using quotes around the text value, though a string can be combined, or concatenated, with other variables to form a complex string. You can define a string like this:

```
var myText:String = "Hey, Flash!";
```

Again, the `var` keyword tells Animate CC you are defining a variable, and `myText` is the identifier for that variable. The type of `String` tells Animate CC that this variable will include text data, and `= "Hey, Flash!"` sets the initial value of the variable.

Interestingly enough, you do not need to set an initial value for a variable. Also, after a variable is set, you can reassign it without the `var` keyword or specific class type, as shown here:

```
var myText:String;
myText = "Hello!";
myText = "Goodbye";
```

TIP

Once a variable is declared as a certain type, it remains that specific type. Therefore, when declaring a variable as a string, you can't just stick a number or an array in there.

FUNCTIONS

When programming in ActionScript, you'll sometimes find yourself typing the same series of lines over and over. This is where **functions** will be of use. A function assigns a single command to a block of code. Once it's defined, you need only call the function name to run everything in that block of code and can reuse the function many times in order to simplify the code. Take a look at the following lines of code:

```
myText = "Hey, Flash!";
myNum = 7;
```

You could write a function to combine these two lines into one command:

```
function setBoth():void {
    myText = "Hey, Flash!";
    myNum = 7;
}
```

It's a little more work, but from now on, every time you want to set both of those variables, you only need to type

```
setBoth();
```

In completing this chapter's project, you will use a function to change the values associated with telling time and adjusting visual assets to reflect the current time in both digital and analog form.

EVENTS

Interactive media applications by nature are **event**-driven. When an event occurs, the code reacts to that event as if some object in the application was listening for that event. Numerous event types are built into ActionScript that allow code to be triggered on a variety of activities like mouse clicks, data loading, frame-entering, and even touch gestures on mobile devices. In our clock application you'll use both timer events and mouse events to enable different types of functionality.

Writing ActionScript to Control the Clock

In Animate CC, you can attach code to any frame on any layer of a project. However, there is an active and long-held practice that all frame script code belongs in its own layer in a project's timeline. This helps a great deal in organizing layers and in keeping all of the code where it can be easily located.

1   Create a new layer named **Actions** and lock it, since you don't want any visual assets in it.

2   To begin writing ActionScript, or any code in Animate CC, you must open the Actions panel. Generally, this panel won't be opened by default, so choose Window > Actions from the application menu to do so.

With the Actions panel open and frame 1 of the Actions layer selected, you're ready to continue with the project.

Importing classes

▶ *Video 6.15*
Importing Classes

To use many of the **classes** available in ActionScript, you'll need to import them in the project's code. You do this through use of the `import` statement, followed by the package and class name. Packages are a coding construct that keeps classes of the same name from causing collisions and also helps with organization.

You'll import a number of classes for your project.

Type the following lines of code to import the `Timer`, `Movie Clip`, `MouseEvent`, and `TextField` classes:

```
import flash.utils.Timer;
import flash.display.MovieClip;
import flash.text.TextField;
import flash.events.MouseEvent;
import flash.events.TimerEvent;
```

`Timer` is a utility class that allows you to run a function on a schedule.

`MovieClip` and `TextField` are used in reference to visual objects you have created on the Stage.

`MouseEvent` and `TimerEvent` will allow you to listen for and respond to events of those types.

Declaring Stage variables

With these classes imported, they are available for use in our application. Now you need to declare a number of variables based on those imported classes that correspond to objects already created on the Stage. Notice that you use the exact instance names given to both the **clockFace** symbol instance and **timeDisplay** text block:

```
var clockFace:MovieClip;
var timeDisplay:TextField;
```

Telling time with a timer

The first thing you need is a way to access the system clock. You do this by using the `Date` class in ActionScript. `Date` is one of a handful of classes that you don't import. These classes don't belong to any package and are called *top-level classes*. Create the `currentTime` variable directly beneath the previous ones:

```
var currentTime:Date;
```

Now you'll declare a variable called `ticker` as an instance of the `Timer` class. You set it equal to a new `Timer` instance and pass in the amount of time, in

TIP

Importing classes in ActionScript will also allow Animate CC to suggest properties and values through code completion in the editor.

▶ *Video 6.16*
Declaring Stage Variables

▶ *Video 6.17*
Programming the Clock Face

milliseconds, on which to have the `Timer` cycle run. In this case, the `Timer` will run every 250 milliseconds, or four times every second.

```
var ticker:Timer = new Timer(250);
```

Additionally, you'll add an event listener to the `Timer` to execute a function every time the `Timer` cycle fires. You do this by listening for the `TimerEvent.TIMER` event and execute a function called `onTick` (which you haven't created yet).

```
ticker.addEventListener(TimerEvent.TIMER, onTick);
```

To start the `Timer`, you invoke its built-in `start()` method.

```
ticker.start();
```

Let's create that `onTick` function now. Here's the completed function, followed by an explanation of what it all means.

```
function onTick(e:TimerEvent):void {
    var currentTime:Date = new Date();
    var seconds:uint = currentTime.getSeconds();
    var minutes:uint = currentTime.getMinutes();
    var hours:uint = currentTime.getHours();

    clockFace.secondHand.rotation = 360 + (seconds * 6);
    clockFace.minuteHand.rotation = 360 + (minutes * 6);
    clockFace.hourHand.rotation = 360 + (hours * 30) +
    ➞ (minutes * 0.5);

    var displayMinutes:String = minutes < 10 ? "0" +
    ➞ minutes : "" + minutes;
    timeDisplay.text = hours + ":" + displayMinutes;
}
```

To create any function in ActionScript, you begin with the keyword `function` followed by the function name. In this case, the function name is `onTick`, and it received an argument identified as `e`, indicated in parentheses, of type `TimerEvent` because that is the type of event that has invoked the function. You can get all sorts of data from this argument. A function will also need a return data type declared. In this function, you are doing lots in the function body but are not actually returning any data to the caller, so you declare the return data type as `void`.

The body of the function consists of the lines of code that are wrapped between the two curly braces. In the body of the function, you first refresh your `currentTime` variable with a new `Date`. The `Date` object includes methods for grabbing hours, minutes, seconds, and more so you use specific methods built into that class to set new variables that represent those specific pieces of data.

The next part of the function will visually adjust the `rotation` property of your three clock hands by interpreting the time data gathered and performing some calculations on it to figure out the proper rotation. The math is a bit beyond the scope of this book, but you're basically converting numeric data into a rotation value to adjust the rotation of each clock hand individually. Notice how you can refer to a nested symbol instance through dot notation like `clockFace.secondHand`? This is incredible powerful!

▶ *Video 6.18* Using Dynamic Text

Additionally, you use shorthand logic to prepend a 0 to the minutes gathered for display in the digital readout, but only if the minutes returned are single numerals. This is so the text in our `timeDisplay` text block does not shift around as the time changes.

Creating mouse interaction

Similar to how you added an event listener to your `Timer`, you'll also add two event listeners to your `clockFace` instance. One will detect whether the mouse cursor has entered over the visual object, and the other will detect when it leaves.

▶ *Video 6.19* Creating Mouse Interaction

1   Set the `visible` property of your text block to `false`. You don't want the digital readout to display until a `MouseOver` event occurs.

```
timeDisplay.visible = false;
```

2   Add the proper `MouseEvent` event listeners to your `clockFace` instance:

```
clockFace.addEventListener(MouseEvent.MOUSE_OVER,
→  showDigital);
clockFace.addEventListener(MouseEvent.MOUSE_OUT,
→  hideDigital);
```

3   Follow this with a new function called `showDigital` that sets the text block `visible` property back to `true`:

```
function showDigital(e:MouseEvent):void {
   timeDisplay.visible = true;
}
```

4   Apply the inverse function, setting it once again to `true`:

```
function hideDigital(e:MouseEvent):void {
    timeDisplay.visible = false;
}
```

Audio playback with ActionScript

▶ **Video 6.20** *Audio Playback with ActionScript*

Audio files in the library don't have to be associated with a keyframe to be played. They can also be triggered using simple ActionScript. Since you gave your mechanical.mp3 sound a linkage ID of Mech in the Library panel, you can now refer to that sound as a class called `Mech` and create instances of it through ActionScript:

```
var mechSound:Mech = new Mech();
```

TIP

The ActionScript command `SoundMixer.stopAllSounds();` *is a useful instruction to stop all audio regardless of the source. It can be helpful when you are implementing a mute button or preparing to load fresh audio content.*

Additionally, you can use all of the inherent `Sound` class methods and properties such as the `play()` method. Here you are telling the sound to play, starting at position 0 (the beginning) and to loop forever using `int.MAX_VALUE`. This will create a constantly looping, mechanical background sound:

```
mechSound.play(0, int.MAX_VALUE);
```

Completed code

The full, completed ActionScript code for this project is shown next. If you are having trouble, compare the code you have written with what's shown here. If you're not having any trouble, try modifying the code in your project to achieve different results.

```
import flash.utils.Timer;
import flash.display.MovieClip;
import flash.text.TextField;
import flash.events.MouseEvent;
import flash.events.TimerEvent;
```

```
var clockFace:MovieClip;
clockFace.addEventListener(MouseEvent.MOUSE_OVER, showDigital);
clockFace.addEventListener(MouseEvent.MOUSE_OUT, hideDigital);
var currentTime:Date;
var timeDisplay:TextField;
timeDisplay.visible = false;
var ticker: Timer = new Timer(250);
ticker.addEventListener(TimerEvent.TIMER, onTick);
ticker.start();
var mechSound:Mech = new Mech();
mechSound.play(0, int.MAX_VALUE);

function onTick(e:TimerEvent):void {
   currentTime = new Date();
   var seconds:uint = currentTime.getSeconds();
   var minutes:uint = currentTime.getMinutes();
   var hours:uint = currentTime.getHours();

   clockFace.secondHand.rotation = 360 + (seconds * 6);
   clockFace.minuteHand.rotation = 360 + (minutes * 6);
   clockFace.hourHand.rotation = 360 + (hours * 30) +
   ➝ (minutes * 0.5);

   var displayMinutes:String = minutes < 10 ? "0" +
   ➝ minutes : "" + minutes;
   timeDisplay.text = hours + ":" + displayMinutes;
}

function showDigital(e:MouseEvent):void {
   timeDisplay.visible = true;
}

function hideDigital(e:MouseEvent):void {
   timeDisplay.visible = false;
}
```

Testing an ActionScript Project

★ ACA Objective 5.1

One of the worst things that can happen when you're writing interactive media applications is to release your work for distribution only to have a user discover that a problem exists with your code. Here's some advice on how to avoid that situation and produce a solid application for your client.

ActionScript errors

You can encounter two distinct types of errors when writing ActionScript code. One is the **compilation error** (**Figure 6.36**). This occurs when you compile your code to run in Flash Player or Adobe AIR. This is probably the easiest type of error to catch, because when you try to test your application, it will not compile, and you'll receive detailed information regarding the specific error from Animate CC.

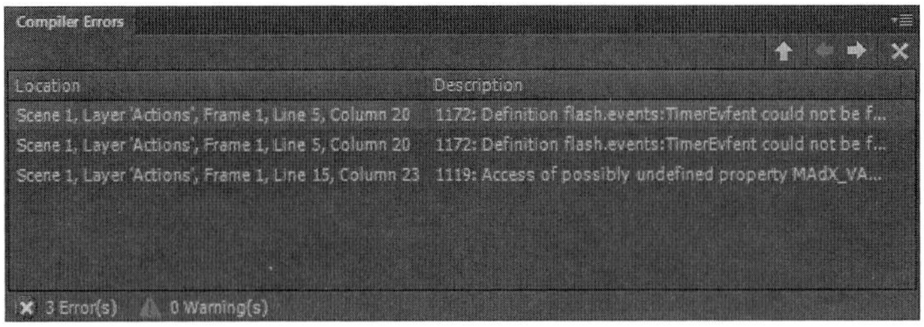

Figure 6.36 Compilation error

The second type of error is a bit more difficult to troubleshoot, because you have to compile and run the application, taking certain steps, to produce the error. These errors are known as **runtime errors** and normally require the use of a code debugger to troubleshoot. Luckily, Animate CC comes with an Action-Script debugger built in. Access this feature by choosing Debug > Debug Movie from the application menu.

ActionScript comments

TIP

You can also comment out pieces of code that might be causing ActionScript errors. This is a good trouble-shooting technique!

ActionScript programming can create some exciting interactive effects, but it can also be difficult depending on what you are programming. Help yourself out by commenting your code. Commenting involves putting notes in your code to help you find your way around at a later date.

There are two main ways of commenting: single-line and block **comments**.

You create single-line comments by starting a line with double slashes:

```
// this is just a short, single-line comment!
```

Block comments start with /* and end with */. This will let you block off larger blocks of text like this:

```
/*
This is a multi-line
comment. Use it to comment
out big chunks of code
or to make lengthy notes
to reference later
*/
```

Trace statements

The last technique we'll explore is how to trace data to the Output panel in Animate CC. The `trace()` command is a versatile way to expose the values of certain variables, or even just to fire off an alert when you hit a specific piece of code.

In your clock project, you could use this command to trace the value of rotation on your minute hand; for instance:

```
trace(clockFace.minuteHand.rotation);
```

The values are then output to the Output panel for us to monitor.

Publishing the Clock for Desktop Installation

The Adobe AIR platform is an exciting addition to the output options in the Animate CC interactive media development environment. It allows the same file to be delivered across a wide variety of platforms, including mobile and desktop devices. Under the Target options in the Publish Settings dialog box, you can choose the appropriate format for the AIR output. You're targeting "AIR for Desktop" with this particular project, but all AIR targets share a similar development methodology since they are all written in ActionScript 3.0, no matter the specific target.

★ *ACA Objective 5.4*

Exploring the AIR Settings dialog box

The AIR Settings dialog box provides additional options related to the publishing and delivery of an AIR file. You can access these options by clicking the wrench icon next to the Target properties in the Publish Settings dialog box. A series of tabbed windows open in an AIR Settings dialog box (**Figure 6.37**). These windows allow you to set up the options for the AIR application.

COMPLETING APPLICATION DETAILS

To complete the final details for publishing the application, choose File > AIR for Desktop Settings from the application menu. The AIR Settings dialog box appears, containing the following areas:

General: This screen contains core information about how you want to package your desktop application. You can choose to generate an AIR file or an operating system–specific installer or use the embedded runtime option. This is also the place to name your application and make decisions about window style and render mode.

Figure 6.37 AIR Settings dialog box

Signature: All Adobe AIR applications must be signed in order to be properly installed on a user's system. This screen allows you to select a code signing certificate from a signing authority, if you have purchased one. You can also use this screen to create a free, self-signed certificate to publish your applications.

Icons: This section allows you to specify a group of custom icons that the user will see on the desktop, on the dock or taskbar, and when the application is running—just like any desktop application. You can create icons of various sizes in an application like Adobe Photoshop.

Advanced: Here is where you can specify associated file types, initial window settings, and the application installation folder. Many applications will not need to have much of anything specified here.

Language: This section is used only for mobile applications and will be disabled when using AIR for Desktop.

▶ *Video 6.21*
General AIR for Desktop Properties

▶ *Video 6.22* *Using a Signed Certificate*

▶ *Video 6.23 Creating Application Icons*

Publish and install

To publish the AIR for Desktop application once you've finalized the Publish Settings, choose File > Publish from the application menu. To use an AIR document, end users must have the Adobe AIR runtime installed on their systems. Once the AIR runtime is installed, they are able to install any AIR application. If the application was published with the embedded runtime option, the user will not even need to install the AIR runtime separately, because it is bundled into the installation package.

 *Video 6.24*
Publishing and Installing an AIR Application

Once installed (**Figure 6.38**), an AIR application can be run, managed, and uninstalled just like any other application on your system. Periodically, Adobe will issue a new version of the AIR runtime. If you're using the runtime separately, you will be prompted to update. However, with an embedded runtime in use, the application will continue to use that version until the author decides to push out an update of her own.

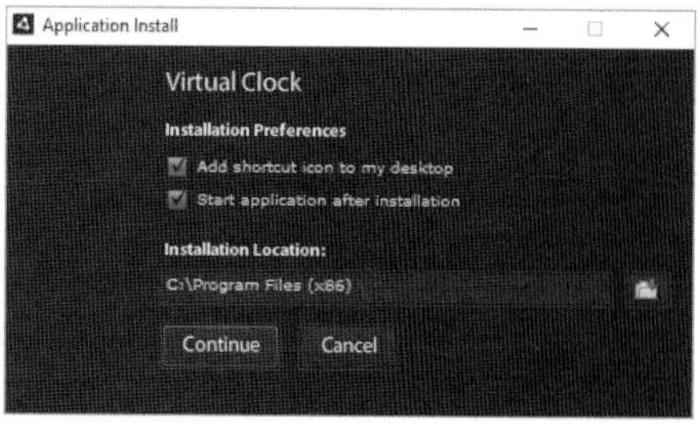

Figure 6.38 The AIR Application Installer

Challenge!

In this project, you're using sounds that are bound to the timeline as well as those initiated through ActionScript. Right now, if you want to mute the clock sounds, you'll have to turn down your computer speakers. The challenge is to create a sound toggle button as part of the interface that will mute all sounds when enabled.

Conclusion

In this chapter, you've moved beyond the web browser to target the Windows and OS X desktop operating systems using ActionScript and Adobe AIR. When working with AIR for Desktop, you're taking everything available to you when targeting Flash Player and injecting it with another layer of functionality and power to create true, installable apps.

We've covered a lot of somewhat advanced concepts in this chapter. You've gone through the process of building a customizable, functional, cross-platform clock application. You've also been given a solid introduction to the fundamentals of ActionScript and how to work with ActionScript code in Animate CC to adjust visual elements on the Stage. Lastly, you've seen how simple it is to integrate sound into an application and how to publish all of this to a Windows or Mac OS X desktop.

CHAPTER OBJECTIVES

Chapter Learning Objectives

- Work with Adobe AIR for Mobile
- Use buttons in Animate CC
- Master object-oriented ActionScript concepts
- Write ActionScript classes
- Ingest and display external data
- Respond to user interaction
- Compile for Apple iOS and Google Android

Chapter ACA Objectives

For more detail on ACA Objectives in this book, see the table on pages 212–215.

DOMAIN 2.0
UNDERSTANDING INTERACTIVE MEDIA DESIGN
2.4

DOMAIN 3.0
UNDERSTANDING ADOBE FLASH PROFESSIONAL
3.2, 3.6, 3.7

DOMAIN 4.0
CREATING INTERACTIVE MEDIA CONTENT USING
FLASH PROFESSIONAL
4.1, 4.3, 4.4, 4.6

DOMAIN 5.0
TESTING, PUBLISHING, AND EVALUATING
INTERACTIVE MEDIA ELEMENTS USING
FLASH PROFESSIONAL
5.4

CHAPTER 7

Develop a Mobile Quiz App

One of the coolest things you can do with Adobe Animate CC is creating a mobile app that can be compiled to either Apple iOS or Google Android using Adobe AIR. In this chapter you'll take a deeper look at ActionScript and build a simple mobile application.

> **NOTE** *Adobe has rebranded Flash Professional CC as Animate CC! They are essentially the exact same application—with absolutely no differences in capability aside from features introduced in the regular update schedule. All future updates to Flash Professional CC will be known by the name Animate CC. If desired, subscribers can run multiple versions of the product—branded as either Animate CC or Animate—but I highly recommend using the latest available version of Animate CC to take advantage of all new features.*

For this project, you'll build a mobile app that can be compiled and distributed in app stores for installation on Apple iOS and Google Android. You'll create a straightforward quiz app that loads in data from a JavaScript Object Notation (**JSON**) file. The loaded data can then be randomized and displayed to the user, prompting a simple decision from the user via the touch of a button (**Figure 7.1**).

> **NOTE** *All of the videos for this book were recorded with a version of Animate CC branded as Flash Professional CC. It is important to note that everything that we demonstrate in the recordings can be applied to Animate CC—even if we refer to the application as Animate CC. They are essentially the exact same application—with absolutely no differences in capability.*

Figure 7.1 The completed project

▶ **Video 7.1** *Project Overview*

Creating an Adobe AIR
for Mobile Document

★ ACA Objective 4.1 Not only can you develop applications for desktop operating systems using Adobe AIR, you can also create apps for the two most popular mobile operating systems in the world today: Google Android and Apple iOS. Depending on which mobile operating system you want to target, you'll choose either AIR for Android or AIR for iOS in the New Document dialog box (which you access by choosing File > New from the application menu).

Adobe AIR for Android

When you tell Animate CC to compile an AIR app for mobile Android, it generates an **APK** file. This is a standard Android app ready for distribution through Google Play, Amazon, or other app stores. Similar to the two different distribution mechanisms for desktop, with Android development you can choose whether to require the user to install the AIR runtime alongside the app or bundle the AIR runtime along with the app in a process called *Captive Runtime*. Just as with desktop solutions, Captive Runtime is preferable since it is much more seamless a process for the user.

GOOGLE PLAY

When distributing your mobile app through the Google Play store, you must sign your app with a self-signed certificate before uploading it to the app store. Additionally, you'll need a Google Developer account, which has a one-time cost of $25: see https://play.google.com/apps/publish/.

Adobe AIR for iOS

When building AIR apps for iOS, you don't have many choices for how to compile or distribute the app you're creating. The compiler builds a native iOS app directly from your Animate CC project since Apple does not allow separate runtimes on iOS. After compilation, you'll have an IPA file ready for testing, distribution, or whatever purpose you choose.

iOS APP STORE

Distributing (or even simply testing) any iOS app is a daunting task. Why? Because Apple has a number of strict requirements for working with iOS as a developer. These requirements include creating and maintaining an Apple Developer account at $99 per year and using Apple's unique arrangement of certificates and provisioning profile management tools. See https://developer.apple.com/programs/.

Setting Up the AIR for Mobile Project Document

▶ *Video 7.2* Setting Up the AIR for Mobile Project Document

To create an Animate document that targets Adobe AIR for mobile devices, you'll make choices that will be very similar to how you've begun other projects in this book.

1 On the Welcome Screen, choose Create New > AIR for Android (or AIR for iOS). Alternatively, choose File > New > AIR for Android (or iOS) from the application menu to launch the New Document dialog box (**Figure 7.2**).

Your document should now be open and ready for you to modify the Stage properties.

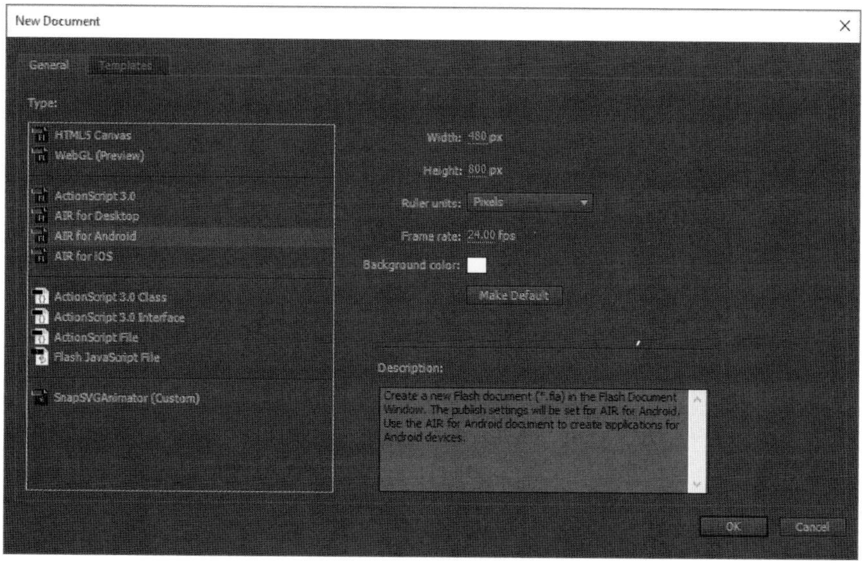

Figure 7.2 Creating a new AIR project

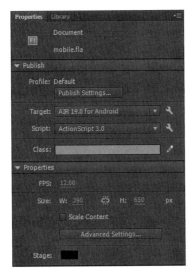

Figure 7.3 Project properties

2 Choose a width of 390 pixels and a height of 650 pixels to form a simulated mobile device view.

On iOS and Android, the application basically takes over the entire screen, so envision the entire Stage as the device screen for this project.

3 Set the background to whatever color you want. I'm using #9999CC in my example project.

4 You could leave the fps at 24 (the default), but you'll be using only a single frame for this project, so I recommend setting this value to 12 (**Figure 7.3**).

Keeping the fps down a bit will save some device resources for the end user.

5 Additionally, if it's available, choose AIR 19 for Android as the publish target. If you use something a bit older, or even a newer version of the AIR SDK, that should be fine as well.

> **NOTE**
> *You won't use any of the new features of recent AIR versions in this project, so just about any of the publish target choices available should be fine.*

Design the App Interface Elements

One of the strengths of Animate CC is that it enables you to use the same tooling and workflows regardless of the target platform. Even though you're building a mobile application for this project, you can still design your entire user interface using the same tools available for asset creation or animation. Animate CC offers a truly unified, creative workspace.

★ *ACA Objective 4.3*

▶ *Video 7.3 Create the App Header*

Create the app header

The first thing you'll do is create an app header using the Text tool (T).

1 Double-click the existing Layer 1 layer and rename it **AppTitle**.

2 Select the Text tool from the Tools panel and use the Properties panel to adjust how your header text will appear.

3 The header text will not be changing during application runtime, so choose Static Text as the text type.

4 For the font family, choose Marker Felt if it's available and Wide as the style. If you need to use a different font, choose a nice big one. Choosing a 75pt font size and a nice, dark color such as #636384 will do fine (**Figure 7.4**).

5 Click anywhere on the Stage and type the header text **Quiz Me!**.

6 Once the text block is created, align it to the center along the x-axis and set the Y position value to 10px.

You should now have a nice, bold app header at the top of the Stage.

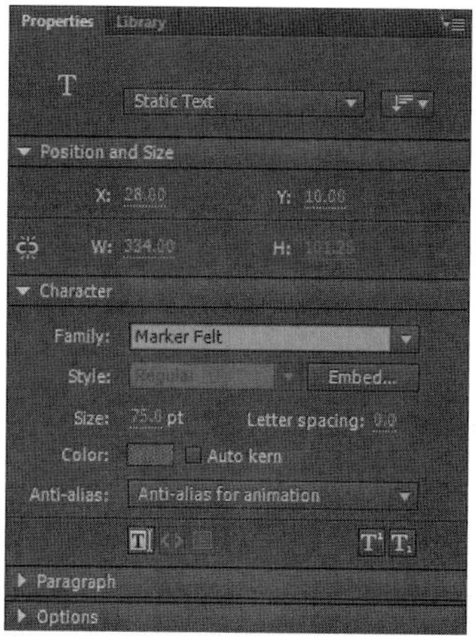

Create a question text element

The next two text blocks you create will be dynamic text because you'll need to change the text values at runtime. You can make them dynamic by providing each text block with an instance name—just like you've done with Movie Clip symbol instances in previous examples.

1 To begin, lock the AppTitle layer and create a new layer called **QuestionText**.

2 In the Properties panel, set the text type to Dynamic Text and for the font family choose Chalkduster.

The font size will be 28pts and the color a neutral gray at #333333.

3 Click and drag out a nice big text block and type **Question Text Here...** for the placeholder text value.

Again, this will be replaced by question text from your quiz bank when the app is running. With the text block created and selected, you'll now modify the instance properties in the Properties panel to finish.

4 Give the text block the instance name **questionText** for ActionScript interactions later on. Make sure the text block measures 375px wide and 257px high.

5 Position the text block at 128px from the Stage top and center it along the x-axis (**Figure 7.5**).

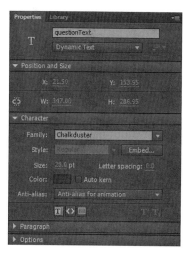

Figure 7.4 Header text properties

▶ **Video 7.4** *Create a Question Text Element*

Figure 7.5 Question text properties

Create a status text element

▶ *Video 7.5* *Create a Status Text Element*

The purpose of the final text element is to provide feedback to users as they make decisions about the questions presented by the app. This will once again be a Dynamic Text object with an instance name for later manipulation through code.

1 Lock all current layers and create a new layer named **StatusMsg**.

2 Choose Chalkduster as your Dynamic Text font once again and set the size to 52pts. Choose a nice off-red color (#993300) for the status message text so that it stands out to the user (**Figure 7.6**).

3 Click the Stage and drag out a text block measuring 320px in width.

4 Type an ellipsis (…) for a placeholder text value.

▶ *Video 7.6* *Embedding Text Outlines*

5 In the Properties panel, set the instance name to **statusMsg**. Set the Y position to 300px from the Stage top and then center the text across the x-axis.

6 Select the Free Transform tool and use it to rotate the text slightly on the Stage (**Figure 7.7**).

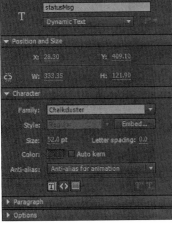

Figure 7.6 Status text properties

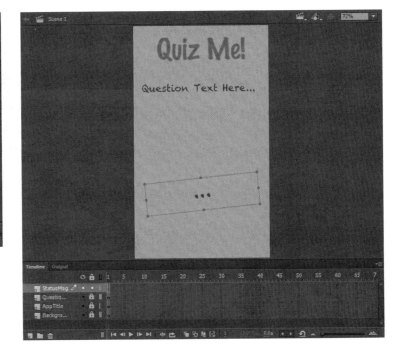

Figure 7.7 Rotating the status text

Designing the buttons

You'll need to provide the user with a means of input. To do so, you'll create a set of buttons: one to indicate a choice of "true" and another for "false." First, you'll create the "true" Button symbol, and then you'll duplicate and edit the new symbol to create a "false" Button symbol.

★ ACA Objective 3.7

Button symbols are unique to Animate CC. They consist of four specific frames: Up, Over, Down, and Hit (**Figure 7.8**). The first three indicate specific states of interaction common to buttons in general, and the Hit state indicates the active area that activates those states.

▶ Video 7.7
Designing a Button

Figure 7.8 Button states

1 Create a new layer in the timeline and name it **Buttons**. Lock all other layers. Next you'll draw a simple visual asset to use in your Button symbols.

2 Choose the Oval tool (⬤) and use the Properties panel to tweak your tool settings.

3 For stroke, choose a color of #333333 and a stroke size of 8. Set the fill color using the green radial gradient swatch from the default swatches (**Figure 7.9**).

4 With these settings in place, hold down the Shift key and drag out a circle of 150px in diameter.

5 With this new shape selected, choose Modify > Convert to Symbol from the application menu.

6 In the dialog box that appears, be sure that the symbol type is set to Button and name it **TrueButton**. Once created, give this object an instance name of **trueBtn** in the Properties panel.

Figure 7.9 Oval tool properties

NOTE

If desired, you can create new keyframes for each of these states and tweak the shape that's created for each specific frame. However, you're targeting a touch screen via mobile devices, so this isn't too great a concern since touch rarely exposes hover events as part of the interaction chain. Often, simply having a default Button symbol state is enough when targeting mobile.

Now that you've created the "true" Button symbol (**Figure 7.10**), you can duplicate it and then tweak a number of properties to create a "false" Button symbol. Duplicating a symbol in this way—no matter what the symbol type—allows you to easily create a uniform look across interactive elements in your application.

First, you'll add a text label to your Button symbol.

7 Double-click the Symbol entry in the project Library to enter and edit the symbol itself. Notice that all four Button symbol frames are available in the internal Button symbol timeline.

8 Choose the Text tool and create a text block with the value of **True**.

9 With this text block selected, use the Properties panel to adjust the font size to 32pt with a color value of #333333 to match the stroke of your shape. Align this text to appear below the shape, centered along the x-axis (**Figure 7.11**).

Figure 7.10 Button symbol in the project Library

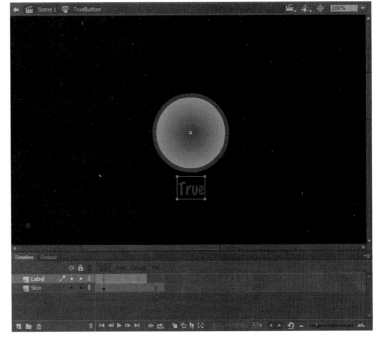

Figure 7.11 Button label

10 With the initial symbol completed, look at the Library panel once again and right-click the TrueButton Button symbol entry.

11 From the menu that appears, choose Duplicate and name the new symbol **FalseButton**.

You'll see the new symbol immediately appear in the Library panel.

12 Double-click that symbol entry and change the text to read **False** instead of True. Additionally, select the shape that already exists. In the Properties panel, choose the red radial gradient swatch from the fill selection area.

Both Button symbols are now completely unique in color and label. With both symbols created, you already have an instance of the TrueButton symbol on the Stage.

13 Click the FalseButton symbol entry in the Library panel and drag an instance out onto the Stage. Name this new instance **falseBtn** and align both instances close to the bottom of the Stage.

These instances should be spaced in equal distance from one another and from each side of the screen (**Figure 7.12**).

▶ *Video 7.8*
Duplicating the Button

Figure 7.12 The completed mobile app interface

Writing the Application Classes

★ ACA Objective 2.4

In the previous chapter, you saw how to build a basic application targeting the desktop with ActionScript in the project timeline. For this project, you'll take a different approach by using the object-oriented class structures that ActionScript provides. Both methods would work for either of the projects in question. We'll use this opportunity to introduce new concepts and approaches.

Writing the QuizGame class

Classes in ActionScript are object-oriented constructs that define a set of **methods** and **properties**, which in turn define a particular object. For instance, `MovieClip` is a class from which all Movie Clip symbols are derived. `MovieClip` includes properties such as x and y and methods like `play()` and `stop()`.

An **object** is a specific **instance** of a class, whereas the class itself is more like a template. Think of the relationship between symbols in the Library and instances on the Stage—it's a similar concept.

You must assign classes, methods, and properties access control namespace attributes. These declarations determine which portions of a program can access the various properties and methods of other classes. Five such attributes are built into ActionScript:

- **internal**: Visible to references inside the same package
- **private**: Visible to references in the same class
- **protected**: Visible to references in the same class and derived classes
- **public**: Visible to references everywhere
- **static**: Specifies that a property belongs to the class, as opposed to instances of the class

You declare these attributes along with variables and functions such as the following:

```
private var myVar:String = "This is private.";
```

Packages are a way to organize classes and preserve them from collisions with other classes that may be named identically. Say, for instance, you've defined a class called `FileEncoder` and you're also using a class named `FileEncoder` from an external library of classes. If you and the library author don't organize or identify the individual `FileEncoder` classes by package, the compiler will have no idea which class you might be referring to at any time.

> **TIP**
>
> *It's common practice to use a reverse-domain naming scheme when defining packages in ActionScript and many other programming languages. For instance, I own the domain "josephlabrecque.com," so for a package name I'd use "com.josephlabrecque."*

CREATING A NEW CLASS

Now you'll begin to create your main class for this project.

 *Video 7.9* *Creating the QuizGame Class*

1 In the Properties panel, check Document Properties to ensure that no objects are selected on the Stage.

2 Note the Class field in the Publish section. On the right is a small pencil icon, signifying the "Edit class definition" function. Click this icon to reveal the Create ActionScript 3.0 Class dialog box (**Figure 7.13**).

Create ActionScript 3.0 Class	✕
Class name: com.josephlabrecque.QuizGame	OK
	Cancel

Figure 7.13 Create ActionScript 3.0 Class dialog box

3 Be sure that the Animate CC radio button is selected, and in the Class name field, type **com.josephlabrecque.QuizGame** (go ahead and use your own domain if you have one).

The following class is created and opened in Animate CC:

```
package com.josephlabrecque {
   import flash.display.MovieClip;
   public class QuizGame extends MovieClip {
      public function QuizGame() {
         // constructor code
      }
   }
}
```

It's important to understand what you've created here. The first line, `package com.josephlabrecque {`, is the package definition for your class. The line `import flash.display.MovieClip;` will make the `MovieClip` class available for your use. Notice how the `MovieClip` class even has its own `flash.display` package? This is a core package definition in Flash Player and AIR.

DEFINING THE CLASS

Next you'll define your class with `public class QuizGame extends MovieClip`. You can tell there's a lot going on here! First, you declare the class as `public`, meaning that it will be visible to other objects in the program. Then you declare your intention to define a class with the `class` keyword, followed by the name of the class. Any class that is the main class of a Animate CC application like this must extend either the `MovieClip` or `Sprite` core class, so in this case, you're extending the `MovieClip` class previously imported. That way, you can make use of everything that `MovieClip` has to offer in terms of properties and methods, while adding your own custom members as well. This is known as *inheritance*, and it's a core object-oriented programming concept.

The last part, `public function QuizGame()`, defines your constructor function. This is a method with the same name as the class that will run by default, meaning you never have to invoke this class. It runs once the class is instantiated. Notice that there's never any return data type declared in a constructor function.

SAVING THE CLASS

Before moving on, you need to save this class as a file:

1 Choose File > Save and navigate to the location of your existing FLA document. From here, you must replicate the package name as a filesystem path.

2 Create a new directory named **com** and enter it. Then create a new directory within that called **josephlabrecque** and enter it as well.

3 Finally, save the file to that directory and name it **QuizGame.as (Figure 7.14)**. Once the file is saved, click the tab in Animate CC that represents your FLA document and save that as well.

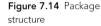
Figure 7.14 Package structure

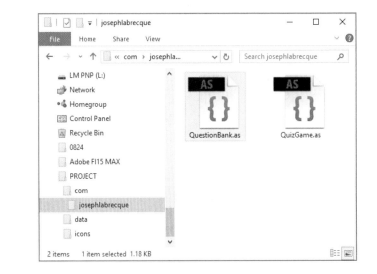

Notice in Figure 7.14 how the package definition and the file structure are identical. Additionally, the name of the class file and the name of the class definition are identical. This is important; your classes won't work unless these items match exactly with one another.

Writing the QuestionBank class

The `QuizGame` class you just created will contain the majority of program logic for your application, but it's useful to delegate specific duties to additional classes whenever possible. Next you'll define an additional class to assist you in handling the loading and management of your question data.

 *Video 7.10* *Writing the QuestionBank Class*

1 To create this new class, choose File > New from the application menu.

The New Document dialog box appears.

2 For document type, select ActionScript 3.0 Class from the menu on the left (**Figure 7.15**).

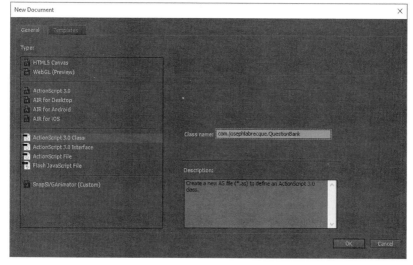

Figure 7.15 Choosing New ActionScript 3.0 Class

3 Note how similar the options presented to you are compared to what you saw when constructing your initial class. Make sure that the Animate CC radio button is selected, and in the Class name field, type **com.josephlabrecque.QuestionBank**. (Again, use your own domain if you have one.) Then click OK.

The following class is created and opened in Animate CC:

```
package com.josephlabrecque {
  public class QuestionBank {
    public function QuestionBank() {
      // constructor code
    }
  }
}
```

Note a number of differences between this class and the previous one. You're not extending any other classes here; this is not a main class and thus isn't bound to any timeline. Similarly, you don't import any classes to extend. You need to save this file as well.

4 Choose File > Save from the application menu and navigate to the location of your existing AS class in the package directory structure you created earlier.

5 Name this file **QuestionBank.as** and save it alongside the QuizGame.as class file.

DEFINING STAGE OBJECT REFERENCES

▶ *Video 7.11*
Defining Stage
Object References

This step isn't exactly necessary, but it provides a lot of benefits to your coding experience, including auto-completion and code hinting. These features won't be available to you unless you import the classes you need and then declare variables with the same instance name as the instances on your Stage.

```
import flash.text.TextField;
import flash.display.SimpleButton;
```

In this example, you have two Button symbol instances on the Stage and two TextFields. All four have instance names. Notice that you declare only the variables; you're not creating new instances of anything, since the instances already exist on your Stage. This is done only to improve the coding experience.

```
public var trueBtn:SimpleButton;
public var falseBtn:SimpleButton;
public var questionText:TextField;
public var statusMsg:TextField;
```

At this point, you can also modify any of your Stage objects. For instance, I'll set the `statusMsg` text to an empty string when initializing the game. You can place this instruction in the `QuizGame` constructor function, and it will run immediately when the app is fired up:

```
public function QuizGame() {
    statusMsg.text = "";
}
```

Creating a Bank of Questions

You could build the data for this application in the ActionScript code, but doing so would mean that every time you wanted to tweak the wording or add new questions, you'd have to edit the code and recompile the app. That's not very convenient, and data doesn't belong with application structures and logic anyway. It's much better to create a service to call over the Internet, or even a local data file (as you'll do next). This approach not only separates the data from the app code but also allows much simpler modification.

Building the JSON file

JSON is a data interchange format created with the intention of being human-readable and at the same time easy for programs to ingest and parse. JSON is a popular data format for the web and has been natively supported in Adobe AIR since AIR 3 and is also available in Adobe Flash Player. For your application, you'll use this format to build a bank of questions and accompanying answers to populate your mobile app.

NOTE
For complete information about the JSON format, visit www.json.org.

▶ **Video 7.12**
Building the JSON File

To create the JSON file, use a simple text editor such as Notepad, TextEdit, or Brackets (http://brackets.io). Begin with a blank text document and enter the following structure:

```
{
    "questions":[
        {"q":"", "tf":""},
        {"q":"", "tf":""},
        {"q":"", "tf":""}
    ]
}
```

TIP
Notice that the final question object in the set does not have a comma after it. If you put a comma here, the code will probably break.

This establishes your JSON structure using standard syntax. The initial curly braces ({}) establish the root object, followed by a **"questions"** array defined with array-syntax braces ([]) that contains a comma-delimited set of additional objects all defined by curly braces. Each object here represents a question-and-answer set. The **question** property of the object is a string that contains the question statement text. The **tf** property is an indicator specifying whether the statement is true or false.

When your JSON file is completed, create the **data** directory in the same location as your FLA document, and in that directory, save the file as **questions.json**.

THE COMPLETED JSON FILE

I've completed the JSON file with a set of 20 statements on Animate CC, Flash Player, ActionScript, and AIR. You can make your version of the quiz on any subject you like. Here is the fully completed JSON structure you'll use in our examples:

```
{
    "questions":[
        {"q":"Animate CC can output to HTML5 Canvas",
        → "tf":"true"},
        {"q":"There is no way to run Animate CC content
        →  on iPad.", "tf":"false"},
        {"q":"Flash Player is an integral component to the
        →  Google Chromebook experience.", "tf":"true"},
        {"q":"The first version of Animate CC was
        →  called FutureSplash Animator.", "tf":"true"},
        {"q":"The Paint Brush Tool was introduced in 2015.",
        →  "tf":"true"},
        {"q":"ActionScript 3.0 is based upon an ECMAScript
        →  standard.", "tf":"true"},
        {"q":"Animate CC cannot output content that will
        →  run in the iPhone web browser.", "tf":"false"},
        {"q":"When targeting HTML5 Canvas, Animate CC
        →  leverages the CreateJS libraries.", "tf":"true"},
        {"q":"Flash Player is built into Google Chrome,
        →  Internet Explorer, and Microsoft Edge.",
        → "tf":"true"},
        {"q":"Using Animate CC, you can build apps which run
        → on iOS.", "tf":"true"},
        {"q":"Animate CC is an industry standard animation
        →  and interactivity tool.", "tf":"true"},
        {"q":"As of September 2015, there have been over
        →  4 BILLION Adobe AIR application installs.",
        → "tf":"true"},
```

```
{"q":"Animate CC content cannot be packaged as
→ OAM files.", "tf":"false"},

{"q":"The current version of ActionScript (as of 2015)
→ is AS4.", "tf":"false"},

{"q":"JavaScript can be edited directly in the Actions
→ Panel.", "tf":"true"},

{"q":"Flash Professional CC (2015) can be used to
→ produce ActionScript 2.0 content.", "tf":"false"},

{"q":"Flash Player cannot access a system webcam or
→ microphone.", "tf":"false"},

{"q":"The final version of Animate CC from
→ Macromedia was Animate CC 8.", "tf":"true"},

{"q":"As of September 2015, Flash Player is downloaded
→ 1.2 BILLION times per month from Adobe.com.",
"tf":"true"},

{"q":"Adobe continues to develop Flash Player for
→ Android.", "tf":"false"}
    ]
}
```

Loading the JSON data

To load the JSON data into your application, you'll leverage the `QuestionBank`
ActionScript class. You'll need to import three additional classes into
`QuestionBank` to deal with loading the JSON file. Add the following lines right
beneath the package definition:

▶ *Video 7.13* Loading
the JSON Data

```
import flash.net.URLRequest;
import flash.net.URLLoader;
import flash.events.Event;
```

Now, immediately after the class definition, you'll enter some variables. Here's a
quick overview of what these variables are named, and their role in the application.

- **JSON_URL**: A constant that defines the location of your JSON file
- **jsonRequest**: A `URLRequest` object that defines the URL you want to load
- **jsonLoader**: A `URLLoader` object that uses the `URLRequest` object to load in
  your JSON
- **questionArray**: The `Array` object you'll use to store all the parsed objects
  from your external JSON

The code will look like this:

```
private const JSON_URL:String = "data/questions.json";
private var jsonRequest:URLRequest;
private var jsonLoader:URLLoader;
private var questionArray:Array;
```

In your QuestionBank constructor function, you'll need to initialize the **Array** object by stating `questionArray = new Array();` and then invoke a method to load in your JSON via `loadJSON();` using the URLRequest and URLLoader objects. The completed constructor function will look like this:

```
public function QuestionBank() {
    questionArray = new Array();
    loadJSON();
}
```

To load the JSON, you must use the loadJSON method that first defines your URLRequest, with the String constant declaring your file path to the JSON file. A URLLoader is then created that's instructed to invoke a method called jsonLoaded when the file load completes. Finally, you tell the URLLoader to load your URLRequest.

```
private function loadJSON():void {
    jsonRequest = new URLRequest(JSON_URL);
    jsonLoader = new URLLoader();
    jsonLoader.addEventListener(Event.COMPLETE, jsonLoaded);
    jsonLoader.load(jsonRequest);
}
```

Once the file has completely loaded into your application, the jsonLoaded method is triggered, which uses the native JSON parser in ActionScript to parse the event target data and save it to a new object named jsonData. This object is then processed in a **for each loop** in order to add each question object to the array you created previously.

```
private function jsonLoaded(e:Event):void {
    var jsonData:Object = JSON.parse(e.target.data);
```

```
for each (var question:Object in jsonData.questions){
    questionArray.push(question);
  }
}
```

Integrating the QuestionBank class

Now you've created two completely independent classes. Your `QuizGame` class is tied to the FLA document, but the `QuestionBank` class isn't connected to anything. To have a working application, you'll need to integrate the `QuestionBank` class into your main `QuizGame` class so that it can be used from there.

▶ *Video 7.14*
Integrating the QuestionBank Class

PREPARING THE QUIZGAME CLASS

The way you use one class from within another is something you've already done, though you may not fully realize it yet. Basically, any time you've imported classes and then instantiated variables from those classes, you've taken the same steps needed to integrate your `QuestionBank` class into `QuizGame`.

1 In the QuizGame.as file, import the core `Event` class from the `flash.events` package. You'll use this to listen for events broadcast from your `QuestionBank` class.

2 Import the `QuestionBank` class from the `com.josephlabrecque` package:

```
import flash.events.Event;
import com.josephlabrecque.QuestionBank;
```

3 Declare two objects: one as a `QuestionBank` instance and one as an `Array`. Place these lines of code alongside the previous import commands:

```
private var questionBank:QuestionBank;
private var questionArray:Array;
```

Now in the `QuizGame` constructor function, you'll perform some setup operations. You already have a line of code that clears out your status message text.

4 Right below that line of code, set `questionArray` to a new `Array` object. This action makes the `Array` object available for use.

5 Below that, set `questionBank` as a new `QuestionBank` object. The `questionBank` variable has now been instantiated, and you're able to read properties from it or invoke the methods that belong to it.

NOTE

Simply declaring the variables like this does not instantiate them or make them available for use in the application. It merely provides the intention to use named variables as specific data types.

6 Listen for an event to be broadcast from the `questionBank` instance so that you know exactly when the question data has been retrieved and made available for use.

7 Add an event listener of type `Event.COMPLETE` to your instance.

When this event is detected, an additional method called `dataReady` will execute:

```
public function QuizGame() {
statusMsg.text = "";
questionArray = new Array();
questionBank = new QuestionBank();
questionBank.addEventListener(Event.COMPLETE, dataReady);
}
```

8 To create the method, create a new private function, name it **dataReady**, and pass through the `Event` from your listener as an argument.

If any method is invoked with argument data passed through, the receiving function must be configured to accept that data or the compilation will fail. The return data type is set to `void` since this method doesn't return any data.

9 In the body of your function, set `questionArray` equal to `questionBank.buildBank()`.

This will invoke the `buildBank` method, which you have yet to create, from the `questionBank` instance and will return that `Array` data to `questionArray` for your use in the main `QuizGame` class.

10 Grab a question from the bank by invoking a method named `grabQuestion` that doesn't yet exist.

```
private function dataReady(e:Event):void {
    questionArray = questionBank.buildBank();
    grabQuestion();
}
```

FINISHING THE QUESTIONBANK CLASS

▶ Video 7.15
*Finishing the
QuestionBank
Class*

By now you've prepared your main `QuizGame` class to listen for events emerging from the `QuestionBank` class and to respond to such events appropriately. However, the `QuestionBank` class needs to be modified in order to be able to broadcast such events. In the `QuestionBank` class, the first thing you must do is import the `EventDispatcher` class from the `flash.events` package:

```
import flash.events.EventDispatcher;
```

Similar to how you extended the `QuizGame` class from `flash.display.MovieClip`, you'll extend the `QuestionBank` class from `flash.events.EventDispatcher`. That way, your `QuestionBank` class can dispatch events to other parts of the application. On the existing class definition, simply add `extends EventDispatcher` right after `public class QuestionBank` to enable this:

```
public class QuestionBank extends EventDispatcher
```

Now you'll broadcast, or dispatch, your event. In the final line of your `jsonLoaded` method, right after the `for` loop, use the `dispatchEvent` method to broadcast a completion event to the rest of your application. You'll be able to catch this event in your main `QuizGame` class since you've already added an event listener to do so. To your `for` loop, add the following line of code immediately after the closing curly brace:

```
dispatchEvent(new Event(Event.COMPLETE));
```

Additionally, you must create a way of getting all the question data now contained in the `QuestionBank` class over to your main `QuizGame` class for use in the app. To populate your `Array` in `QuizGame`, you're invoking a nonexisting method of `QuestionBank` named `buildBank`. You'll create this method now:

1. Create a new public function named **buildBank** with a return data type of `Array`.

2. In the function body, create a temporary `Array` named **b**.

   This is what will eventually be returned to the `QuizGame` class. Additionally, you'll create another variable, `max`, which is an int.

3. Set the value of this variable to the length of `questionArray`.

   This lets you know how many questions you have to deal with.

The next thing you need to do is to establish a `for` loop that counts from 0 to the value of `max`. For each iteration of this loop, you use the `Array.push()` method to add specific values from your main `Array` into the temporary `Array`. Once all the questions have been added, the `for` loop ends, and you use the `return` command to send the temporary `Array` and all of its data back to the class that invoked this method:

```
public function buildBank():Array {
    var b:Array = new Array();
```

```
      var max:int = questionArray.length;
      for(var i:int=0; i<max; i++){
        b.push({q:questionArray[i].q, tf:questionArray[i].tf});
      }
      return b;
  }
```

THE COMPLETED QUESTIONBANK CLASS

You've now constructed the entire `QuestionBank` class. Yours should appear identical to the class shown here:

```
package com.josephlabrecque {
    import flash.net.URLRequest;
    import flash.net.URLLoader;
    import flash.events.Event;
    import flash.events.EventDispatcher;

    public class QuestionBank extends EventDispatcher {
        private const JSON_URL:String = "data/questions.json";
        private var jsonRequest:URLRequest;
        private var jsonLoader:URLLoader;
        private var questionArray:Array;

        public function QuestionBank() {
            questionArray = new Array();
            loadJSON();
        }

        private function loadJSON():void {
            jsonRequest = new URLRequest(JSON_URL);
            jsonLoader = new URLLoader();
            jsonLoader.addEventListener(Event.COMPLETE, jsonLoaded);
            jsonLoader.load(jsonRequest);
        }

        private function jsonLoaded(e:Event):void {
```

```
            var jsonData:Object = JSON.parse(e.target.data);
            for each (var question:Object in jsonData.questions){
              questionArray.push(question);
            }
            dispatchEvent(new Event(Event.COMPLETE));
          }


          public function buildBank():Array {
            var b:Array = new Array();
            var max:int = questionArray.length;
            for(var i:int=0; i<max; i++){
              b.push({q:questionArray[i].q, tf:questionArray[i].tf});
            }
            return b;
          }
        }


      }
```

App Logic and Flow

You have the interface designed, the basic classes written, and the data load-ing in. Your mobile app is nearly finished! You do have an essential task to com-plete, though: the interactive part. You must have the app respond to user input, check the choices the user provides, and give feedback once this all has occurred. You'll establish all of this functionality through modifications to your main `QuizGame` class.

★ ACA Objective 4.6

Showing questions to the user

To manage your set of questions, you'll define a number of variables in the applica-tion. Directly below the other variable declarations that exist in the `QuizGame` class, you'll define an additional set of variables for this purpose. `questionMax` is an int and a constant, meaning that once a value has been set, it should never change. This defines how many questions, from the full pool of questions, you want to show your user. The `questionCount` variable keeps track of how many questions

▶ Video 7.16
Showing Questions to the User

have been asked so far, and the `currentAnswer` variable holds the answer data, gathered from your internal `Array` of questions.

```
private const questionMax:int = 5;
private var questionCount:int = 0;
private var currentAnswer:String;
```

In your `dataReady` function, you're invoking a method called `grabQuestion` to pull a question object from the pool and show it to the user. This isn't something you've written yet, so you'll define a new private function with the name of `grabQuestion`, which returns nothing, typed as `void`. In this function, you'll look to see if your current question count is less than the maximum amount of questions you want to ask in the app. If it is, then you'll pull a random question from the `Array` by using a randomization Math function.

You're pulling the question object from the Array by using the `Array.splice()` command, which will remove the object completely from the `Array`, making the length of the `Array` one index shorter each time `grabQuestion` is run. This ensures that you never present the user with the same question twice. The question data is placed in a temporary `Array` named `ta`, and the question statement is immediately pulled from this `Array` and placed in the `questionText` text block on the Stage, effectively making the statement visible to the user in the app. You do this by setting the value of `questionText.text` equal to `ta[0].q`. When you see something like `[0]` in ActionScript, this is `Array` syntax, simply requesting the data at position 0 of your `Array`.

Your `currentAnswer` variable will always contain the exact answer data pulled from this `Array` so you can easily check the user response against the correct answer. Similar to how you retrieve the question statement text from your temporary `Array`, you'll once again use this syntax to retrieve the correct answer to the statement. You do this by setting the value of `currentAnswer` equal to `ta[0].tf`. This will set the value of `currentAnswer` to a `String` of either `"true"` or `"false"` for each specific question statement.

Lastly, you increment your `questionCount` variable by 1, keeping a tally of how many questions you've presented to the user. This allows you to determine when to invoke your `gameOver()` method.

```
private function grabQuestion():void {
    if(questionCount < questionMax){
```

```
        var max:int = questionArray.length-1;
        var rq:int = Math.floor(Math.random() * (max - 0 + 1));
        var ta:Array = questionArray.splice(rq, 1);
        questionText.text = ta[0].q;
        currentAnswer = ta[0].tf;
        questionCount++;
    } else{
        gameOver();
    }
}
```

The `gameOver()` method is fairly simple. You define a new private function with the name of `gameOver`, which accepts no arguments and returns nothing as well. In the body of this function, you display the number of calculated points from the `currentScore` variable and change the `questionText` text value to read **Game Over!**.

```
private function gameOver():void {
    statusMsg.text = currentScore+"/100 points";
    questionText.text = "Game Over!";
}
```

As for keeping track of the score, this is something done with each button press from the user, and it's the last bit of code you need to write.

Building button interactivity

You've now arrived at the final part of this project: allowing the user to interact with the mobile app and then reacting to choices the user has made in the application flow.

The first thing you need to do is import a couple more classes. The `MouseEvent` class will allow you to set up event listeners in response to mouse and touch events; `setTimeout` will enable you to perform a delayed function call following the user interaction.

```
import flash.events.MouseEvent;
import flash.utils.setTimeout;
```

▶ *Video 7.17*
Building Button
Interactivity

To keep score based on user choices, you'll establish a new variable called `currentScore`. This will start with a value of 0 and be updated every time the user correctly responds to each statement.

```
private var currentScore:int = 0;
```

Back in the `QuizGame` constructor function, you'll add an event listener to both of the `SimpleButton` instances on the Stage. Each will invoke a method to respond to the user's choice, based on the `currentAnswer` variable, determining whether to add to the user's score, and proceeding with the next question.

```
trueBtn.addEventListener(MouseEvent.CLICK, truePressed);
falseBtn.addEventListener(MouseEvent.CLICK, falsePressed);
```

Scroll down in the class and add a method to control responses to your user interaction. First, you create a new private function named **truePressed**. This method fires off whenever the user selects the **trueBtn** instance on the Stage. In the body of this function, you first check to see whether a status message is present. If a status message exists, it means that you should not allow the user interaction to count, because you're between questions.

Then you check whether the user's choice matches the `currentAnswer`. If it matches, then you increment the score based on how many total questions you'll be displaying and set the status message text to **CORRECT!**. If it's incorrect, you set it to **WRONG!**. No matter which answer is chosen, you then use the `setTimeout` method to be sure the status message stays on the screen for a full second before invoking the `newQuestion` method to retrieve the next statement.

```
private function truePressed(e:MouseEvent):void {
    if(statusMsg.text == ""){
        if(currentAnswer == "true"){
            currentScore += 100/questionMax;
            statusMsg.text = "CORRECT!";
        }else{
            statusMsg.text = "WRONG";
        }
        setTimeout(newQuestion, 1000);
    }
}
```

Basically, you do the same thing for the `falsePressed` function. The only real difference is that you're checking whether `correctAnswer` is false. Everything else is practically identical.

```
private function falsePressed(e:MouseEvent):void {
  if(statusMsg.text == ""){
    if(currentAnswer == "false"){
      currentScore += 100/questionMax;
      statusMsg.text = "CORRECT!";
    }else{
      statusMsg.text = "WRONG";
    }
    setTimeout(newQuestion, 1000);
  }
}
```

The last method you need to build is the `newQuestion` function, which gets called from each button press method. All this does is clear out the status message text and then invoke the `grabQuestion` method. Again, this `newQuestion` method call is delayed by one full second to ensure that users will see the status message feedback to their selection before it's cleared and the new question appears.

```
private function newQuestion():void {
  statusMsg.text = "";
  grabQuestion();
}
```

THE COMPLETED QUIZGAME CLASS

That completes all of your ActionScript code for this project! The completed code for QuizGame.as is included here for your reference.

```
package com.josephlabrecque {
  import flash.display.MovieClip;
  import flash.text.TextField;
  import flash.display.SimpleButton;
  import flash.events.Event;
  import com.josephlabrecque.QuestionBank;
  import flash.events.MouseEvent;
```

```
import flash.utils.setTimeout;

public class QuizGame extends MovieClip {
  public var trueBtn:SimpleButton;
  public var falseBtn:SimpleButton;
  public var questionText:TextField;
  public var statusMsg:TextField;

  private var questionBank:QuestionBank;
  private var questionArray:Array;
  private const questionMax:int = 5;
  private var questionCount:int = 0;
  private var currentAnswer:String;
  private var currentScore:int = 0;

  public function QuizGame() {
    statusMsg.text = "";
    questionArray = new Array();
    questionBank = new QuestionBank();
    questionBank.addEventListener(Event.COMPLETE, dataReady);
    trueBtn.addEventListener(MouseEvent.CLICK, truePressed);
    falseBtn.addEventListener(MouseEvent.CLICK, falsePressed);
  }

  private function truePressed(e:MouseEvent):void {
    if(statusMsg.text == ""){
      if(currentAnswer == "true"){
        currentScore += 100/questionMax;
        statusMsg.text = "CORRECT!";
      }else{
        statusMsg.text = "WRONG";
      }
      setTimeout(newQuestion, 1000);
    }
  }
```

```
private function falsePressed(e:MouseEvent):void {
    if(statusMsg.text == ""){
        if(currentAnswer == "false"){
            currentScore += 100/questionMax;
            statusMsg.text = "CORRECT!";
        }else{
            statusMsg.text = "WRONG";
        }
        setTimeout(newQuestion, 1000);
    }
}

private function dataReady(e:Event):void {
    questionArray = questionBank.buildBank();
    grabQuestion();
}

private function newQuestion():void {
    statusMsg.text = "";
    trace(currentScore);
    grabQuestion();
}

private function grabQuestion():void {
    if(questionCount < questionMax){
        var max:int = questionArray.length-1;
        var rq:int = Math.floor(Math.random() * (max - 0 + 1));
        var ta:Array = questionArray.splice(rq, 1);
        questionText.text = ta[0].q;
        currentAnswer = ta[0].tf;
        questionCount++;
    }else{
        gameOver();
    }
}
```

```
        private function gameOver():void {
            statusMsg.text = currentScore+"/100 points";
            questionText.text = "Game Over!";
        }


    }


}
```

Publishing the App for Distribution

★ ACA Objective 5.4

Now that you've completed the application and made it ready for distribution, consider some additional options. The AIR Settings dialog box provides settings related to the publishing and delivery of an Android or iOS app. You can access these options by clicking the wrench icon next to the Target properties in the Publish Settings dialog box. A series of tabbed windows opens in an AIR output dialog box. These windows allow you to set up the options for the AIR mobile app.

Completing application details

▶ Video 7.18
Publishing the App
for Distribution

To complete the final details for publishing the application, choose File > AIR for Desktop Settings from the application menu. The AIR Settings dialog (**Figure 7.16**) opens, containing the following areas:

- **General**: This screen contains core information about how you package your mobile application. You can choose to generate an AIR file, use an OS-specific installer, or use the embedded runtime option. This is also the place to name your application and make decisions about aspect ratio, orientation, and render mode.

- **Signature**: All Adobe AIR applications must be signed in order to be properly installed on a user's device. This screen allows you to create a free, self-signed certificate to publish your applications to Android. If you're targeting iOS, you can input all the information about your provisioning profile and certificate from Apple.

- **Icons:** This section allows you to specify a group of custom icons that represent the mobile application. You can create icons of differing sizes in an application like Adobe Photoshop.
- **Permissions:** This is a list of permissions you can check off, indicating which specific permissions are needed for Android. This screen does not appear if you're targeting iOS, since it handles permissions differently.
- **Language:** In this section you indicate the languages used in your mobile application.

Figure 7.16 AIR Settings dialog box

Challenge!

There are a *lot* of different resolutions and aspect ratios to deal with when targeting mobile devices. The way you've built this project doesn't take this fact into account, but using ActionScript, you can make the user interface elements completely responsive in regard to different screen sizes. It requires many of the concepts you've learned so far: instance names and the ability to adjust X and Y positions and other attributes through code.

Conclusion

In this chapter, you've worked in Animate CC to create a mobile app that can be compiled to either Apple iOS or Google Android using Adobe AIR technology. You spent a lot of time with ActionScript and had a deeper look at the object-oriented syntax and rich capabilities of the language structures needed to build a real, cross-platform mobile app.

You've dug deeper into ActionScript to properly organize your code into packages and classes, all while learning more of the functionality available to you when ingesting external data and forming complex data structures. You've also learned how to listen for and respond to user interaction through something as straightforward as button presses.

CHAPTER OBJECTIVES

Chapter Learning Objectives

- Edit and evaluate your interactive media content
- Test usability and accessibility
- Work with focus groups and beta testers
- Identify useful web resources for Animate CC users

Chapter ACA Objectives

DOMAIN 5.0
TESTING, PUBLISHING, AND EVALUATING INTERACTIVE MEDIA ELEMENTS USING FLASH PROFESSIONAL

5.1 Conduct basic technical and usability tests.

5.3 Make a Flash document accessible.

CHAPTER 8

Wrapping It Up!

Congratulations! You've made it to the end of this book—and by now you should be pretty good at using Adobe Animate CC to create interactive media projects targeting a variety of publishing targets and formats. As you've seen through the projects we've worked on, Animate CC is capable of a diverse array of project types.

Before we close, let's tie things up with a few words about content evaluation and testing, along with some resources for exploring more of what Animate CC has to offer.

> **NOTE** *Adobe has rebranded Flash Professional CC as Animate CC! They are essentially the exact same application—with absolutely no differences in capability aside from features introduced in the regular update schedule. All future updates to Flash Professional CC will be known by the name Animate CC. If desired, subscribers can run multiple versions of the product—branded as either Animate CC or Animate—but I highly recommend using the latest available version of Animate CC to take advantage of all the new features.*

Evaluating Interactive Media Content

★ ACA Objective 5.1

Interactive content created in Animate CC can be complex depending on the type of project you're working on. Being able to properly evaluate and test a project is a task that you should always undertake before you consider a project complete. Be prepared for several rounds of editing in your project plan. Define your procedures and processes to make editing as painless as possible.

Many people are drawn to interactive media development because it is dynamic and flashy. Evaluating, proofing, and editing interactive media files isn't as glamorous as creating cool interface elements or manipulating video, but it's essential to getting your work out the door. You may be tempted to try passing this tedious task off to others. That isn't a good idea. Remember that no one else knows the files like the designer or developer who put it all together.

Types of evaluation

You can evaluate interactive media content from multiple vantage points, but in any case it's best to keep your objectives specific. Your evaluation process can involve testing technical aspects of an interactive media document to search for bugs, broken links, and other glitches. You can perform a separate round of evaluation on the contextual information to make sure it accurately reflects the intent of the storyboards. Usability should always be the final evaluation in each cycle, to test to see how end users receive the interactive media document. A good starting point is to evaluate the technical, content, and usability aspects of your interactive media piece.

TECHNICAL EVALUATION

To conduct a technical evaluation of interactive media content, you'll examine the work for any coding errors, playback issues, and deployment problems. This evaluation doesn't include addressing usability or proofreading the content against the working documents. Breaking down the tasks for this technical evaluation will help you focus on specific problems and not get overwhelmed. You also may find that solving one issue will fix other issues. Conversely, you might create or find new problems as you attempt to resolve issues.

There is always some overlap in the evaluation processes, but when evaluating an interactive media application for technical issues, you should be focusing on the functionality of the content delivery system, not the content itself. Errors and warnings in the ActionScript or JavaScript, bugs, broken links, excessive load times, and navigation errors are some of the issues that fall into this category.

INITIAL EVALUATION

You can perform your initial technical evaluation on the development platform, but as you enter the final cycles of editing, make sure that the content is running on the actual target platform. This is especially important if the interactive media content is to be delivered via mobile devices.

Bugs are the major target of a preliminary technical evaluation. Test the interface and functionality thoroughly to determine if any errors were made in scripting or naming of instances. It's never acceptable to ship a final version of a product with a **bug** or error in the ActionScript or JavaScript. To prevent this from happening, you'll need to schedule enough time with testers to test every element in every way that it might be used (or misused).

This is a good time to call others in to help. Because you're familiar with the code and functionality, you may never even imagine how the interactive media content could be misused. Another set of hands on the keyboard and mouse can reveal issues that you may not have considered when you were building the project.

TIP

Do your preliminary technical testing before you perform any usability testing, because a technical bug may skew the usability results.

DEPLOYMENT TESTING

Most interactive media content designers and developers have powerful machines that let them quickly create and manipulate video, animations, and sound files. However, when it comes to evaluating how your interactive media application will run in the real world, all this horsepower can actually be a bad thing.

Depending on your target user, you may want to test on a machine with minimum specifications. Even running the Flash Player–based SWF file from an integrated version of Flash Player instead of running it from the browser (and even multiple browsers) can reveal unexpected results.

CONTENT EVALUATION

Content is king, and even the slickest interface can't save you if your content is inaccurate or poorly implemented. At some point in the evaluation process, a meticulous editor must proof the content. The editor should look for inconsistencies and typos by comparing the working documents to the onscreen content. Subject matter experts (SMEs) can also be called in at this point to make sure the intended concepts reflect accurately in the interactive media format.

WHAT TO LOOK FOR

During the content evaluation, look for errors in the text, proper use of imagery, correct navigation points, and so on. It all begins with basic proofreading. There are other considerations, too. Recall our discussion of using type specifications, graphic treatment, placement, and color to reinforce the purpose of elements in an interactive media application. During the content evaluation, make sure that the style guide outlining those treatments is followed consistently. Look not only at the text and images but also at how those images appear and whether their appearance conforms to the style guidelines.

SPELLING CHECK

Checking spelling is the single easiest form of evaluation and can reveal problems that may have occurred while the text was imported or pasted from the working documents. Animate CC does not include an integrated spell check, so you must do this manually.

Usability evaluation

Many aspects of technical evaluation and content evaluation may be executed concurrently, but the **usability** evaluation should always be the last evaluation in the cycle (or cycles).

Poorly proofed and executed interfaces will affect how your audience perceives the experience, and they can increase the end user's sensitivity to how the interactive media is presented. Suddenly that very cool interface element may appear too complex or busy. Or maybe the background graphic that was just perfect for the content now seems distracting.

It is best for your project to be clean, error-free, and functioning seamlessly by the time you test it for usability so that the testers focus on just usability and don't get distracted by anything else.

WHAT TO LOOK FOR

Usability includes not only testing the interface to see how end users operate the interactive media application but also evaluating how users react and work with the content. You could have a fantastic interface that is crippled by content that isn't properly organized. Even the delivery device could cause some unintended problems, like buttons that are accidentally pressed because of proximity or something being obstructed because you need to hold the device in a certain way. You may not spot this type of issue unless you throw it out there and let the testers start beating on it.

There isn't a set checklist for usability, because the content and audiences vary. However, you could make some general guidelines to follow in your evaluation as you assess the interface, the content, and the experience.

EVALUATE ACCESSIBILITY

★ ACA Objective 5.3

Accessibility is important. Although it's challenging to work with certain Animate CC projects in an accessible way, it's not impossible to do so. When targeting Flash Player, you have access to the accessibility portion of the Properties panel (**Figure 8.1**) when working with the document or movie clip properties. The choices allow you to make the entire project and specific child objects accessible.

You can input metadata regarding object name and description and, in the case of Movie Clip symbol instances, choose keyboard shortcuts and tab order. It's important to note, however, that there are many commonsense ways of making any piece of interactive media more accessible. These include consistent navigation, color choices, and the typefaces used.

Figure 8.1 Accessibility in the Properties panel

INFORMAL TESTING

How you execute the usability testing depends on the scope of the project and its intended audience. For smaller projects, a simple random group from around the office may suffice. Have your colleagues run the application and take notes as they go. Be sure that the people selected are representative of the target end users. For instance, if special subject knowledge is required to understand the content, make sure the informal group has that knowledge.

FOCUS GROUPS

A focus group can be a big help in understanding how end users will react to an interactive media experience. When an organization conducts a focus group, they invite individuals from the target audience to sit in and evaluate a product. They use the product and are encouraged by a facilitator to make comments on their experience. You may need to pay each evaluator or offer them a free gift to entice them to participate.

NOTE

Many people think it's their job to criticize. In this case, they would be correct. Don't let it get to you, and don't lose sleep if only one member of the group has a problem with something. You're looking for patterns in the opinions.

Observe your evaluators via video or through a one-way window. The point is not to spy on them as much as it is to get an honest reaction. Many people will not tell you what you need to hear when you're standing right in front of them. The anonymity of a focus group allows people to loosen up and express what they really think. A focus group also shows you how users react to the interface. You understand it because you created it, but someone viewing it for the first time may have a different reaction.

BETA TESTING

Beta testing is another valuable tool in determining usability. This involves getting potential users to agree to use preliminary releases of a product and report back with their recommendations. The big benefit of beta testing is that it involves real end users using the product in a real environment. Feedback from beta testing can be gathered via phone calls, interviews, questionnaires, or other means.

Revisions

No matter how carefully you plan or proof an interactive media application, you'll always have room for improvement. The evaluation process doesn't stop after you deliver the product. Many interactive media applications are delivered without any physical medium; this means that making improvements and revisions can be an ongoing process.

But just because you can revise it later doesn't excuse you from thoroughly evaluating an application before it goes out the door. You have only one chance at making a good first impression.

If you do a great job creating interactive media content, the development path is circular, not linear.

Where to Go Next

You may be wondering what is next for Adobe Animate CC and how you can stay up to date on all things "Flash." Like many of the Adobe Creative Cloud desktop applications, Animate CC receives a number of major updates every year.

Animate CC resources

Adobe has a number of web-based resources that are designed to serve the Animate CC user and developer community, including the following:

- **Adobe Animate CC Team Blog** (*http://blogs.adobe.com/flashpro/*): Here you'll find the latest news, tips, and insights directly from the Adobe Flash team.

- **Adobe AIR and Adobe Flash Player Team Blog** (*http://blogs.adobe.com/flashplayer/*): This blog offers news, commentary, and insights from the Flash Player and Adobe AIR product and engineering teams.

- **Animate CC | Product Page** (*http://adobe.com/products/flash.html*): "Create animations for any device or platform."

- **Animate CC | New Features** (*http://adobe.com/products/flash/features.html*): "With Animate CC, you always have access to new features as soon as they're released."

- **Animate CC | Learn** (*https://helpx.adobe.com/flash.html*): "Get started or go deeper with our library of tutorials, projects and articles."

- **Animate CC | Release Notes** (*https://helpx.adobe.com/flash/flash-professional-releasenotes.html*): Here you'll find release notes by version.

- **Animate CC |ActionScript Reference** (*http://help.adobe.com/en_US/FlashPlatform/reference/actionscript/3/*): "The ActionScript 3.0 Reference for the Adobe Flash Platform contains the ActionScript language elements, core libraries, and component packages and classes for the tools, runtimes, services, and servers in the Flash Platform."

Goodbye!

I hope you've had fun learning about interactive media with Animate CC and that you now have a deeper understanding of what can be accomplished with this powerful, modern application. You can achieve an enormous variety of projects using Animate CC—so have fun!

ACA Objectives Covered

continues on next page

continued from previous page

DOMAIN OBJECTIVES	CHAPTER	VIDEO
DOMAIN 3.0 Understanding Adobe Flash Professional		
3.1 Identify elements of the Flash Professional interface and demonstrate knowledge of their functions, including Panels, the Timeline, and Document Properties dialog.	**Ch 1** The Animate CC Workspace, 6 **Ch 1** Major Interface Features, 9	**1.1** The Animate CC Workspace **1.2** The Properties and Tools Panels **1.4** Managing Panels
3.2 Define the functions of commonly used tools, including selection tools, the Pen tool, other drawing tools, and shape tools.	**Ch 1** Commonly Accessed Tools, 12 **Ch 2** Additional Vector Creation Tools, 27 **Ch 4** Laying Out the Background Elements, 73 **Ch 5** The 3D Rotation and 3D Translation Tools, 112 **Ch 6** Building the Basic Clock Visual Elements, 144	**1.3** The Animate CC Timeline **1.6** Common Keyboard Shortcuts **2.4** Drawing the Floor **2.5** Drawing a Ball **2.6** Use the Align Panel **2.7** Testing the Project **4.3** Drawing the Background **4.4** Decorating with Art Brushes **4.8** Shaping with the Selection Tool **5.9** 3D Tooling Introduction **6.4** Build the Clock Body
3.3 Navigate, organize, and customize the workspace.		
3.4 Use design tools in the interface, such as rulers and guides.	**Ch 2** Preparing the Project Stage and Timeline, 20 **Ch 3** Setting Up Your Project, 49	**2.3** Preparing the Project Stage and Timeline **3.3** Rulers and Guides
3.5 Use the Motion Editor.	**Ch 5** Creating the Rotation Effect for Your Headshot, 114	**5.10** Creating the Rotation Effect
3.6 Demonstrate knowledge of layers and masks.	**Ch 2** Setting Layer Properties on the Timeline, 22 **Ch 3** Dealing with the Timeline and Layers, 54	**3.6** Break Apart an Image
3.7 Understand Symbols and the Library.	**Ch 3** The Project Library, 51 **Ch 4** Convert to a Graphic Symbol, 79 **Ch 7** Designing the Buttons, 179	**4.10** Creating a Graphic Symbol **4.11** Editing Symbols and Symbol Instances **4.12** Preparing the Symbol **7.7** Designing a Button

continues on next page

continued from previous page

DOMAIN OBJECTIVES	CHAPTER	VIDEO
4.6 Add simple controls through ActionScript 3.0, JavaScript for HTML5 Canvas, and WebGL.	**Ch 7** App Logic and Flow, 195	**7.16** Showing Questions to the User
4.7 Create masks.	**Ch 3** Hiding Content with a Mask, 57 **Ch 5** Creating Dynamic Backgrounds with Animated Shape Masking, 106	**3.8** Hiding Content with Masking **5.4** Create a Star Mask
4.8 Import and use sound.	**Ch 6** Using Imported Audio in an ActionScript Project, 155	**6.13** Inserting Audio
4.9 Add and export video.	**Ch 5** Video in Animate CC, 130	
DOMAIN 5.0 Testing, Publishing, and Evaluating Interactive Media Elements Using Flash Professional.		
5.1 Conduct basic technical and usability tests.	**Ch 6** Testing an ActionScript Project, 168 **Ch 8** Evaluating Interactive Media Content, 206	
5.2 Understand Flash file types and file sizes.	**Ch 2** Setting Document Type and Properties, 19	
5.3 Make an a Flash document accessible.	**Ch 8** Evaluate Accessibility, 209	
5.4 Publish and export Flash documents.	**Ch 2** Publishing for Flash Player, 39 **Ch 3** Generating an Image, 64 **Ch 4** Publishing Your Project for HTML5 Canvas, 98 **Ch 5** Rendering and Converting the RAW Video, 127 **Ch 6** Publishing the Clock for Desktop Installation, 169 **Ch 7** Publishing the App for Distribution, 202	**2.14** Publish for Flash Player **2.15** Generate a Projector **3.12** Exporting a Static Image **3.13** Additional Publish Options **4.22** Publishing for HTML5 Canvas **4.23** Converting to WebGL **5.21** Rendering the Video **6.21** General AIR for Desktop Properties **6.24** Publishing and Installing an AIR application **7.18** Publishing the App for Distribution

Glossary

3D Three-dimensional image or video that gives the viewer a perception of depth. To achieve this using the tools in Animate CC, a third position axis, "z," is added to the x and y axes.

accessibility Software designed with specific or general people with disabilities in mind.

ActionScript An object-oriented programming language based upon the ECMAScript standard and originally developed my Macromedia before being acquired by Adobe. ActionScript is the programming language used to build interactive and dynamic projects for Flash Player and Adobe AIR.

additive color Created by combining light.

AIR Adobe AIR allows the creation of standalone applications using Flash technology for installation on Microsoft Windows, Apple OS X, Apple iOS, and Google Android.

alignment Indicates how the lines are aligned on the right and left edges, such as left, centered, and right.

all caps Uses only uppercase letterforms for each letter.

analogous Colors that are side by side on the color wheel. They create gentle and relaxing color schemes.

Animate CC Adobe Animate CC is the rebranded version of the revered animation and interactivity application known as Flash Professional CC. Animate CC retains all of the functionality present in Flash Professional CC...and even more.

anti-aliasing A software rendering technique of which the primary goal is to soften or eliminate jagged lines. Often applied to text.

API Application Programming Interface: A documented set of functions and protocols that allows one piece of software to communicate with another or allows one piece of code to take advantage of another in its execution.

APK Android Application Package: An APK can be installed on an Android device as an executable program. The iOS equivalent is IPA.

armature An armature in Animate CC allows for movement through inverse kinematics. Armatures can be composed of multiple Movie Clip Symbol instances or through a simple shape.

array An array is a structured, index-based object type that allows a number of different values or references to be stored in a single object. Arrays in ActionScript begin with index 0.

asymmetrical Achieves balance with different elements with different weights on each side (or the top and bottom) of an image.

attribution Written acknowledgment provided with the name of the original copyright holder of the work. Creative Commons and other licenses feature different kinds of attribution requirements.

balance Evenly distributed, but not necessarily centered or mirrored.

beta Considered an unstable program. Generally, when a program is in beta, it must be tested in various ways before being considered stable.

bitmap Images represented by stored pixel data within a grid. Scaling a bitmap will degrade the visual representation of the image.

blackletter fonts Also known as old English, Gothic, or Textura. Feature an overly ornate style. Convey a feeling of rich and sophisticated gravitas.

blank keyframe A keyframe with no content whatsoever. Represented in Animate CC with an unfilled circle.

bug Generally an error, fault, or failure in a piece of code that needs to be addressed.

canvas An HTML5 element that allows the rendering of complex graphics and interactivity through JavaScript.

cast shadow The shadow cast on the ground and on any objects that are in the shadow of the form. Shadows fade as they get farther from the form casting the shadow.

chaotic lines Look like scribbles and feel unpredictable and frantic. Convey a sense of urgency, fear, or explosive energy.

class A class is a template through which code instances can be created. This is very similar to the relationship between Symbols and instances in Animate CC.

color The perceived hue, lightness, and saturation of an object or light.

color harmonies Color rules that are named for their relative locations on the color wheel.

comments Commenting code will prevent that code from being executed. Comments can also be added to code for reasons of documentation.

complementary Colors that are opposite each other on the color wheel. They are high in contrast and vibrant.

contrast Creates visual interest and a focal point in a composition. It is what draws the eye to the focal point.

Creative Commons Ways that artists can release their works for limited use and still choose the way the works are used and shared: Public Domain, Attribution, ShareAlike, NoDerivs, and NonCommercial.

curved (line) Expresses fluidity, beauty, and grace.

decorative fonts Also known as ornamental, novelty, or display fonts. They don't fall into any of the other categories of fonts. Convey a specific feeling.

deliverables A predetermined list of items that will be delivered to the customer.

demo reel A video or audio presentation meant to showcase your work. Almost like a portfolio of work but specific to video and audio formats.

deprecation A status applied to a piece of code or other functionality that is meant to steer people away from using a particular feature. Most often, the user will be urged to adopt a replacement.

design elements The building blocks of art defined by artists to provide a framework for creating art.

design principles The essential rules or assembly instructions for art.

diagonal (lines) Lines traveling neither on a vertical nor on a horizontal path. Express growth or decline and imply movement or change.

dingbat fonts Also known as wingdings. They are a collection of objects and shapes instead of letters.

direction A common way to describe lines, such as vertical, horizontal, diagonal.

DRM Digital Rights Management: A general term referring to protections and licensing enforcement upon a piece of media.

ECMAScript A scripting language specification standardized by ECMA International. Both ActionScript and JavaScript are implementations of the ECMAScript standard.

elements of art The building blocks of creative works. They are the "nouns" of design, such as space, line, shape, form, texture, value, color, and type.

emphasis Describes the focal point to which the eye is naturally and initially drawn in a design.

event Events can generally be listened for, and reacted against, in various programming languages. Some common events to listen for are those broadcast when a mouse is clicked or a key is pressed.

fade-in Sometimes referred to as a "dissolve" or simply a "fade." A fade-in is a basic transition technique where the opacity of one layer is changed over time to either transition to or reveal additional content.

fair use A set of rules that specify how and when copyrighted material can be used and that make sure copyright protection doesn't come at the cost of creativity and freedom.

feedback loop A system set up to continually encourage and require input and approval on a project's direction.

filters Filters in Animate CC can be added to certain object types to apply different effects like glows or drop shadows. Filters can be stacked, and one object can have multiple filters applied to it.

Flash Player The web browser plugin that has pushed creativity forward on the Internet—even when web standards stagnated. While much functionality can be achieved with native web technologies, Adobe Flash Player is still an integral technology for games, premium video, and even more.

Flash Professional CC For nearly 20 years now, Adobe Flash Professional CC has enabled rich creativity on the web and beyond. In early 2016, Adobe will release a rebranded version of this application named Animate CC.

flow A category related to the energy conveyed by lines and shapes.

focal point What the design is all about. The call to action or the primary message you are trying to get across.

fonts The whole collection of a typeface in each of its sizes and styles.

form Describes three-dimensional objects, such as spheres, cubes, and pyramids.

frame Frames are a unit of measurement in Animate CC. An animation will run at a specific FPS (frames per second), and how many frames exist across the timeline, along with the FPS, determines the length of animation.

function A defined group of commands and logic that can be invoked by a program to fulfill a certain task.

geometric (lines) Tend to be straight and have sharp angles. Look manmade and intentional. Communicate strength, power, and precision.

geometric shapes Predictable and consistent shapes, such as circles, squares, triangles, and stars. They are rarely found in nature and convey mechanical and manufactured impressions.

GIF Graphics Interchange Format: A lossless bitmap image format limited to 256 colors. Best used for simple images due to the limited palette. GIF images can also be animated.

glyph Each character of a font, whether it is a letter, number, symbol, or swash.

gradients A gradient in Animate CC is a type of color swatch consisting of two or more colors that visually blend into one another via a transition of properties.

H.264 MPEG-4 Part 10, Advanced Video Coding: The most common video format for web-based video. Sometimes referred to as "AVC" or "MPEG-4 AVC."

hand-drawn lines Appear as though created using traditional techniques, such as paints, charcoal, or chalk.

handwritten fonts Also known as hand fonts, they simulate handwriting.

headshot A realistically photographed portrait used for branding, casting, and social media.

highlight The area of a form that is directly facing the light and that appears lightest.

horizontal Moving from left to right; for example, the horizontal line in an "H." Expresses calmness and balance.

horizontal scale Describes the function of stretching letters and distorting the typeface geometry.

HTML5 Version 5 of the Hyper Text Markup Language. HTML defines the page markup elements used for layout and content and can be interpreted and displayed by a web browser.

hyphenation Determines if and when words should be split with hyphens when wrapping to the next line.

ideographs (ideograms) Images that represent an idea, such as a heart representing love.

implied lines Lines that don't really exist but are implied by shapes, such as dotted or dashed lines, people waiting in lines, or the margins of a block of text.

indent Settings that determine how far an entire paragraph is indented from the rest of the text on each side or in just its first line.

instance When a class is instantiated with the "new" keyword in ActionScript, a new instance of that class is created that we can then work with.

instances Instances are objects used within a project that are based upon Symbols created and stored within the project Library. Instances can have many properties adjusted individually, apart from the Symbol itself.

inverse kinematics At times this is referred to as IK. Inverse kinematics is a model of movement employed by Animate CC for use upon armatures. It is a system of bones and joints that all interact with one another, creating natural movement.

iterations New versions of a design that successively become closer to the desired result.

iterative work Work that is shared as it is completed, allowing the customer to chime in with comments while it is still easy to make a change.

JavaScript The programming language used for the native web. Alongside HTML and CSS, JavaScript is an essential technology component for the modern web. Animate CC allows the use of JavaScript in project types that support it through the Actions panel.

JPG Joint Photographic Experts Group: A lossy bitmap image format used heavily on the web. Suitable for complex images like photographs. Also represented in the form JPEG.

JSON JavaScript Object Notation: A human-readable way to structure data that is also easily ingested and parsed by software.

justified Aligns text to a straight edge on both the right and left edges of a paragraph.

kerning The space between specific letter pairs.

layer Layers exist as part of the Animate CC timeline and serve the dual functions of containing image, sound, code, and other data as well as to provide a mechanism to arrange the visual stacking order of content.

leading The amount of space between the baselines of two lines of text.

licensing A way to legally use copyrighted material for a certain time and in a certain way, usually associated with paying a fee established by the copyright holder.

ligatures Special characters used to represent letter combinations, such as "fi."

light source The perceived location of the lighting in relation to the form.

line A mark with a beginning and an end point.

loop A programming construct that repeats a certain piece of code a certain number of times depending upon some logical operator.

mask Layers in Animate CC can use their contents to mask other layers grouped beneath them. Any content covered by the mask object will appear visible, while any content outside of that overlay will not be visible.

meme An idea, often expressed on the Internet through images and video, which spreads from person to person, often becoming culturally significant.

metadata Information that is included in a document but is hidden, such as copyright, lens information, location via GPS, camera settings, and more.

methods Methods are functions that exist as members of a class in ActionScript.

model releases The permission that is required when a person's face is identifiable in a photo and the image will be used to promote something—whether it's a product or idea.

monochromatic Different shades and tints of the same color. Communicates a relaxed and peaceful feeling.

monospaced fonts Fixed-width or non-proportional fonts that use the same amount of horizontal space for each letter.

movement Visual movement within an image, such as the natural tracking of the eye across an image as the eye moves from focal point to focal point.

MP3 MPEG-2 Audio Layer III: A lossy audio file format and the most common audio file format on the web.

negative space Blank areas in a design. Also known as white space.

NoDerivs (ND) Creative Commons licensing. Requires that you not change material when you incorporate it into your own work. It can be used freely, but you must pass it along without change.

NonCommercial (NC) Creative Commons licensing. Means you can use work in your own creative work as long as you don't charge for it.

number The most flexible and general numeric data type in ActionScript. Used to store numeric data within variables.

object A generic object type in ActionScript that can have properties and data values assigned to it.

object shadow The area of the form that is facing away from the light source and appears darkest.

organic lines Lines that are usually irregular and imperfect. Found in nature.

organic shapes Are random or generated by something natural. They are usually asymmetric and convey natural, homemade, or relaxed feelings.

package Using packages in ActionScript is a way to organize your classes and ensure that no code collisions are possible between properties or methods that may share the same name.

PNG Portable Network Graphics: A lossless bitmap image format useful for complex photographic elements and simpler images as well. PNG may include a full alpha channel, allowing for nuanced transparency.

primary colors Red, blue, and green. These can be combined to create every other color in the visible spectrum.

project deadlines Dictates when work needs to be completed.

project scope Outlines the amount and type of work to be completed.

properties Properties are variables and constants that exist as members of a class in ActionScript.

proportion (scale) Describes the relative size and scale of elements.

public domain Creative Commons licensing. When copyright is expired or released and no longer applies to the content or when an artist releases their work. It can be used without worrying about infringement.

radial Circular type of balance that radiates from the center instead of the middle of a design.

Raw Whether talking video or any other medium, the term "raw" refers to the fact that the data has not been compressed, encrypted, or processed by any means.

reflected highlight Area of a form that is lit by reflections from the ground or other objects in a scene.

repetition Repeating an element in a design.

representative shapes Shapes used to represent information. They are helpful in communicating with multicultural and multilingual audiences.

rhythm Creative and expressive, rather than a consistent pattern or repetition in a design.

rule of thirds A technique for laying out the space of your page to provide a focal point. Two vertical and two horizontal lines evenly divide the space into nine equal boxes, as in a tic-tac-toe board.

Runtime A piece of software that executes specifically targeted code. The Adobe Runtimes include both Flash Player and AIR.

sans serif fonts Text without serifs. Often used for headlines and titles for their strong, stable, modern feel.

scale *See* proportion.

script fonts Mimic handwriting. They convey a feeling of beauty, grace, or feminine dignity.

SDK Software Development Kit: A set of tools and software packages or frameworks that allows the development of applications or games based upon a specific platform.

secondary colors Created when you combine primary colors.

serif fonts Associated with fonts created by typewriters. They convey tradition, intelligence, and class.

shape An area enclosed or defined by an outline, such as circles, squares, triangles, or even clouds.

ShareAlike (SA) Creative Commons licensing. Allows you to use an item (design) in any way you want as long as your creation is shared under the same license as the original work.

sketches Representative drawings of how to lay out a document or web page. These are sometimes one of the deliverables of a project.

slab serif fonts Squared-off versions of a typical serif font. Also known as Egyptian, block serif, or square serif. Convey a machine-built feel.

small caps Uses only uppercase letterforms for each letter and appears in a smaller size.

space The canvas, or working area. Its dimensions are determined by the resolution of the page you are creating.

specifications Detailed written goals and limits for a project. These are sometimes one of the deliverables of a project.

spritesheets In order to require as few server calls as possible, bitmap images can be packed together into a single image that is loaded only once. The loaded image can then be parsed in accordance with an accompanying data file.

stock photos Images for which the author retains copyright but for which a license for use is available.

string A sequence of characters assigned to a variable. Generally, a piece of text.

style (line) An effect applied to a line, such as varying width, hand-drawn, and implied.

subtractive color Created by subtracting light.

SVG Scalable Vector Graphics: An XML-based scalable vector format used for the representation of image data. Can be viewed on the web and may include animation and interactivity.

swashes Special characters with flowing and elegant endings for the ascenders and descenders.

Symbols Symbols in Animate CC primarily allow the re-use of assets as instances within a project. Symbols are stored within the project Library. Editing a Symbol will edit all instances of that Symbol.

symmetrical Occurs when you can divide an image along its middle, and the left side of the image is a mirror image of the right (or the top reflects the bottom). Conveys an intentional, formal, and mechanical feeling.

tertiary colors Created by mixing primary and secondary colors.

texture Describes the actual tactile texture in real objects or the appearance of texture in a two-dimensional image.

tracking The overall space between all the letters in a block of text. It allows you to compress or expand the space between the letters as a whole rather than just between specific pairs, as you do with kerning.

transcode Encoding a piece of media from one format to another. Animate CC works in conjunction with Adobe Media Encoder to encode and transcode video files from one format to another.

type size A font's height from the highest ascender to the lowest descender.

typeface Specific letterform set, such as Helvetica, Arial, Garamond, and so on. It is the "look" of letters.

unity Also known as harmony and sharing similar traits. Low contrast. Things that go together should look like they belong together. The opposite of variety.

usability The ease of use or learnability of a piece of software.

value Describes the lightness or darkness of an object. Together with color, value represents the visible spectrum, such as a gradient.

variety High contrast. The opposite of unity.

varying width lines Expresses flow and grace.

vector Graphics generated through mathematical expressions. Vectors can be infinitely scaled without any loss in visual fidelity.

vertical Moving from top to bottom. Vertical lines tend to express power and elevation.

vertical scale Describes the function of stretching letters and distorting the typeface geometry.

WebGL A graphics language that is able to render GPU-accelerated 2D and 3D content using HTML5 Canvas.

weight (line) The thickness of a line.

Welcome Screen A special user interface element that provides quick access to recent documents and the creation of new documents.

XML Extensible Markup Language: HTML and other content delivery formats are often based upon this simple, node-based structural language.

Index

G

gameOver() method, 196–197
GIF files, 65
Google Play, 174
GPU-acceleration, 100
Gradient Transform tool, 78, 79
gradients
    shapes and, 78–79
    strokes and, 126
Graphic symbols, 81, 83, 93
greeting card. *See* animated greeting card project
grid, 50
Group command, 147
grouping layers, 77
guides, 50

H

H.264 video format, 130, 131
Hand tool, 12
Hardware acceleration option, 43
HDS streaming protocol, 134
headers, app, 176–177
headshot movie clip, 109–118
    creating, 109–111
    fade-in effect, 117–118
    filter applied to, 115–117
    rotating, 112–115
hidden layers, 42, 99
hints, shape, 35, 109
HLS streaming protocol, 133
Hosted Libraries option, 99
HTML sample file, 43–44
HTML5 Canvas
    document creation/setup, 70–72
    Dynamic Text used in, 71, 92
    filters available in, 94, 95
    publishing projects for, 98–100
HTML5 video element, 130
HTTP Dynamic Streaming (HDS), 134
HTTP Live Streaming (HLS), 133

I

icons
    desktop, 170
    mobile, 203
Illustrator files, 52–53
image generation, 64–67
import statement, 162

Import

Import Video command, 132
importing
    audio files, 156–157
    background images, 105, 143
    bitmap images, 51–53, 145
    video as a guide, 132
informal testing, 209
inheritance, 184
initial evaluation, 207
Ink Bottle tool, 31, 111
input text, 62
instances
    class, 182
    symbol, 82
interactive buttons, 197–199
interactive media content
    evaluation process, 206–210
    revisions process, 210
interface
    features overview, 6–7, 9–13
    See also workspaces
internal attributes, 182
inverse kinematics, 85–86, 88
iOS apps, 174, 175

J

JavaScript
    ActionScript vs., 138–139
    panels for working with, 96–97
    Publish Settings related to, 99
    stopping animations using, 97–98
JavaScript libraries, 70
JPEG Deblocking option, 42
JPEG images
    exporting stills as, 64–65
    quality settings for, 41–42
JSON files, 173, 187–191
    building, 187–188
    code example, 188–189
    loading, 189–191
jsonLoaded() method, 190

K

keyboard shortcuts, 13
keyframes
    adjusting, 37
    audio attached to, 158
    blank, 32, 89
    copying/pasting, 34

explained, 13, 32
inserting, 33–34, 37
labeling, 160
See also frames

L

labels, frame, 160
Land, Edwin, 6
Lasso tool, 30
Layer Options menu, 23
Layer Properties dialog box, 23
layers, 13
    Actions, 97, 140, 162
    armature, 86–88
    deleting, 84
    grouping, 77
    hidden, 42, 99
    icons for managing, 22
    mask, 57–58
    outline mode for, 54
    setting properties for, 22–23
    stacking order of, 26
    visibility of, 54
Library panel, 57
Line tool, 27, 123, 150
linear gradients, 78, 79
Linkage ID, 52, 157
Linux systems, 141
`loadJSON()` method, 190
Local playback security option, 43
Lock Guides option, 50
lock icon, 22

M

Magic Wand tool, 30
Manage Adobe AIR SDK dialog box, 143
masks
    animating, 107–109
    drawing shape, 106–107
    hiding content with, 57–58
meme image project, 47–67
    black vector shape creation, 58–59
    Challenge! exercise, 67
    document creation/setup, 48–50
    importing bitmap images, 51–53
    managing bitmap images, 54–58
    still image generation, 64–67
    text elements, 59–64

Merge Drawing mode, 25
methods, ActionScript, 182
mobile quiz app project, 173–203
    Adobe Air document creation, 174–176
    button interactivity, 197–199
    Challenge! exercise, 203
    code example, 199–202
    interface element design, 176–181
    logic and flow description, 195–197
    publishing for distribution, 202–203
    question bank creation, 187–195
    writing the classes for, 182–187
Motion Editor, 114, 115, 116–117
motion guides, 122–125
motion presets, 120
motion tweens, 90–91, 122
mouse interaction, 165–166
`MouseEvent` class, 163, 197
Movie Clip symbols, 80
    ActionScript and, 160
    animated greeting card project, 90–91
    Graphic symbols distinguished from, 83
    promotional video project, 111, 121
    virtual clock project, 149
`MovieClip` class, 163, 182
MP3 file format, 156
MP4 file format, 130, 131
Multiframe bounds option, 100

N

name animation, 118–120
    motion presets for, 120
    movie clip creation, 119
New Document dialog box, 71, 142
New Layer icon, 21, 72
number variable, 160

O

Object Drawing mode, 25, 73
objects, class, 182
onion skinning, 37
Options area, 12
outline text, 92, 100
Output File option, 41
Oval Primitive tool, 24, 89, 146
Oval tool, 24, 78, 146, 179